KV-704-650

1987

1972

OUR EXCUSE FOR BEING

It will be the aim of the publishers to present to its subscribers

a succinct epitomization of the most important happenings

and events occurring in the women's wear industry. The scope

of the publication will be to cover the factors between the

mill and the merchant.

There is probably no other line of human endeavor in which

there is so much change as in the product that womankind wears.

This brings about an enormous amount of traveling, and

the result is that important men in all departments of women's

wear are scattered everywhere over the earth's surface

and lose track of events and happenings, which it will be our

purpose to to try and chronicle as briefly as possible, so

that these men can pick up and at a minimum of time and

expense keep posted. A knowledge of what has transpired is

most important, and *Women's Wear* will aim to do this.

—WOMEN'S WEAR, JUNE 1910, VOL. 1, NO. 1

WOMEN'S WEAR

JUNE 1910

PUBLISHED QUARTERLY BY

Women's Wear Company

42 East 21st Street, New York

Vol. 1, No. 1.   50c A Year

746 920922 WWD

WWD

100 Years | 100 Designers

FAIRCHILD BOOKS | NEW YORK

1972

WWD

100 Years | 100 Designers

2009

1992

2007

FOREWORD

A preview at a European house with Mr. Fairchild was a rare and special opportunity for this reporter, having arrived at *WWD* sometime after the legendary publishing genius began his retreat from day-to-day interaction with all but a few senior staff members.

Mr. Fairchild had long since relocated to New York from his beloved Paris, where during his five-year stint as bureau chief, he took creative command of his family's rag trade paper, shaping it into a powerful force within the fashion industry. At the same time, he crafted his own reputation as a razor-sharp, often prickly and always witty chronicler of popular culture.

We were at Fendi headquarters in Milan, where Karl Lagerfeld and some fraction of the five famous sisters for whom he worked, would take us through a wondrous collection.

Either coming or going, I don't recall which, we bumped into then-editor of French *Vogue* Joan Juliet Buck, who earlier in her career had worked for *WWD* in its Paris and Rome bureaus. She greeted Mr. Fairchild, her deep voice full of theatrical warmth. "John!"—familiar invocation of Mr. Fairchild's given name by a staff member, current or former, was not something the rank-and-file heard every day of the week—"You know, John, I wish all of my staff could have been trained by you. I tell them, you can write the caption *and* stamp the envelope."

Thus Joan Juliet Buck captured in two sentences the essence of life at *WWD*: You roll up your sleeves, and if a job needs doing, you do it. Just don't miss the story while getting those envelopes out.

From the beginning until now, that story could be about virtually anything, from major world events

(the Titanic; the rise of Hitler; 9/11) to the latest social and celebrity dish (near-stalking of Jackie O; news of an unknown singer, Lady Gaga) to random industry musings (precrash plans for a golf course atop 498 Seventh Avenue in 1929; the establishment in 1951 of a summer corsetry course at New York's City College). Hence, this volume's decade-by-decade snapshots, which reflect the paper's general coverage. But from the beginning, *WWD* recognized that when it comes to fashion, the most essential stories spring most often from the great designers, the men and women whose work we not only wear, but which also impacts and inspires us, and at times shocks us, forcing us to challenge our presumptive values. Thus, to celebrate its 100 years, *WWD* here celebrates 100 designers whose work has helped define the eras in which they lived.

1968

1987

1968

It's popular in media today to speak of the fusion of fashion and culture. Editors and bloggers at countless titles and Web sites love to stress that their purpose is to cover the point of intersection between the two as if it were a newfangled, watershed concept, as if until our current, uber-enlightened age, fashion somehow existed on its own ancillary track, removed from the greater culture. What a fiction. Go back as far as you will, all the way to that most notorious of DIY garments itself, the fig leaf, which emerged in direct response to a societal event.

More recently, during the 100 years of *WWD*'s existence, virtually all of the major movements in fashion have had a cultural trigger—a single visionary designer or a group of designers acting in reaction to, anticipation of, or revolt against particular stimuli. Poiret didn't ditch the corset in a vacuum, nor did Coco Chanel advance her chic, simplified sportif unaware that sartorial options reflected women's changing lives. And when Christian Dior brazenly rid his collection of then-de rigueur austerity in favor of the flamboyant New Look, he did so as a predictor of the excitement that would accompany the end of World War II. And on through the designing generations: Yves Saint Laurent, who translated the mood of the street into the stuff of couture; Giorgio Armani, who dressed an upwardly mobile generation of women bound for newly opened careers; the great social designers; the minimalists; architects; deconstructionists; artistic souls; and those who are now marshaling social media as a tool of fashion.

From the beginning, *WWD* treated these creators as stars of their craft. In the years that followed under Mr. Fairchild's brilliant tutelage, the paper elevated designers further still, to full-on celebrity status, examining not only their professional pursuits, but their private passions: visiting their homes, chronicling their off-duty exploits—nightlife, holidays, feuds, obsessions. The reasoning: Along with traditional celebrities, socials and business leaders, designers were, he said, "people who made the world tick."

They did so—and continue to do so—for the way they lived, but most especially for their work, even at its craziest, a point that continues at the core of *WWD* today. As the great surrealist Elsa Schiaparelli, by then an elder icon of her milieu, told the paper in 1969, "I think the future is going to be for the wearable things and some stunts...sometimes from stunts comes the real fashion."

—BRIDGET FOLEY

1972

— Suffragettes take to the streets to help secure passage of the 19th Amendment, clearing the way for women to vote.

— Retail dynasties Macy's, Lord & Taylor, Gimbels and Filene's flourish.

— In the wake of the devastating Triangle Shirtwaist Factory fire, which kills 146 working women and girls, new laws are passed to protect garment workers. "The lesson for the sewing trades to learn

from the tragic fire at Washington place [sic], New York, the terrible loss of life, seems to lie in the necessity of more discipline and less selfishness which is concealed under the guise of personal rights." (*WWD* 3.27.11)

—— The unsinkable Titanic sinks. Macy's and Abraham & Straus stores close in mourning for drowned owner Isadore Straus and his wife, Ida. Designer "Lucile,"

Lady Duff-Gordon, survives, as does *WWD*'s Paris correspondent, Edith L. Rosenbaum.

—— Silent films reflect a new sexiness that ranges from "The Vamp" to "America's Sweetheart."

—— Designers start incorporating versatile, less-expensive fabrics like jersey into their work. "Gabrielle Chanel has on display some extremely interesting sweaters

which embrace new features. The material employed is wool jersey in the most attractive colorings...." (*WWD* 7.27.14)

—— During WWI, the Burberry trench becomes popular, women tone down accessories and hemlines reach mid-calf.

—— High society throngs to the south of France and embraces resort wear designs.

Chanel Sports Suit

ready for all Emergencies

Whether facing the Hun or facing the Weather, the most efficient and comfortable Safeguard is a

BURBERRY TRENCH-WARM

Practical in every detail, smart and soldierlike in appearance, and designed in two parts which can be worn separately or together, it supplies the services of

THREE COATS IN ONE GARMENT.

The outside, worn alone, provides a **WEATHERPROOF** that is thoroughly reliable, yet self-ventilating and healthful. It excludes anything in the form of wet, yet is entirely free from rubber, oiled-silk or other airtight fabrics. The inside makes a capital

BRITISH WARM. Made of luxuriously soft Camel Fleece, it is warm in chilly weather, yet very light. A most comfortable coat for wear in dug-outs or when off duty. The two parts together form the finest

TRENCH-COAT available. A staunch double-breasted safeguard that withstands a steady downpour or blizzard and engenders abundant warmth.

Officers under Orders

for Europe or the Far East, can obtain at Burberrys, Uniforms in suitable materials, and every detail of kit

READY-TO-PUT-ON

Perfect fit is assured, as each garment is made in more than 50 different sizes. Complete kits to measure in 2 to 4 days.

BURBERRYS

HAYMARKET S.W. 1 LONDON

ARTCRAFT PICTURES

MARY PICKFORD IN JOHANNA ENLISTS

BY RUPERT HUGHES
SCENARIO BY FRANCES MARION
DIRECTED BY WILLIAM D. TAYLOR

AN ARTCRAFT PICTURE

DAILY   DAILY
Retailers   Fashion,
Jobbers and News and
Manufacturers Ideas

Women's Wear

PUBLISHED EVERY BUSINESS DAY
(Copyright, 1917, by the Women's Wear Co.)

VOL. 15. NO. 87.   NEW YORK, SATURDAY AFTERNOON, OCTOBER 13, 1917.   PRICE TWO CENTS.

Poiret's Ideas for Year 2017
SHOWN AT THE THEATRE MICHEL

COSTUME in Culotte Style Made of Yellow Velvet. Corsage Shows Alternate Stripes of Cloth of Gold and Black Velvet. Cold Lace in Sleeves.

COSTUME in Culotte Style of Bright Red Velvet. Corsage Made of Paillettes of Jet and Silver.

COSTUME in Culotte Style Showing Skirt of Emerald Green Velvet Striped With Black Velvet. Corsage of Black Velvet, Sleeves Edged With Skunk Fur. Hat of Black Lace With Cross Pompon.

PAJAMAS Worn by Mlle. Spinelly Made of Marian Printed Silk in Black and White Trimmed With Bands of Black Silk.

COSTUME Worn by Mlle. Spinelly in Culotte Style Skirt of Cloth of Silver Corsage of Jet Spangles. Headdress of Brilliants With Black Ostrich Pompon.

Sketched in Paris Especially for Women's Wear

FUNSTEN FUR SALE PASSES $3,000,000 MARK

Final Day's Total of $1,051,260 Brings Aggregate to $3,350,429 — Attribute Success to Healthy Business Conditions.

NEW CLOAK UNION HALTS PAYMENT OF DUES OF WORKERS

Coats Longer, Pleats and Belts Featured, Chicago Designers Report

Spring Models Show No Shortage of Materials

DO WOMEN WANT TIGHT FITTING BONED BODICE?

POIRET DESIGNS COSTUMES WORN IN NOVEL REVUE

Bubbles

Fitting the Whole Family and the Weather

Crepe Paper Display Models Suggested

Chicago Ladies' Tailors' Union May Call Strike

In the wake of WWI, the '20s roar with jazz, flappers and defiance against convention —and Prohibition. Simpler silhouettes, home-sewing and knockoffs make it easier for more women to become "fashionable."

Accessories are back with a vengeance: fringe, head wraps, cloche hats, long strings of pearls, slave bracelets, fur wraps, silk flowers and more fringe.

WWD copyrights the title of its recurring feature, "They Are Wearing."

The excitement surrounding the burgeoning aviation industry and the styles of Amelia Earhart and Charles Lindbergh influence design.

Women begin to wear trousers in public, starting with beach pajamas. "But now comes the word from Palm Beach to the effect that fashionable females are walking around the hotel lobbies and shopping centers of the resort arrayed in Pajamas; I am now asking myself how many moons will wax and wane before the women wear trousers

on the streets of New York?" (WWD 1.27.26)

— Clara Bow becomes the original "It" girl when she appears in the silent film, *It*.

— Developments in photography allow designers' creations to be shared in a striking new way.

— As more women take up sports like swimming, golf and tennis, designers respond by creating sporting costumes.

— By the end of the decade, lower hemlines and curves are back in style.

— The stock market crash of 1929 brings what F. Scott Fitzgerald called "the greatest, gaudiest spree in history" to an end.

— Hollywood and its affordable entertainment take center stage during the Great Depression; women yearn for the designs worn by movie stars.

— Despite the financial hardships of the time, women continue to follow fashions by making their own clothes or adding embellishments like jeweled clips, clutches, corsages and hats.

— A handy fastener finds a place in fashion: the zipper.

— Evening gowns become sexier—

women embrace the backless and the bias-cut.

— The DuPont chemical company creates and patents nylon, the "miracle fiber" that saves generations of women from sagging stockings.

— Androgynous styles take off—women begin wearing trousers and menswear-inspired fashions, following the lead of actresses like Katharine Hepburn.

— Surrealism infiltrates the art and design world, insinuating itself into fashion through Elsa

Schiaparelli's designs—including her collaborations with Salvador Dali.

— Dashing King Edward VIII abdicates the throne for stylish Wallis Simpson, and as the Duke and Duchess of Windsor, they influence popular imagination *and* fashion. "To millions of women throughout the world today the question of what the bride wore was of great importance. She wore the "Wallis blue" (a pale shade like hyacinth) gown by Mainbocher...." (*WWD* 6.3.37)

At the Opening of the Waldorf Roof — Four Striking Ways of Widening Shoulders

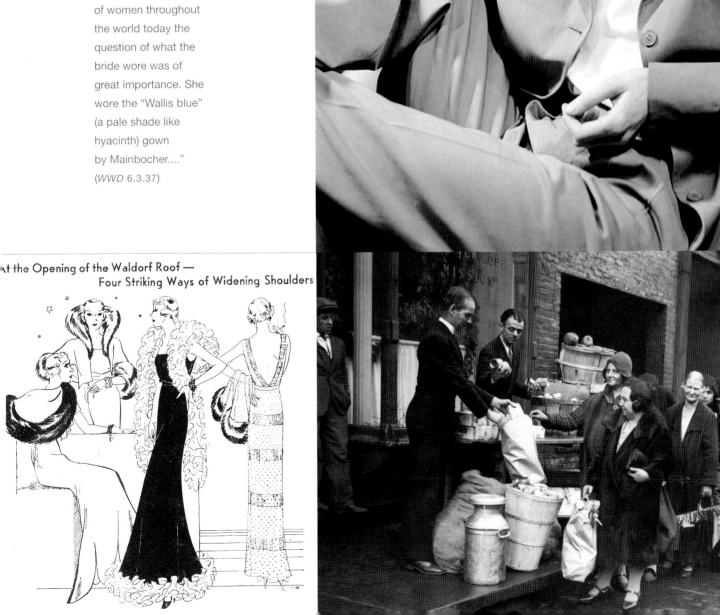

Claire McCardell Makes Resort Clothes
Fitted or Loose, but Always Straight

— Rationing and shortages during WWII lead to simpler designs and greater use of rayon and viscose.

— As women replace men in the workplace, the prevalence of practical dressing grows. "'Kerchief' Hats: ...Certain costume fabrics, especially cottons, linens, suggest the informality of the kerchief theme in real hats to be stocked in millinery, not neckwear, departments." (*WWD* 3.27.40)

— During the war, fashions are also influenced by military styles, featuring epaulettes, insignias and sailor-inspired dresses.

— Soldiers overseas pine after the idealized female form, popularized by "sweater girls" and "pin-up girls," like Lana Turner and Betty Grable.

— "Torpedo" or "bullet" bras and girdles become the underwear of choice for many women.

— The U.S. is cut off from Parisian fashions during the war, resulting in the rise of American sportswear.

— The American concept of "separates" is widely embraced, allowing women to mix, match and extend their wardrobes.

IN THE 1940s

— Men return from the war, and women are urged to "re-feminize" and focus on the home.

— In a bid to restore themselves to center stage and promote their designs post-war, French designers create the *Théâtre de la Mode*, a traveling exhibition of couture-attired dolls.

— To create his uber-feminine New Look, Dior emphasizes small waists and uses many yards of no-longer-rationed fabric for full skirts.

IN THE 1950s

— As war babies come of age, teenagers embrace Elvis Presley, *American Bandstand* and James Dean—and become sought-after consumers. "Teen-Age Charge Accounts Seen as Growing Potential." (*WWD* 7.18.58)

— Television sets proliferate, prompting women to buy "screen styles" worn by stars like Lucille Ball—and advertisers discover a new and powerful medium.

— An all-American Hollywood "It" girl becomes a princess: the nation is obsessed with the courtship and marriage of Grace Kelly and Prince Rainier of Monaco.

— The suburbs, with their spacious houses and sprawling malls, begin to lure people away from "downtown" and inspire fashions suited for in-home entertaining.

— Polyester is introduced as the no-iron fabric, and synthetic textiles become increasingly popular.

First Paris Opening Sketches:

The Cocktail Dress: Top Fashion

— The curvy Marilyn Monroe look is in — and the lingerie market grows.

— The Cold War adds a soupçon of fear to an otherwise optimistic decade; kids learn to "duck and cover," and retailers are urged to plan for disasters. "Shadow of Sputnik Darkens Retail Scene: Sputnik is likely to have an effect on retail business in the United States in the next couple of years." (*WWD* 10.17.57)

— Inspired by writers of the Beat Generation, "Beatniks" embrace black turtlenecks, black berets, black glasses and brooding looks.

— *WWD* copyrights the phrase "Fashion Flash."

One of the Fairchild Publications

Women's Wear Daily

Printed in U. S. A.   THE RETAILER'S DAILY NEWSPAPER

Vol. 101   No. 8   ★ ★ ★   NEW YORK, N. Y., WEDNESDAY, JULY 11, 1960   TEN CENTS

We're Fifty Years Old

Aid to Firms Hit by Imports, Wider FLSA in Platform
By JOHN T. NORMAN

Report Japan To Use 'Secret' Quota Figures
By SHELDON WENSON

Fashionable Kennedys Big Paris Customers
By JOHN B. FAIRCHILD

Rome Showings On Against Backdrop Of Political Unrest
By J. W. COHN

Kitten Britches
Fits the Market...
Purr-fectly

READY SOON!!
Preview of our HOLIDAY SWEATER COLLECTION
Rosanna

50 YEARS AGO

IN THE 1960s

—— Jackie Kennedy's influence on fashion begins with JFK's bid for the presidency and continues for years after.

—— Andy Warhol's Pop Art impacts fashion and leaves everyone yearning for *their* fifteen minutes of fame.

—— Babe Paley and her fellow "Ladies Who Lunch" dine in designer-wear and influence style.

—— Civil unrest, spurred by the struggle for civil rights, the Vietnam War and the assassinations of John F. Kennedy and Dr. Martin Luther King, Jr., leads to sit-ins, protests and the growth of counterculture.

—— The British Invasion: Swinging London's Carnaby Street, Mod Mary Quant and bobbed Twiggy are all the rage on both sides of the pond.

—— Popular culture and music are forever changed by the rise of groups ranging from The Beatles to the The Supremes.

—— Women gain access to the Pill, embrace feminism, and to the dismay of the lingerie biz, reject wearing bras.

—— WWD introduces the term "sportive" to describe casual looks from Paris.

—— Fashions become cheaper and more disposable—literally, in the case of chic dresses made of paper. "Paco Rabanne—the Plastics Pioneer—is leading the way again. Now with paper dresses...." (*WWD* 1.9.67)

—— The space race and moon landing inspire new frontiers and far-out looks.

—— When she marries Aristotle Onassis, or "Daddy O," WWD is the first to dub a certain someone "Jackie O."

—— Hippies from far and wide gather at Woodstock, wearing bell-bottoms, Indian-influenced styles, tie-dyed shirts, headbands, sandals—and sometimes nothing at all—to celebrate sex, drugs and rock 'n' roll.

IN THE 1970s

—— As the "Me Decade" tries to find itself, hemlines go up and down and up and down and up—from minis to maxis to midis to the short shorts that *WWD* coins "hotpants."

—— African-Americans increasingly influence the cultural scene, as models, designers, performers and arbiters of cultural style and taste.

—— The oil crisis leads to long lines at the pumps, and retailers fear a slump in business.

—— Everybody wears, designs and adores T-shirts—even New York City sanitation workers, whose version reads "Sanitation Man."

—— Women enter the workplace in greater numbers, pantsuits take off and Diane Keaton's menswear-inspired *Annie Hall* look becomes popular.

—— In with the new: women trade staid classics for the extreme silhouettes and loud colors of designers like Kenzo Takada.

—— The supersonic Concorde becomes the jet-set fashion shuttle.

—— Sequins meet Lycra meets Lurex in the splashy, shiny world of disco nightlife. "Regine's, Cafe Reginette and Studio 54 are the best places to catch a glimpse of New York's Nightcrawlers, fashion claques and young arbiters in their new nighttime looks." *(WWD 12.9.77)*

—— Punk rock trickles up from the streets of London to the work of designers.

—— Denim goes up-market: designer jeans make their debut.

—— Pierre Cardin's company becomes one of the first to capitalize on China's new openness to the West.

IN THE 1980s

— The fairy-tale wedding of Lady Di and Prince Charles captures the imaginations of the masses, inspiring many a lavish nuptial.

— MTV adds visuals to rock, making musicians' images as important as their sounds.

— Bright, big-shouldered power suits grace everyone from actresses on *Dynasty* to powerbrokers on Wall Street.

— With a little help from Jane Fonda's Workout, *Flashdance* and Olivia Newton-John getting physical, dancewear takes to the streets.

— The Material Girl appears on the scene—and continues to crib and create styles for decades.

— Designers discover a new promotional opportunity as the red carpet becomes another runway.

— The disease that comes to be called AIDS is identified in 1981. Within a few years it affects thousands and ravages the fashion community, spurring fund- and awareness-raising efforts.

— A booming economy leads to the conspicuous consumption, extravagant parties and excesses of "Nouvelle Society" (a *WWD* term). "The talk of Paris is still the townhouse that Susan Gutfreund, Hubert de Givenchy and Philippe Venet own with the Bemberg family on the Rue de Grenelle. Not only have the occupants built an underground 16-car garage but the garage has reportedly been equipped with a car wash." (*WWD* 2.9.87)

— Vertical retailers like The Gap, Benetton and The Limited seem to sprout on every corner, challenging department store dominance.

— Merger lust sweeps the fashion industry, creating huge corporations, such as LVMH Möet Hennessy Louis Vuitton.

— Designers like Ralph Lauren and Calvin Klein build megabrands, becoming megarich in the process.

— The Cold War ends, the Berlin Wall comes down and international markets open up.

31

— Seattle-spawned grunge, with its emphasis on the unkempt flannel thrift-store look, goes mainstream.

— The tragic and untimely deaths of Jackie O, Maurizio Gucci, Gianni Versace, Princess Diana, Liz Tilberis, JFK, Jr., and Carolyn Bessette-Kennedy shock the fashion community and the world.

— Supermodels become celebrities, dominating the runway and the media; superskinny Kate Moss evokes "heroin chic."

— Even everyday looks become more casual as the corporate world embraces "dress-down Fridays." "The spread of casual Fridays has been the most radical change in career fashions since the Seventies, when women began wearing pants to work." (*WWD* 9.20.95)

— Celebrities including Gwyneth Paltrow, Nicole Kidman and Julia Roberts become designers' muses and champions, further blurring the lines between fashion and Hollywood.

— Allegations that Kathie Lee Gifford's clothing line was manufactured by sweat-shop labor shed light on international labor rights.

— Hip-hop's influence is seen on the runway and on the street: bling, backward baseball caps, baggy jeans and polo shirts.

Women's Wear Daily • The Retailers' Daily Newspaper • July 19, 1999 Vol. 178, No. 12 $1.75

WWDMONDAY

Paradise Lost

NEW YORK — Fashion appears to have lost its newest and brightest fashion icon — the only real successor to her mother-in-law, Jacqueline Onassis.

At press time Sunday, authorities still held out a rapidly-dimming hope that Carolyn Bessette Kennedy and her husband, John F. Kennedy Jr., and sister Lauren Bessette may have somehow survived the crash of their small private plane off the coast of Martha's Vineyard last Friday evening. Developments have been slow to come, but increasingly pessimistic.

The news media's focus has largely been on John's fate — the latest in a long history of Kennedy family tragedies. But in the

Carolyn Bessette Kennedy and John F. Kennedy Jr.

— IPO fever (which strikes designers such as Ralph Lauren, Tommy Hilfiger and Donna Karan) and bankruptcies (for retailers including Barneys and Macy's), put fashion on Wall Street's map.

— Dot-coms come and go—but the Internet is here to stay.

— Globalization continues apace for "instant fashion" retailers like Zara and H&M.

33

MILAN
Men's collections/fall '09

with Giorgio Armani, Versace, Alexander McQueen and more, pages 8 to 13.

► FINANCIAL: Burberry joins wave of luxury layoffs, page 2.

Fashion Pre-fall looks from Chloé, Givenchy and Emilio Pucci Akris, page 7.

Women's Wear Daily • The Retailers' Daily Newspaper • January 21, 2009 • $3.00

WWD WEDNESDAY

Sportswear

At Last

WASHINGTON — The Etta James tune soulfully sung by Beyoncé Knowles at the Neighborhood Inaugural Ball Tuesday night perfectly summed up the mood of the day that saw the swearing in of the nation's first African-American president. Knowles sang as President Barack Obama, clad in a custom Hart Schaffner Marx tuxedo with white tie, and his wife, Michelle, in an off-the-shoulder long white dress by Jason Wu, took to the dance floor. As for the new First Lady's gown, it got praise from one important quarter: "How good looking is my wife?" her husband said to the crowd. For more on the inauguration and surrounding parties, see pages 4 to 6.

IN THE 2000s

—— The attacks of September 11th usher in a decade of terrorism and anxiety— and mark a shift in the global landscape.

—— *Sex and the City*'s Sarah Jessica Parker and her co-stars leave viewers green with fashion- and lifestyle-envy. "[*Sex and the City*] became known as the most fashion-savvy show in television history." (*WWD* 12.7.04)

—— Access to the inside world of fashion gets easier thanks to reality TV shows like *Project Runway*.

—— Designers like Mizrahi and Lagerfeld create affordable collections for Target and H&M.

—— Celebrities are addicted to launching their own clothing lines— no fewer than eight stars debuted designs in 2004 alone! "Celebrities are increasingly usurping the traditional role of the fashion creator...." (*WWD* 9.11.04)

—— Consumer-side markets emerge in China, India, Brazil and Russia, affecting the global economy—and creating growth potential for the fashion industry.

—— As consumers become more health- and environmentally-conscious, all-natural and sustainable fashions, designs and materials hit the mainstream.

WWD WEDNESDAY

STATE OF SIEGE

NEW YORK — At four o'clock on Thursday, Donna Karan's fashion show should have been held there. But instead, by early afternoon on Tuesday, the Lexington Avenue Armory was being patrolled by armed National Guardsmen and tanks, and was serving as a hospital and triage center. The set for the show had already been partially constructed and the benches were converted into beds for the injured. In the wake of the terrorist attacks on New York and Washington, the American collections had been cancelled. Here, the Armory under guard. For more on the effects of the horrific events on New York and the fashion industry, see inside pages.

—— The worldwide recession marks the end of the ultraluxury market as it existed in the 1980s and 1990s.

—— Michelle Obama inspires women—and retailers—by mixing off-the-rack fashion with the work of both young and established designers, symbolizing an accessible "you-can-do-it-too" image.

—— Lady Gaga's intriguing style and dance-pop music are a hit in the fashion world: A new fashion icon is born.

—— Constantly connected: Digital innovation and social networking fundamentally change the way people shop, consume media and interact, allowing fashion and designers to become even more integrated into daily life.

ADOLFO

Every season Adolfo has **just what the ladies are looking for.**

—*WWD* 9.14.70

1983

"Women need **EVENING CLOTHES** that will be just as good-looking at the end of the evening as at the beginning."
—ADOLFO; *WWD* 1.4.78

1972

1972

1985

" I don't dictate my designs to my ladies. Often, I take their ideas and use them with some of my own. "
—ADOLFO; *WWD* 12.30.71

39

2003

1984

...ZIPPERS,
TOP-STITCHING,
KICK PLEATS
pinched with a single
grommet and accented with
wide elbow-high gauntlets.
—*WWD* 4.6.82

Probably the
most copied and
influential designer
of the early Eighties.... —*WWD* 10.17.86

Alaïa defined an era of **sensational, skin-tight shape** with a genius for cut and seamed-in sex appeal....

— *WWD* 10.17.86

AZZEDINE ALAÏA

2003

"After all the extravagance, people want **something clean and simple.**"

—GIORGIO ARMANI; *WWD* 6.25.92

" I love...to take existing forms and then take them out of their context. I think that is probably the direction of modern fashion. "

—GIORGIO ARMANI;
WWD 10.9.79

GIORGIO ARMANI

2010

The Italians adore pants, perhaps none more so than Giorgio Armani who cuts them feminine "for a woman, not a superwoman."

—*WWD* 3.9.88

1985

2010   1978

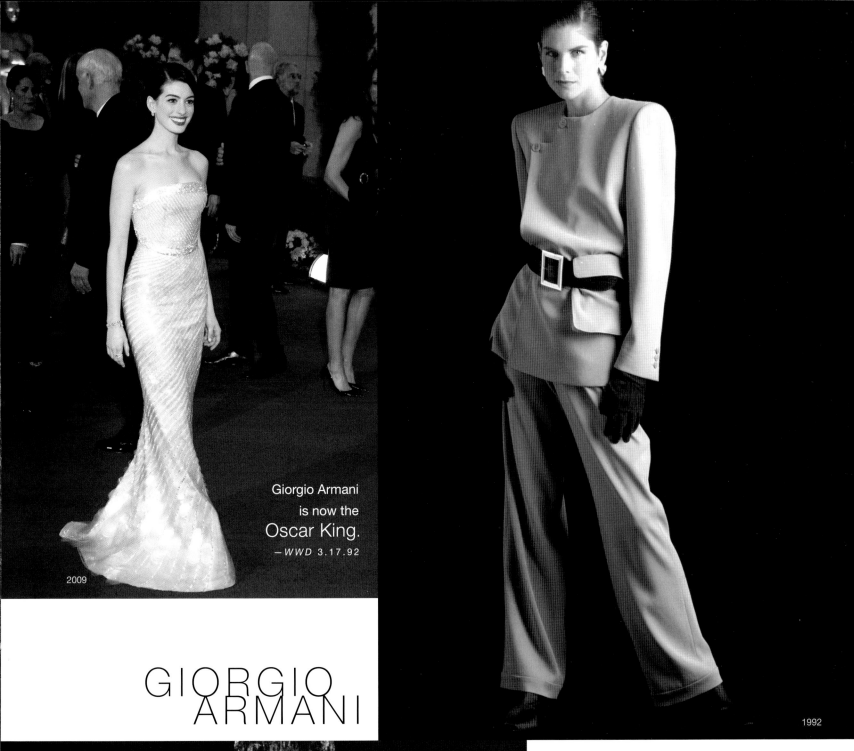

Giorgio Armani
is now the
Oscar King.
—*WWD* 3.17.92

2009

GIORGIO ARMANI

1992

The Designer Laureate
of Milan's new sensuality
takes his cue from
Italian haberdashery and
adds lots of leg...
AN EROTIC BLEND
OF RAGAZZO INSOUCIANCE
WITH WOMANLY
ELEGANCE.

—*WWD* 10.11.84

2009

2009

BAILEY'S
STRENGTH
in his work
lies in subtlety....
—*WWD* 2.24.05

2004

...there's something
delightfully British
about Bailey's first take:
well-bred but
just a little naughty
in its casual
compilations of parts,
as if a young
Miss Marple took
shopping advice from
Nancy Spungen.

—*WWD* 3.6.02

2008

2002

Bailey's ability to keep his retro-Brit-"It"-girl looking fresh season in and season out is an **honest-to-goodness marvel of modern fashion.**

—*WWD 9.26.06*

CHRISTOPHER BAILEY

IMAGES ON PAGES FOR BURBERRY PRORSUM.

CRISTÓBAL
BALENCIAGA

1964

The fashion world lives off his ideas....
All Paris couturiers are influenced by him.
—*WWD* 7.9.58

1963

1964

The King can iron,
sew, cut, baste—
just everything.
He has been known to
embroider a sample
before sending it to the
embroiderer.

—WWD 2.1.62

1962

1962

Balenciaga was the Father of the chemise . . . the Father of tough chic . . . the Father of great tailoring.

LIKE SO MANY FATHER FIGURES, HE WAS DIFFICULT, PROUD, ARROGANT. *—WWD* 5.23.68

1964

CRISTÓBAL
BALENCIAGA

PIERRE BALMAIN

Balmain has a certain
taste for elegance
which cannot be found
in any other house.

—WWD 1.9.59

1956

"I have nothing to do with Seventh Avenue and Seventh Avenue has nothing to do with me . . .

MY CLOTHES AREN'T 'VULGAR' ENOUGH FOR SEVENTH AVENUE."

—PIERRE BALMAIN; *WWD* 10.31.60

"Fashions are no longer set by definite seasons. With planes making travel a matter of hours it brings all the world close to Paris and in many parts of the world the seasons do not correspond to our seasons."

— PIERRE BALMAIN; *WWD* 12.5.46

1950

53

1977

1973   1981

The Elegant Mr. Beene...
    bursts on the fall scene...
leaping into the Couture Concept of
        pure shape, pure fabric, pure fashion.

— WWD 6.11.63

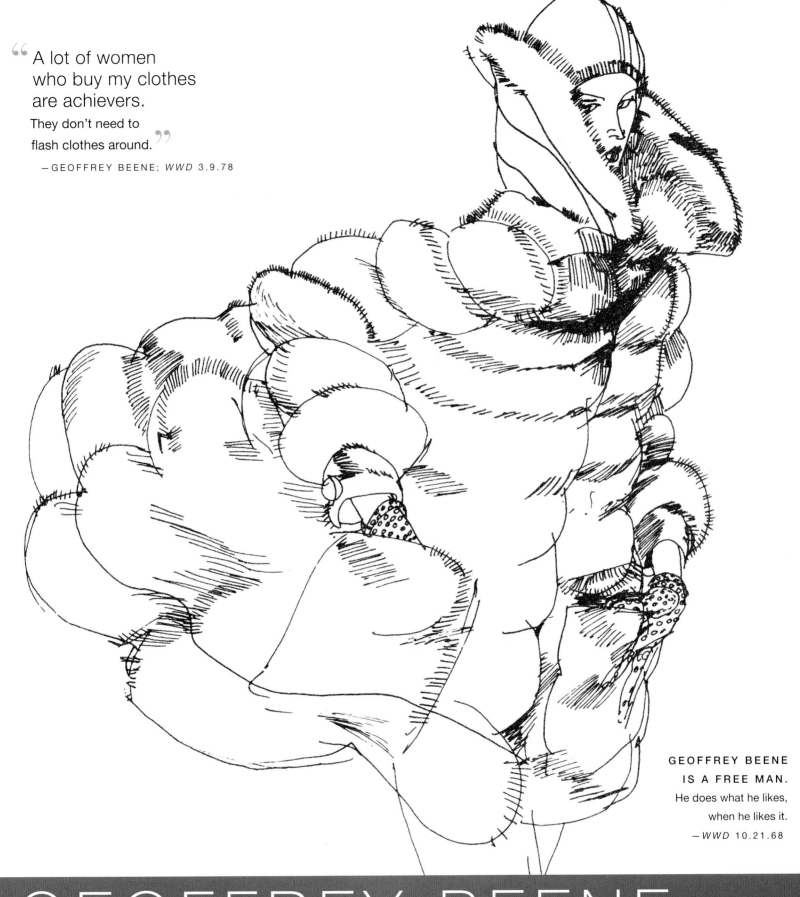

"A lot of women who buy my clothes are achievers. They don't need to flash clothes around."
—GEOFFREY BEENE; *WWD* 3.9.78

GEOFFREY BEENE
IS A FREE MAN.
He does what he likes,
when he likes it.
—*WWD* 10.21.68

GEOFFREY BEENE

1972

BILL BLASS

" To think fashion
should take
one direction
is all wrong.
We've existed for
two decades now
on two looks,
Chanel and Balenciaga.
There should be
several acceptable
ways of dressing.
Maybe the New Look is No Look. "

—BILL BLASS; *WWD* 9.8.64

1972

Mr. Glamor is never better than when he interjects
his Cole Porter-ish sense of romance
into distinctly contemporary,
sporty silhouettes. —WWD 4.29.80

1982

1982

1973

"**Ready-to-wear** is part of general democratization....It's part of a bigger evolution. Couture remains the work of artisans." —MARC BOHAN; *WWD* 1.27.75

1965

1964

1966

Today, Bohan has conquered the fashion world—the **BOHAN FLARE IS EVERYWHERE**— and more to come. —*WWD* 4.27.61

"I make clothes for real women— not for myself, not for mannequins and not for fashion magazines. I gladly leave the abstract creations to others."

—MARC BOHAN;
WWD 1.24.83

MARC BOHAN

1973

IMAGES ON PAGES FOR CHRISTIAN DIOR.

CALLOT
SOEURS

1918

Callot combines the
richest of fabric and embroidery
with lines of formal simplicity. —WWD 9.26.18

1913

1926

1917

1978

1962

1972

> " For me, fabric is nearly secondary. I believe first in shape, architecture, the geometry of a dress. " —PIERRE CARDIN; *WWD* 2.26.79

NUMBER 208---THIS IS THE BEST COAT FROM CARDIN---PINK WITH CAMPY COLLAR

THE HOODED CAPE---LIKE A RUSSIAN "BABA" DOLL---IN SHOCKING PINK WOOL.---OVER PAILLETTED PINK DRESS WITH HUGE BLACK DOTS

BICOLOR WOOL---BEIGE TOP, BROWN BOTTOM---BIAS WAVED CUT---BROOCH IN TOPAZ AND BROWN STONES...BROWN TEXTURED STOCKINGS

WHITE CREPE EVENING SHEATH---FLARING SLEEVES WITH HANDKERCHIEF POINTS---BIG BLACK ROSE

LONG SLEEVED PINK CHIFFON---PURPLE AND RED EMBROIDERED CHOKER AND CUFFS

BLACK SATIN HALTER DRESS---ORGANZA ROSE AT FLOUNCE

BICOLOR DRESS---TURQUOISE TOP, BRONZE BOTTOM---DEEP GREEN STOCKINGS AND SHOES---ENAMEL NECKLACE FROM JEANNE PERAL

1965

PIERRE CARDIN

Geometrics everywhere—
bi-color and tricolor, diamond, circle,
square insets in jackets center
or off-center of skirts and hembands.
Skirts six inches above knee and
those sheer matching, textured stockings.
—PARIS BUREAU, *WWD* 1.31.66

1968

He has done his damnedest to see that as much of the Earth as possible bears in some form his stamp....
his commercial and cultural ventures have reached into **EVERY CORNER OF THE INHABITED WORLD**, including China and the Soviet Union.
—PARIS BUREAU, *WWD* 3.7.85

1951

Carnegie is famous for
her sixth sense of spotting
winning silhouettes
and for her
daring use of color.

— *WWD* 3.11.45

HATTIE CARNEGIE

...ONE OF
THE GREAT
INDIVIDUALISTS
OF THE
FASHION WORLD,
both professionally and personally.

—*WWD* 2.23.56

1941

> "All I want is to speak simply in my designing. I don't want the gilt and the glamour. I don't want to gussy it up."
>
> —BONNIE CASHIN; *WWD* 10.14.64

1969

BONNIE
CASHIN

HER DESIGNS STEM FROM HER PHILOSOPHY OF LIVING—

she doesn't change her ideas, she lets them evolve. "My collections don't reflect the '20s or '30s or '40s. They are for the women living today."

—BONNIE CASHIN; *WWD* 5.4.71

1973

1974

1964

1973

1962

OLEG CASSINI

"I'm an original thinker.

I'm very learned, more than I appear to be.

I am courageous and honest....

I have the kind of wealth that

many other people don't have —

I am pleasing to the opposite sex."

—OLEG CASSINI; *WWD* 7.12.72

1962

"...IT WAS DIGNITY, NOT NOVELTY THAT MRS. KENNEDY WANTED.

The most difficult thing during the whole episode was restraint." —OLEG CASSINI; *WWD* 2.24.64

1965

When I was a young fellow
in Rome…I wanted to go to
America and be a famous designer,
marry a beautiful woman—
a big star maybe—
and to be a millionaire.
All these things came true in the end.
**I HAVE MADE ONLY ONE
MISTAKE IN MY WISH LIST.**
I should have wished
to be a billionaire.

—OLEG CASSINI; *WWD* 5.15.03

1972

> "Fashion in this moment needs color and fantasy. I think people are tired of black, black, black."
>
> —ROBERTO CAVALLI: *WWD* 2.4.98

2010

ROBERTO CAVALLI

The image of the
woman he wants to convey
never changes—
sexy, powerful and
plucky.
—*WWD* 4.13.09

2003

2001

2005

2009

...A DESIGNER KNOWN
FOR HIS EXPERIMENTAL
RUNWAY SHOWS,
replete with mechanical dresses
and LED effects....
— *WWD* 7.30.09

2008

2010

2009

In a season rife with
futuristic gestures, perhaps
no one has
been more forward
thinking than
Hussein Chalayan....
— *WWD* 10.5.06

Trippy, indeed.
—*WWD* 3.8.10

HUSSEIN
CHALAYAN

2007

GABRIELLE CHANEL

CHANEL

CHANEL

1962

1959

Chanel is more
than a look—
it is an institution—it is a
belief and a way of life—
which this clever and very
crafty artiste has done.
She knows that her ever
hungry Fashion Babies
are women and girls who
eat and drink and dance—
and love. —*WWD* 8.2.65

CHANEL

GABRIELLE CHANEL

MLLE. CHANEL IS A VIVACIOUS, ATTRACTIVE BRUNETTE. The travel costume which she wore debarking from the Europa embodies style points which she explained convey HER CURRENT IDEAS FOR DAYTIME. She drew attention to the length of her beige tweed skirt which was about 14 inches from the ground, as a correct version for the suit....Her draped turban of the same fabric as the jacket suit was caught at the right side of the front with large pear-shaped pearl pins....She wore a multi-strand necklace of graduated pearls.

—WWD 3.4.31

1917

1927

1929

1931

1937

THE BEST TIME TO BE A CHANEL-WATCHER IS WHILE SHE IS ACTUALLY MAKING A COLLECTION.
Just when a suit or dress looks perfect to you, Chanel rips off a sleeve, chews out her assistant tailors, reduces the mannequin to tears, and starts all over again. —*WWD* 12.18.69

1958

1959

1960

1966

1977

1983

"When I was designing, I would close my eyes and picture my customer's closet. I would think, 'What does she have in there and what does she need?'... That's the beginning."

—LIZ CLAIBORNE; *WWD* 8.4.86

> "I envision my clothes for working women, although that's not always the case. Actually, they're for **active, young-minded women** who want to put themselves together for under $150."
> —LIZ CLAIBORNE; *WWD* 10.30.76

1971

1970

LIZ CLAIBORNE

Costa sees DESIGN AS AN "INTELLECTUAL RESOLUTION," a place where beauty, society, practicality and service intersect. —WWD 7.28.09

2007

FRANCISCO COSTA

"There's nothing to be reinvented here. We just have to keep bringing the essence of Calvin Klein forward."
—FRANCISCO COSTA;
WWD 9.16.04

2010

2010

" I like simplicity.

In Brazil, life was so simple and everyone was living easily in jeans and T-shirts. There's a great relevance to that in what I do. "

— FRANCISCO COSTA;
WWD 9.13.03

2006

2007

2006

2005

IMAGES ON PAGES FOR CALVIN KLEIN.

ANDRÉ COURRÈGES

COURRÈGES LIFTS SKIRTS to 3 inches above the knee and dares boots for hot summer and evenings. Boots are always white kid with low flat heels just like American cowboy boots in shape. — *WWD* 2.3.64

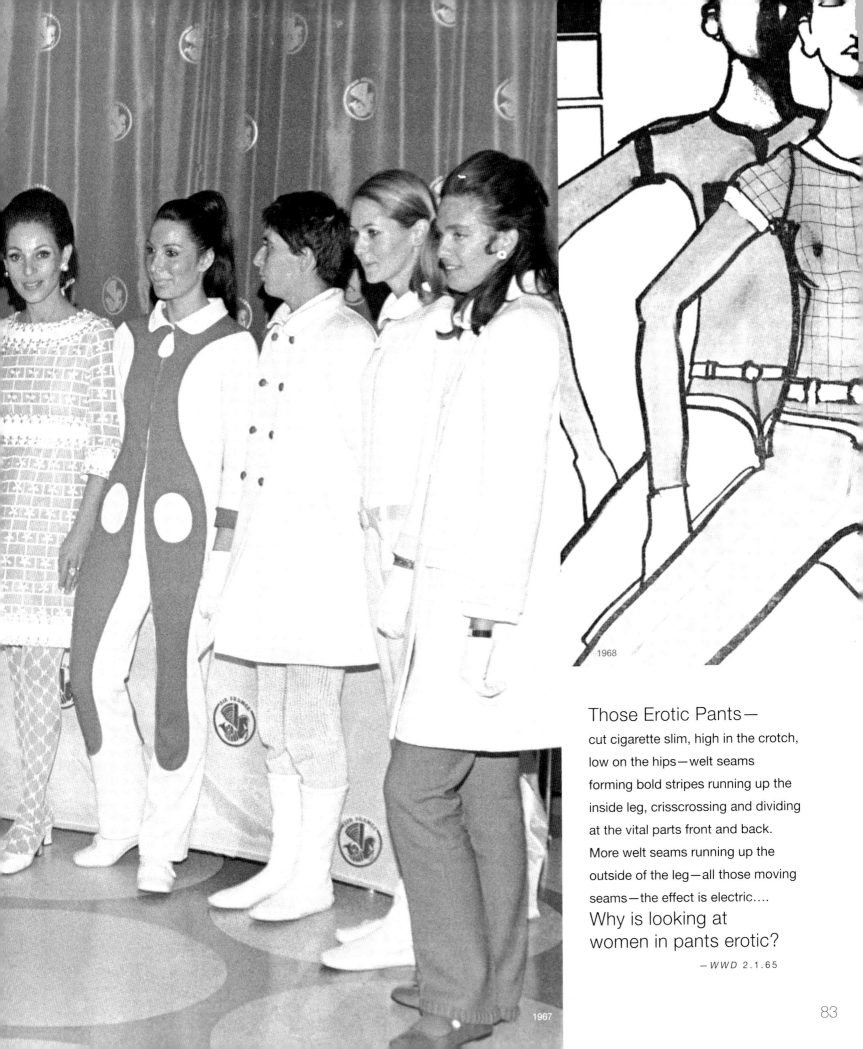

1968

1967

Those Erotic Pants—

cut cigarette slim, high in the crotch,
low on the hips—welt seams
forming bold stripes running up the
inside leg, crisscrossing and dividing
at the vital parts front and back.
More welt seams running up the
outside of the leg—all those moving
seams—the effect is electric....
Why is looking at
women in pants erotic?

—*WWD* 2.1.65

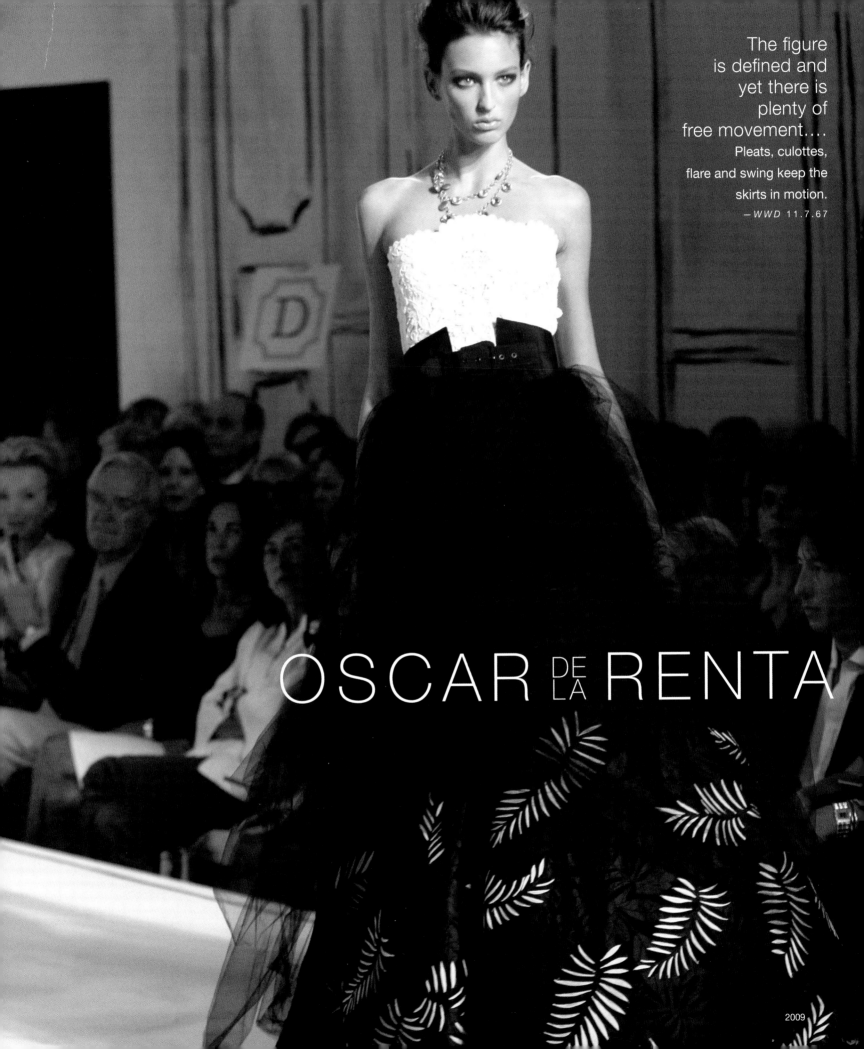

The figure
is defined and
yet there is
plenty of
free movement....
Pleats, culottes,
flare and swing keep the
skirts in motion.
— *WWD* 11.7.67

OSCAR DE LA RENTA

2009

A slim, elegant young man, whose 32nd birthday is coming up next month, Oscar de la Renta is one of the most popular escorts in town. He turned up at almost every ball and opening last winter. "I feel I have to see what people are wearing and what they need," he said.

— *WWD 6.10.65*

OSCAR DE LA RENTA

2010

"IT'S NOT FASHION when it's on the runway; it's only fashion when it's on the woman's back."

—OSCAR DE LA RENTA; *WWD* 10.3.95

2008

"There are two classes of designers — those who make such a strong impact on a certain period that it's difficult to get out of it, and the survivors. I like to think I'm a survivor."

—OSCAR DE LA RENTA; *WWD* 4.3.79

2010

2009

Dior firmly believes,

"You can't make women wear something they don't want—

but you must feel what they are tired of— what they want to wear even though women themselves may not be aware of it."

—PARIS BUREAU, *WWD* 1.2.57

1950

1947

The new silhouettes are
elegant and wearable.
The "corolle" or corolla line
is newest for it lengthens skirts to
cover midcalf for daytime and nearly
reaches ankle for restaurant dining
but gives bell fullness to skirts. Many
are apparently slightly stiffened to
hold the crisp rounded outlines;
even when pleated, accentuating the
hips below ultra-slim waists.

—PARIS BUREAU, *WWD* 2.13.47

CHRISTIAN
DIOR

A man who started out to be a
diplomat heads an around-the-world
fashion producing organization.
A MAN WHO CONSIDERS
FRIDAY UNLUCKY, DISLIKES
ODD NUMBERS AND
BELIEVES EVEN NUMBERS,
PARTICULARLY 8,
BRING HIM GOOD FORTUNE,
has determined more than any other
single figure, the way women dress in
countries of three different continents.

—*WWD* 7.14.53

Stefano, the savvy northerner, and Domenico, the smoldering southerner, have a single vision of Italian sensuality.... "The sexiness in our clothes comes from showing the woman's shape."

—DOMENICO DOLCE;
WWD 12.1.96

DOLCE & GABBANA

2010

"We're not about minimalism.
We're massimalismo."

—STEFANO GABBANA; *WWD* 9.30.05

2009

"Luckily, there are two of us," quipped Gabbana. Indeed, with a great-minds-think-alike approach,
THE TWO ARE PERFECTLY COMPLEMENTARY. — *WWD* 12.03.07

2000   2005   2003   2001

2006   2004

> " Lanvin was all about cut,
> all about detail, all about beauty.
> Also, there was a sense of fragility.
> The clothes had
> something that was
> very emotional. "
>
> —ALBER ELBAZ; *WWD* 3.6.02

2007   2008

"When it comes to fashion,
we are still stuck on two words:
sexy and glamour. And I ask
whether sexy can be smart.
CAN WE INTRODUCE SMART
DESIGN TO FASHION?"
—ALBER ELBAZ; *WWD* 11.12.08

ALBER ELBAZ

IMAGES ON PAGES FOR LANVIN.

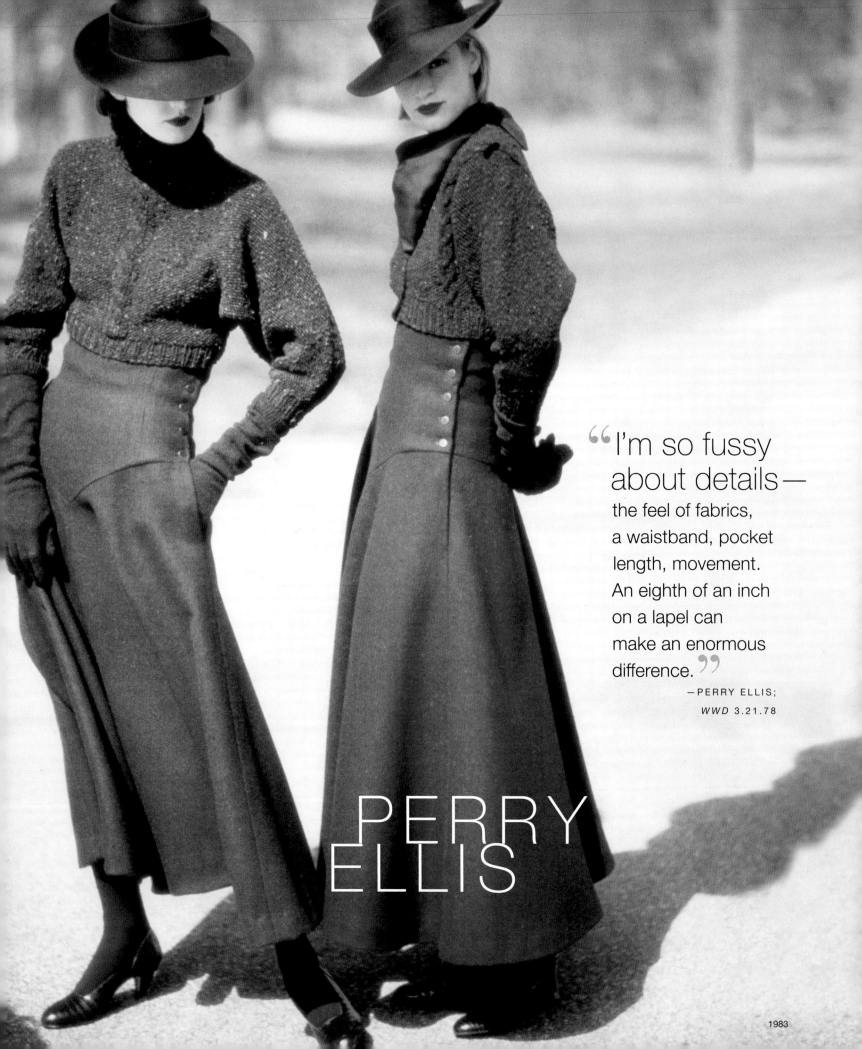

"I'm so fussy about details— the feel of fabrics, a waistband, pocket length, movement. An eighth of an inch on a lapel can make an enormous difference."
—PERRY ELLIS;
WWD 3.21.78

PERRY ELLIS

1983

"We all change and evolve, thank God....
I HAVE A MATURITY AND A CONFIDENCE THAT FEELS GOOD."
—PERRY ELLIS;
WWD 4.9.86

1982

1986

Ellis always flirts with a range of saucy new proportions.
—*WWD* 11.11.83

1981   1978   1979

Jacques Fath calls his silhouette
"the column line."

—PARIS BUREAU, *WWD* 7.28.50

His clothes
continue to fit snugly
over the midriff,
define the waist sharply,
and curve the bust...and
many of the prettiest dresses
have fine gather drapes
for further accent, or deep front
necklines filled in with drapes.

—*WWD* 8.2.54

1949

Jacques Fath put his collection under the sign of the 18th Century, believing that women are tired of uniforms,
seeking femininity and ESCAPE FROM WARTIME AUSTERITY. —*WWD* 9.7.45

1954

1957

JACQUES FATH

...his influence
is clearly evident
all over Milan. — *WWD* 3.18.82

FERRÉ'S CLOTHES
ARE MEANT FOR
A STRONG WOMAN.
His signatures are sleekly
sculptured silhouettes—
often marked with such
details as big bows at the
neck or obi belts—
and stunningly simple
white blouses.
— *WWD* 5.8.89

> " It is not difficult to identify, in the various collections over the years, **my love of the figurative arts, the great classical painters....** The references to worlds and cultures I have experienced personally.... "
> —GIANFRANCO FERRÉ;
> *WWD* 6.18.07

1990

1990

1990

GIANFRANCO FERRÉ

IMAGES ON PAGES FOR GIANFRANCO FERRÉ AND CHRISTIAN DIOR.

2003

"I don't *do* vulnerable."

—TOM FORD; *WWD* 6.5.97

2004

2003

"Hollywood is now more influential in fashion than New York or Europe."

—TOM FORD; *WWD* 6.5.97

TOM
FORD

Many industry observers
cite Gucci's creative director,
Tom Ford, as
**THE ARCHETYPE OF A
MODERN DESIGNER
WHO CAN BALANCE
BUSINESS AND BUZZ.**
He not only designs headline-generating
collections, he is said to pore
over sales reports daily and visit
Gucci stores frequently, engineering
the image at all levels to drive sales.
— *WWD* 2.18.99

2003

IMAGES ON PAGES FOR GUCCI AND YVES SAINT LAURENT.

His evening dresses...look **clean, classic and simple.** But, each is a masterpiece of detail.

—*WWD* 2.7.72

1961

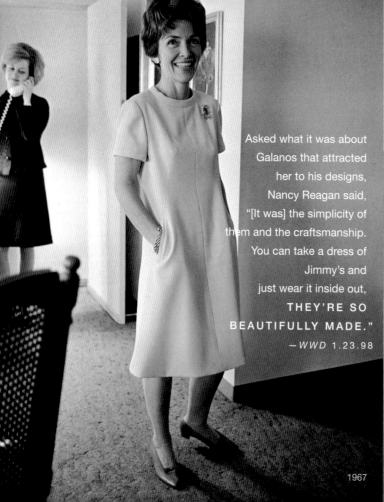

Asked what it was about Galanos that attracted her to his designs, Nancy Reagan said, "[It was] the simplicity of them and the craftsmanship. You can take a dress of Jimmy's and just wear it inside out, **THEY'RE SO BEAUTIFULLY MADE."**

—*WWD* 1.23.98

1967   1967

Love of classic simplicity with emphasis on the bodice and hipline (like the torso definition in Grecian statuary) can be considered inherent with this designer who is of Greek parentage.

—*WWD* 4.21.54

JAMES GALANOS

Too Elegant

.... because a woman must attain this look. They are not pretty sweet little clothes — they are a challenge to a woman to look this way... only the Fashion Intellectual and the trained eye can see this cut and the details... you must feel these clothes... how the clothes are put together is the news.

1963

1963

JOHN GALLIANO

Season after season, he offers
spellbinding proof...
of fashion's ability to transport....

— WWD 7.8.03

2002

2004

2005

2004

2008

IMAGES ON PAGES FOR JOHN GALLIANO AND CHRISTIAN DIOR.

Imagine a child trying to recreate the pleasures of a holiday carnival with backyard ingenuity. Now imagine the child has **the vision and talent of an artist, all still unfettered by convention.**

— *WWD* 3.6.00

2009

" I do have the discipline. **Maybe it's that my appearance is a bit wild.** "

— JOHN GALLIANO;
WWD 5.23.95

JOHN GALLIANO

2010

"It is important to work with old techniques and use them as a springboard toward the future. I see that as a return to **GLAMOUR AND CONSTRUCTION.** Otherwise, we'll lose all of that tradition."
—JOHN GALLIANO;
WWD 6.13.94

2010

2010   2010

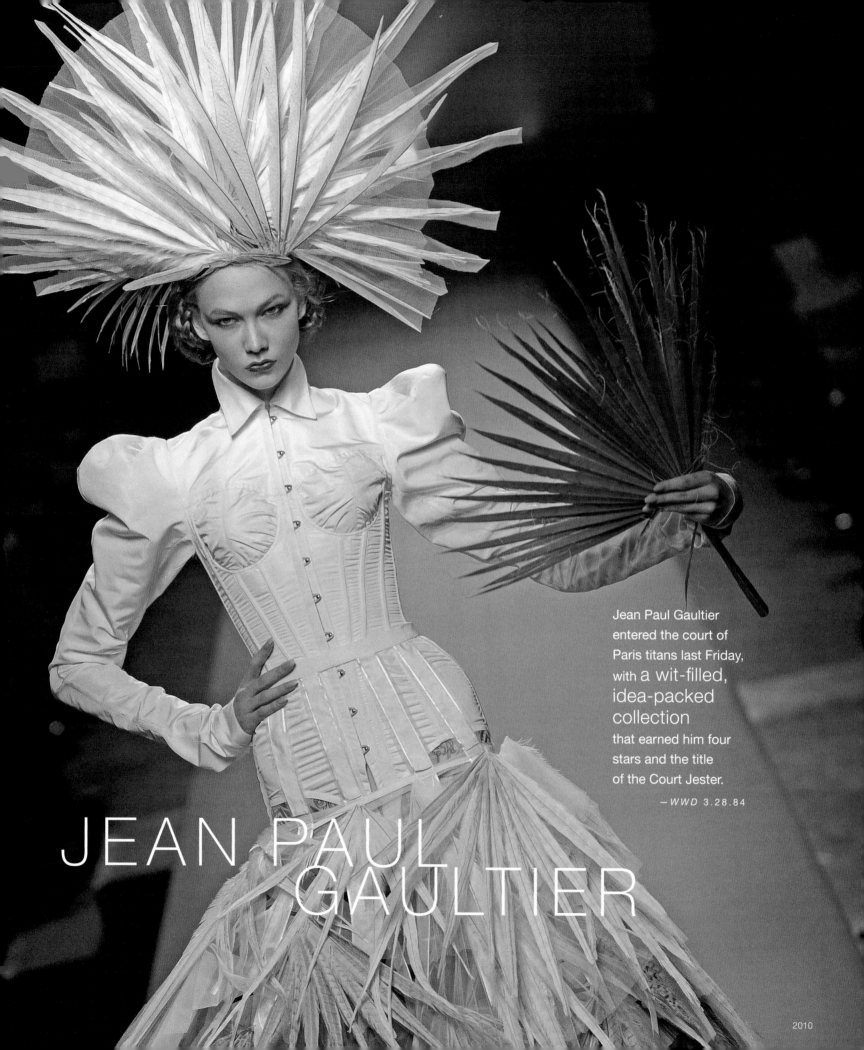

Jean Paul Gaultier entered the court of Paris titans last Friday, with a wit-filled, idea-packed collection that earned him four stars and the title of the Court Jester.

—*WWD* 3.28.84

JEAN PAUL GAULTIER

2010

2002

2010

2010

He's done corsets and lingerie for day and put men in skirts,
earning him the title of FRENCH FASHION'S BAD BOY.
But...the 54-year-old designer is—like any true rebel—
still resisting labels. "I am no longer the 'enfant terrible.'
My age indicates it clearly."
—JEAN PAUL GAULTIER; *WWD* 9.8.06

Jean Paul
Gaultier
loves to
mix it up....
—*WWD* 3.20.92

2009

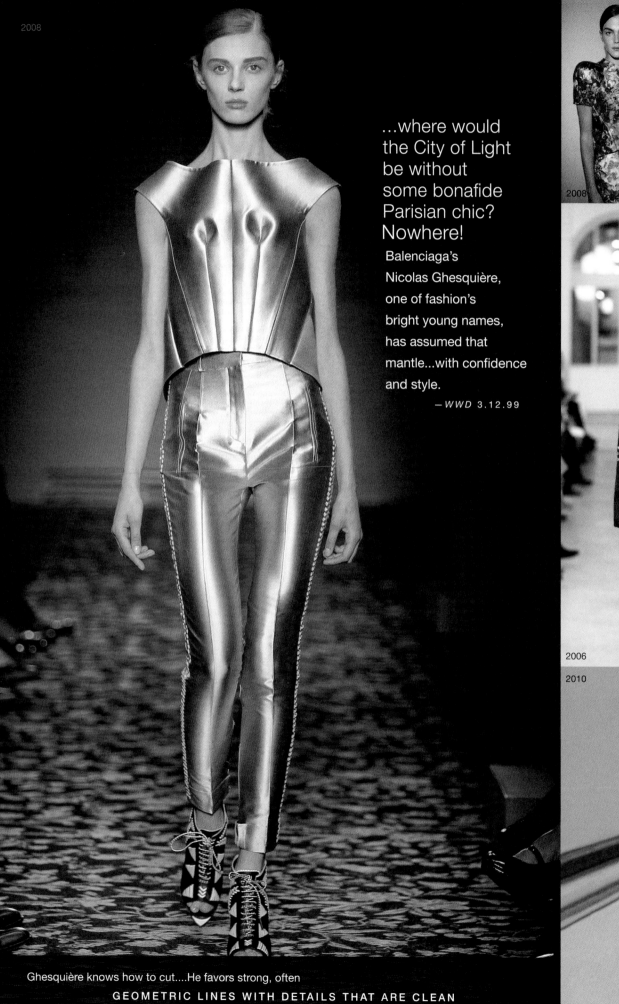

2008

...where would
the City of Light
be without
some bonafide
Parisian chic?
Nowhere!
Balenciaga's
Nicolas Ghesquière,
one of fashion's
bright young names,
has assumed that
mantle...with confidence
and style.

—*WWD* 3.12.99

2008   2006

2006

2010

Ghesquière knows how to cut....He favors strong, often

GEOMETRIC LINES WITH DETAILS THAT ARE CLEAN
BUT SOMETIMES FLAMBOYANT. —*WWD* 3.17.98

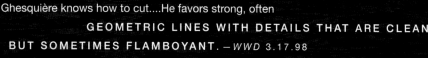

"You have to try until it looks perfect. What is very important at Balenciaga is the perfectionism and the innovation."

—NICOLAS GHESQUIÈRE;
WWD 11.16.05

IMAGES ON PAGES FOR BALENCIAGA.

2008

NICOLAS GHESQUIÈRE

"I applied the same technique
I used for the accessories—
finding new icons and
mining the archives for
prints and color schemes,
obviously reinterpreted
**TO CREATE A
MOOD BASED ON
INNOVATION AND
TRADITION.**"
— FRIDA GIANNINI;
WWD 6.5.06

...it seems the
Gucci Girl
is turning down
her dosage of
**high-voltage
sexuality,**
and perhaps not
taking herself
quite so seriously.
—*WWD* 6.14.05

FRIDA GIANNINI

IMAGES ON PAGES FOR GUCCI.

2010

2010 2007

" I would like to imagine a woman who can play with her life, but always sophisticated and rich because obviously we are still Gucci. " —FRIDA GIANNINI; *WWD* 6.14.05

2008

2009 2010

1974

"I still believe above all in elegance...."
—HUBERT DE GIVENCHY; *WWD* 1.13.70

Hubert de Givenchy's clothes have the chic which comes from **handsome fabrics and cleancut lines....**
—*WWD* 2.4.53

1954   1958

1976

AUDREY HEPBURN
AND HUBERT DE
GIVENCHY...
AN UNBEATABLE
FASHION TEAM....
—*WWD* 6.23.61

date?

HUBERT DE
GIVENCHY

Her clothes have a kind of **subtle sexiness** that restores women to adult status.
— PARIS BUREAU, *WWD* 1.29.68

Tight, fine drapings which have a classical grace and call for a wearer with a figure as faultless as a Grecian goddess continue to be favorites with Mademoiselle Alix.
— *WWD* 3.27.36

1977

1960

Grès does not work
with patterns or toiles,
but still cuts directly
on the fabric,
**EASING, TWISTING,
SOMETIMES
TORTURING IT**
into singular constructions
that are never à la mode,
but never démodé.

— *WWD* 8.12.77

ALIX GRÈS

1966

"One thing I know for sure, sexy sells." —HALSTON; *WWD* 1.3.77

HALSTON

The undisputed **MR. CLEAN** of American fashion....
—*WWD* 9.30.81

1975

Halston takes
a look, believes
in it strongly
enough to do it
over and over and
still makes
you want to
see more.
—*WWD* 6.6.69

1981

1973

He loves the
BARE LOOK....
—*WWD* 5.24.72

1975

CAROLINA
HERRERA

She describes her point of view as
"very feminine with a
certain chic; classic
in a modern way."

—WWD 3.2.87

1992

1987

2011

She doesn't
stint on details
in clothes that are
replete with discreet
curves, ruffles and
wickedly feminine bows.

— *WWD* 8.16.83

2007

1989

...VERY
SOCIABLE
clothes....

— *WWD* 8.18.86

Welcome
to Tommy's world.

— *WWD* 12.16.99

2009

2003

66 Young people
are global thinkers.
They watch the same MTV,
drink the same
Coca-Cola, listen to the
same music, use the same
Internet—and buy **99**
the same Tommy Hilfiger....

— TOMMY HILFIGER; *WWD* 7.16.99

2002

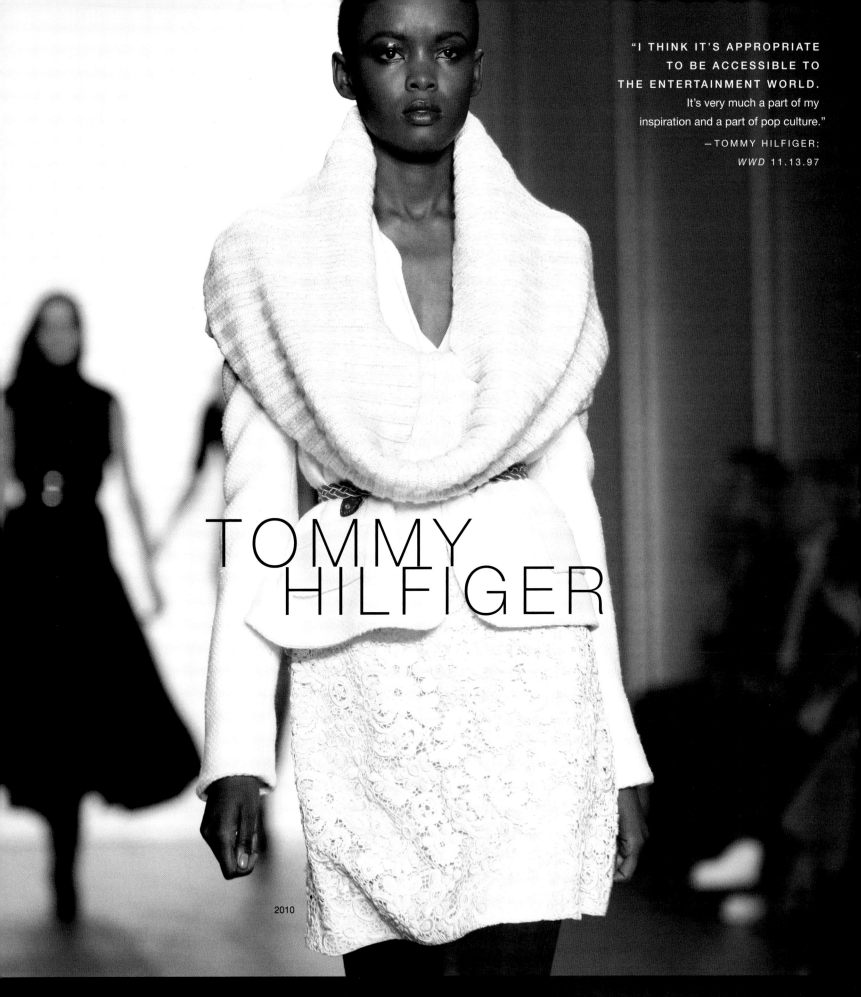

"I THINK IT'S APPROPRIATE TO BE ACCESSIBLE TO THE ENTERTAINMENT WORLD. It's very much a part of my inspiration and a part of pop culture."
—TOMMY HILFIGER; *WWD* 11.13.97

TOMMY HILFIGER

2010

"THIS ENTIRE BUSINESS IS ABOUT EVOLUTION. It's continually changing. One has to be very aware of what is going on in the world, in my particular case, in pop culture, in music, art and film." — TOMMY HILFIGER; *WWD* 10.23.98

"You make
it new somehow;
you make her want to buy it,
whether you do it with
humor, color or texture. "
—MARC JACOBS; *WWD* 4.4.88

MARC JACOBS

IMAGES ON PAGES FOR MARC JACOBS AND LOUIS VUITTON.

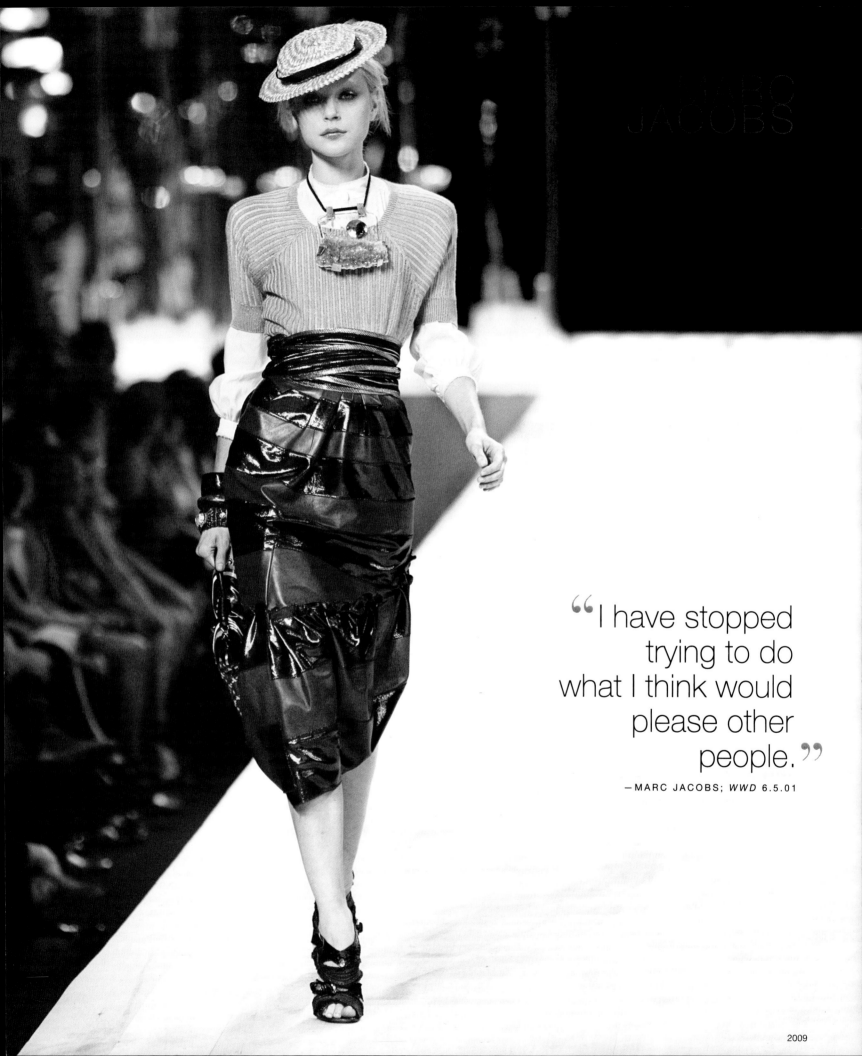

"I have stopped
trying to do
what I think would
please other
people."

— MARC JACOBS; *WWD* 6.5.01

...Jacobs has consistently
made some of
the most luxe clothes
anywhere, clothes
that can tread both sides
of the taste divide,
but are almost always
**intriguing
and exquisitely
beautiful.**

—*WWD* 4.1.96

1985

2009   2010

The long fitted bodices, the longer skirts, and taffeta afternoon frocks which have been seen in Charles James models for several years, are evident again....

—*WWD* 6.12.47

1951

CHARLES JAMES

"The couturier is the author, the manufacturer is the publisher.
But in America, the manufacturer often presumes to be both."
—CHARLES JAMES; *WWD* 5.27.63

1944

1946

1948

That very special something about the cut is achieved without darts to give a **tiny look to the body from the shoulder to midriff.**

—*WWD* 12.22.65

2006

2002

2001

66 It's the young people who are the best designers today...

the kids who put it all together themselves. 99

—BETSEY JOHNSON; *WWD* 2.18.69

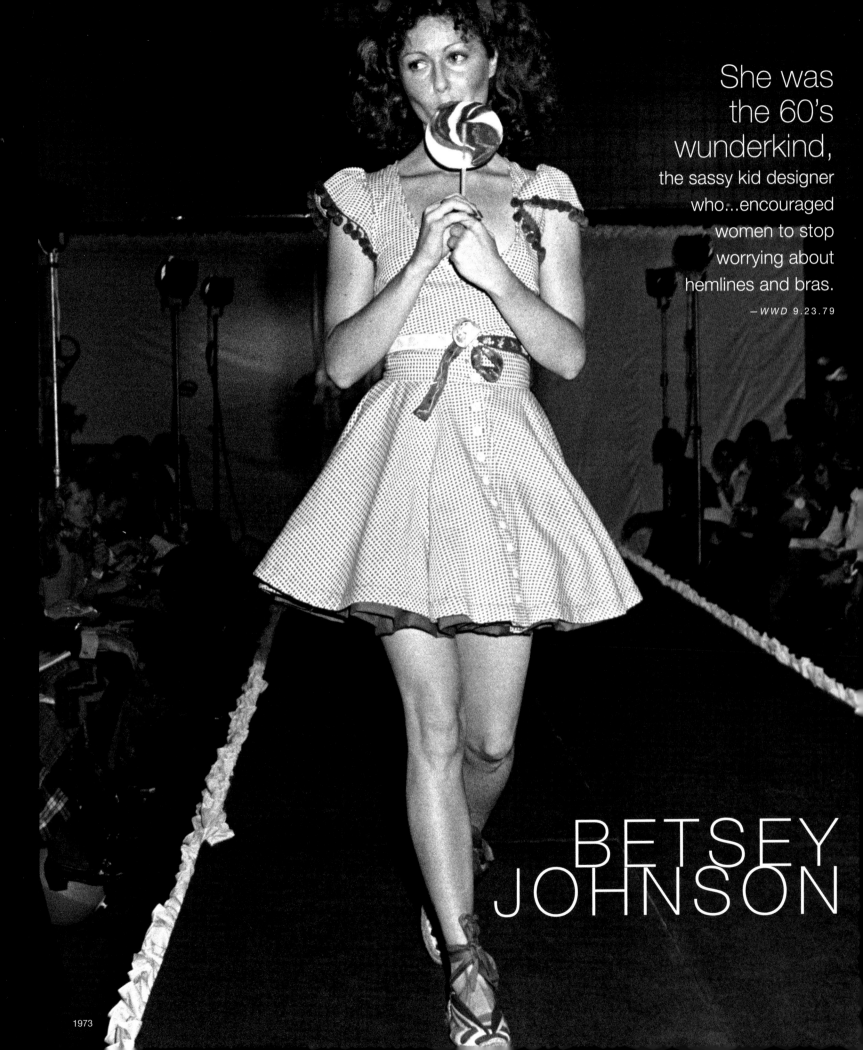

She was
the 60's
wunderkind,
the sassy kid designer
who...encouraged
women to stop
worrying about
hemlines and bras.

—WWD 9.23.79

BETSEY
JOHNSON

1973

66 I don't care whether people love it or hate
I want them to react. 99
— NORMA KAMALI, *WWD* 2.24.82

"The fitting process
is very long and very
tedious, but for me
it's the most important
part of designing,
because HOW
CLOTHES DRAPE
AND FEEL ON
THE BODY is what is
important in the end."
— NORMA KAMALI;
WWD 10.28.85

1976

1981

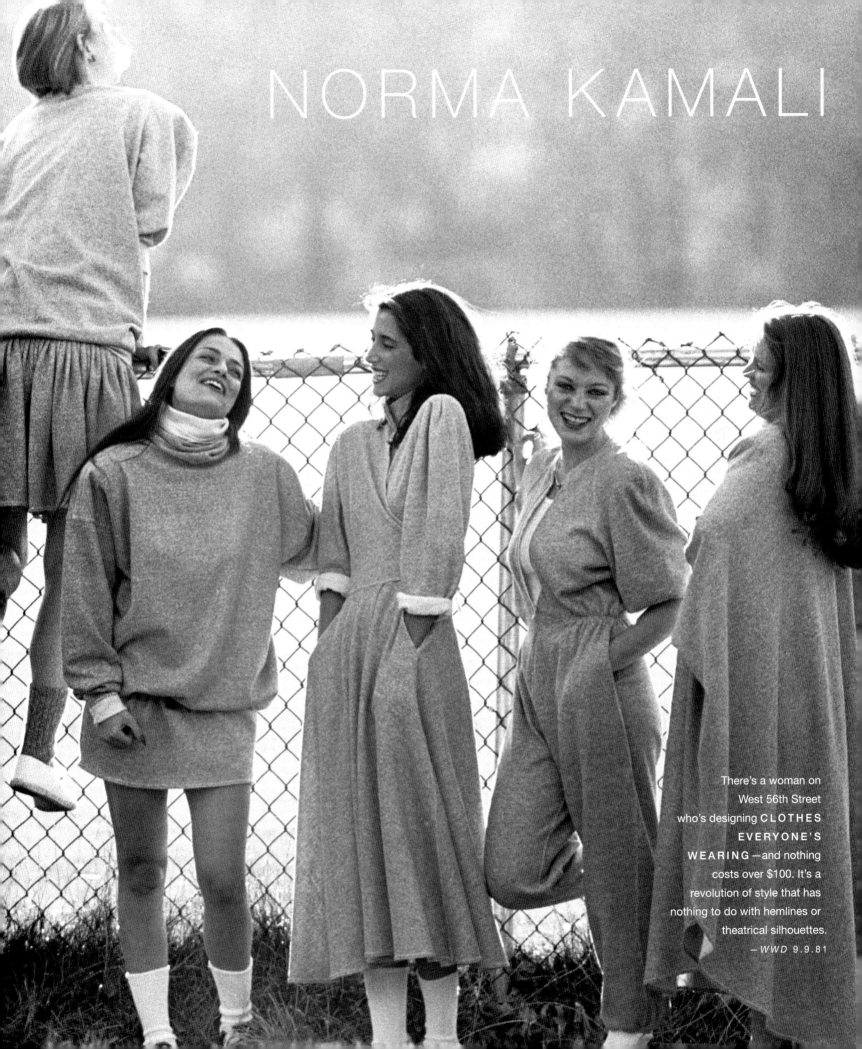

NORMA KAMALI

There's a woman on West 56th Street who's designing CLOTHES EVERYONE'S WEARING—and nothing costs over $100. It's a revolution of style that has nothing to do with hemlines or theatrical silhouettes.

—*WWD* 9.9.81

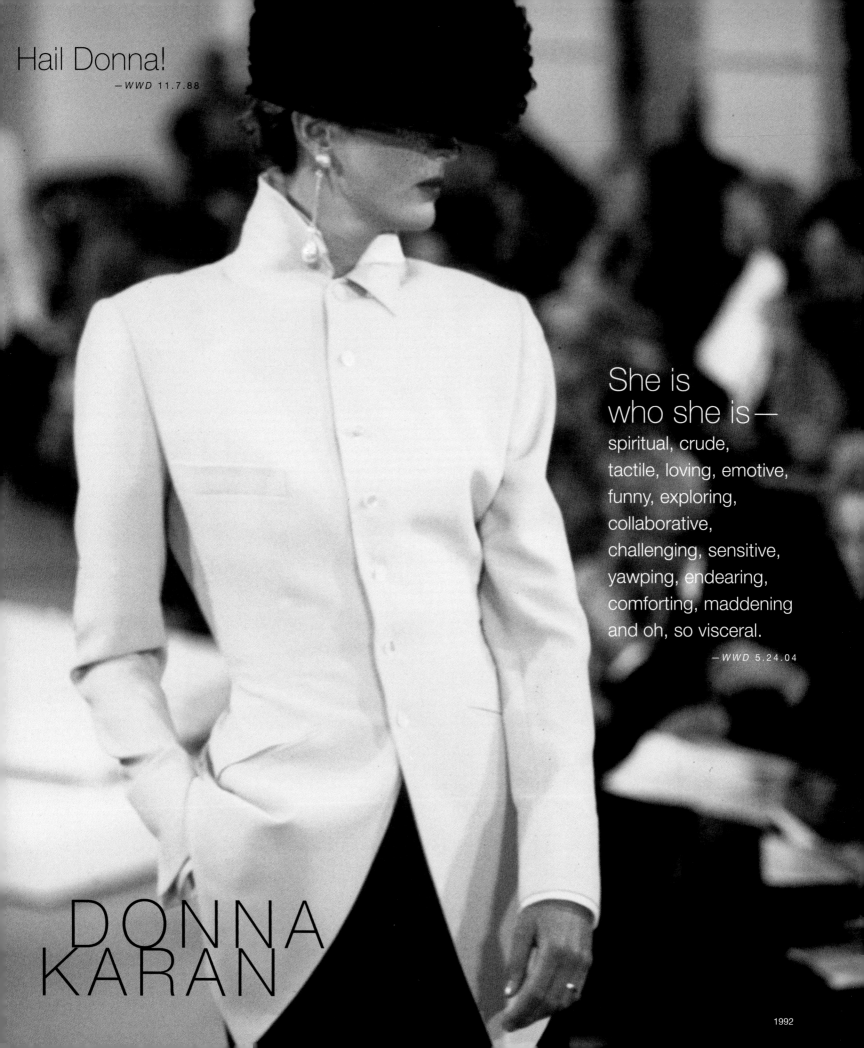

Hail Donna!
—WWD 11.7.88

She is
who she is—
spiritual, crude,
tactile, loving, emotive,
funny, exploring,
collaborative,
challenging, sensitive,
yawping, endearing,
comforting, maddening
and oh, so visceral.

—WWD 5.24.04

DONNA
KARAN

1992

" I see my customer as I see myself....
I will design only clothes and
accessories that I myself would wear. "

—DONNA KARAN; *WWD* 10.31.84

2010

1986

1989

With its center of gravity based on the bodysuit—until now a not very
intriguing piece of fashion outside of exercise class—
KARAN HAS PARED DOWN A WOMAN'S WARDROBE....

—*WWD* 7.10.85

"I find simple shapes more refreshing. I like to balance the softness with the severe."
—REI KAWAKUBO;
WWD 12.6.85

2009

2010

"You have
to know
me through
my clothes."
—REI KAWAKUBO;
WWD 3.19.82

REI KAWAKUBO

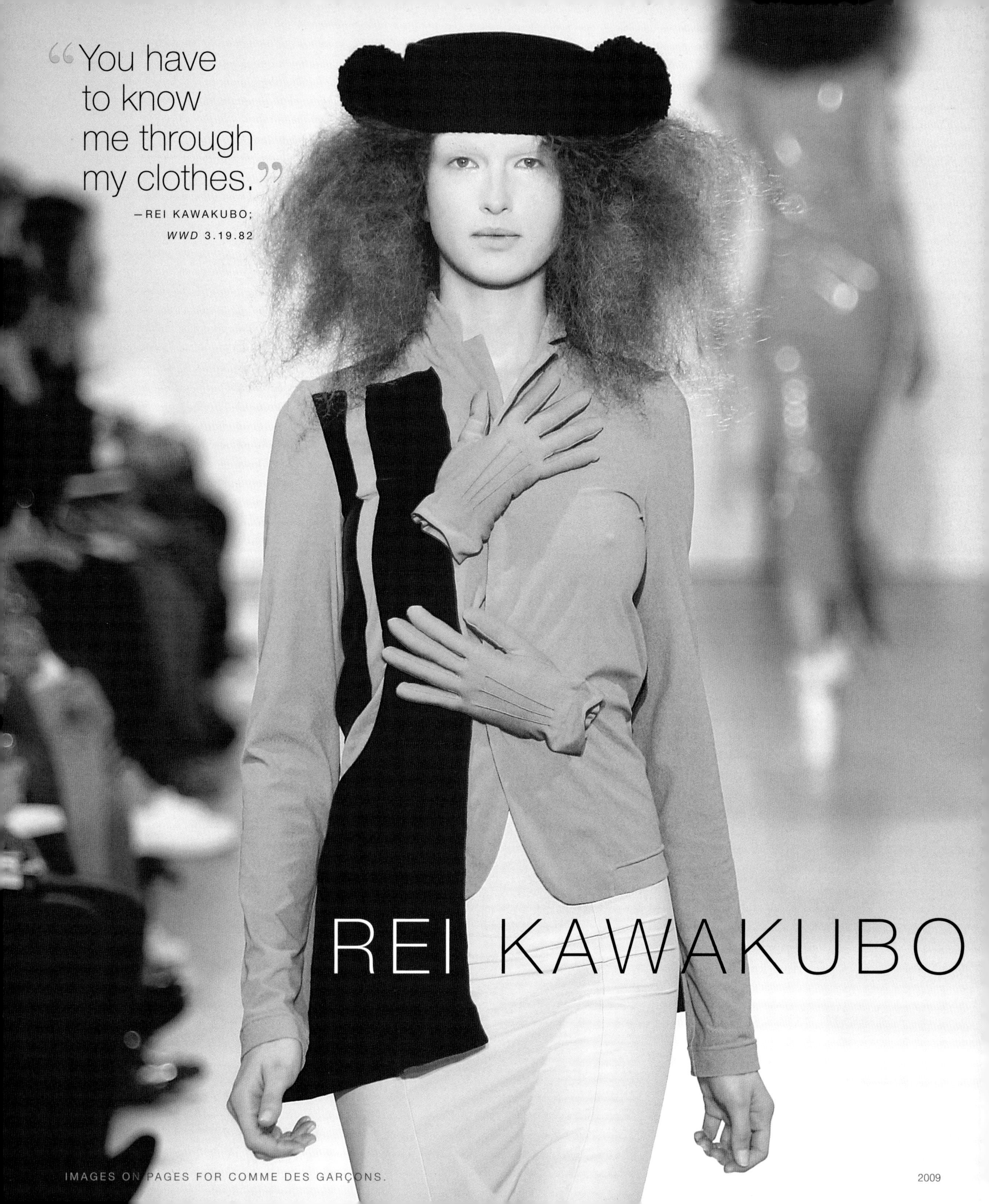

Anne starts with
color that
is dramatic and
uncompromising...
and builds a story
that is threaded
throughout the collection.
— WWD 9.19.73

ANNE
KLEIN

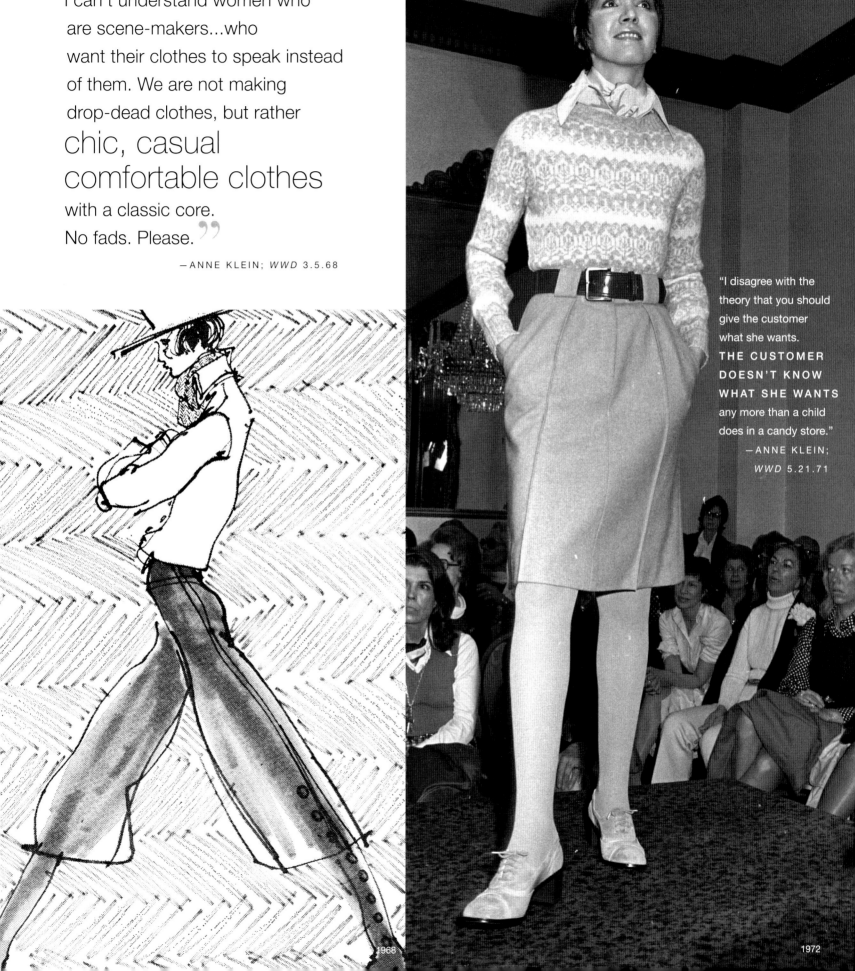

"I can't understand women who are scene-makers...who want their clothes to speak instead of them. We are not making drop-dead clothes, but rather **chic, casual comfortable clothes** with a classic core. No fads. Please."

—ANNE KLEIN; *WWD* 3.5.68

"I disagree with the theory that you should give the customer what she wants. **THE CUSTOMER DOESN'T KNOW WHAT SHE WANTS** any more than a child does in a candy store."

—ANNE KLEIN; *WWD* 5.21.71

1968

1972

Calvin Klein
may stand
on neutral
ground when
it comes
to color,
but not when it
comes to shape....
And the shapes
[his fabric] takes
are decidedly
**loose, easy
and soft.**
— *WWD* 8.12.77

1981

CALVIN
KLEIN

1982

1997

The current
watchwords
in Klein's conversation
about his clothes
are pure, simple
and clean—
words you may
remember from
descriptions of the
collections
that made his name.

—*WWD* 8.8.83

1991

1992

"WHAT WE'RE SELLING IS AN IMAGE, AN ATTITUDE....

I just want the image to be consistent in all markets."

—CALVIN KLEIN; *WWD* 8.9.82

Calvin's clothes
are real—no color
gymnastics, no fuss,
no backward glances.
He just keeps
**redefining
the meaning
of spare.**
—*WWD* 10.31.90

CALVIN KLEIN

1987

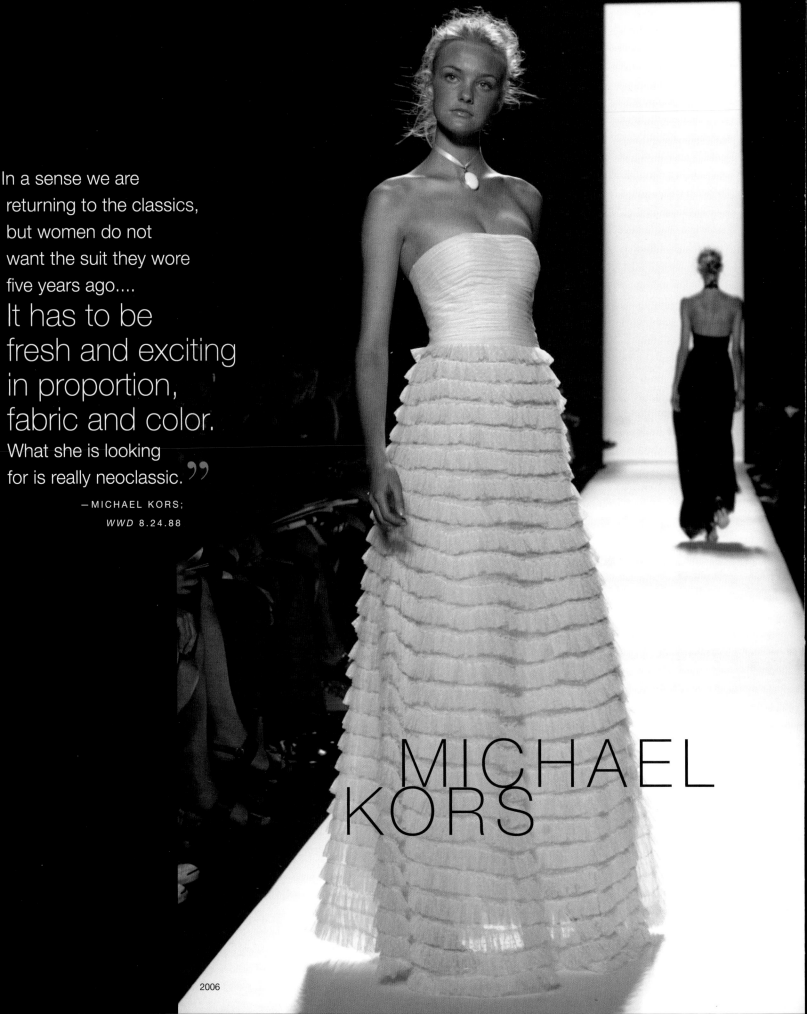

In a sense we are returning to the classics, but women do not want the suit they wore five years ago.... It has to be fresh and exciting in proportion, fabric and color. What she is looking for is really neoclassic. "

—MICHAEL KORS;
WWD 8.24.88

MICHAEL KORS

2006

Kors promises a decidedly
"PARK AVENUE
COLLECTION"....
— *WWD* 3.30.90

His customer
is a city gal
at heart....
— *WWD* 9.21.01

2009   2010

Christian Lacroix hit the ball out of the park Sunday with his first couture collection under his own name. France and the world of fashion have a new star— no question— Christian Lacroix.

—*WWD* 7.27.87

CHRISTIAN LACROIX

HIS PALETTE ranges from the ripest raspberries, banana yellows and sunbaked oranges and reds to the palest pinks and blues....floral and lace prints, polkadot and stripe mixes and enough seashells, straw and fish **TO RIVAL THE RIVIERA ITSELF.**

— WWD 1.25.88

Christian Lacroix, author of fun couture, will introduce **THE NEW POUF** at his Patou show on Monday....

— WWD 1.23.87

1987

2009

2009

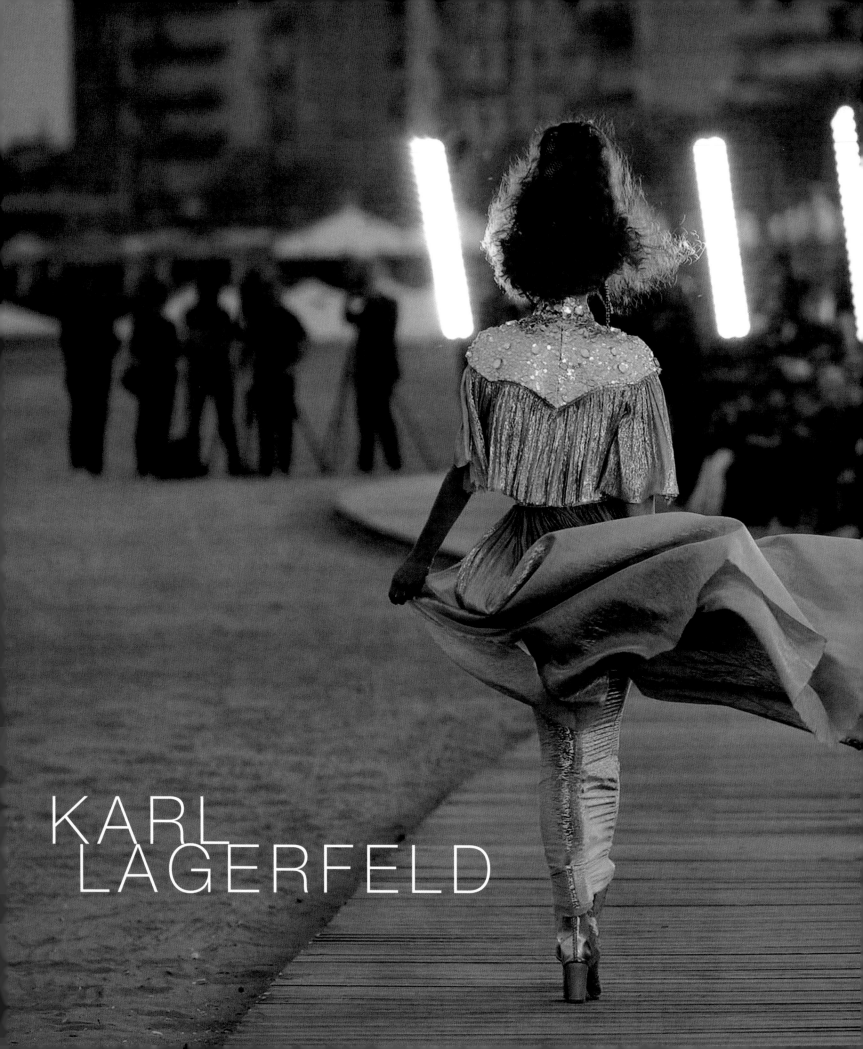

KARL
LAGERFELD

And what was the moment
of his greatest triumph?
"The greatest day, I hope,
is still ahead of me."

—KARL LAGERFELD; *WWD* 11.20.91

2010

"For me,
every collection
is a first
collection....
I take what the
Germans call
the zeitgeist and
cook it my way
but not sitting
down saying we
do this, this and
this. I improvise,
let's try this,
let's do this."
—KARL LAGERFELD;
WWD 11.17.03

2009

2010

2010

2008

1983

"Of course I like—
shall we say—
ECCENTRIC
THINGS FROM TIME
TO TIME.
But I strongly believe
in a mode that can actually
be worn."
—KARL LAGERFELD;
WWD 9.23.77

He used to be The Kaiser.
Now he's le Roi.
Karl Lagerfeld is the master of the couture milieu.

—*WWD* 7.8.05

IMAGES ON PAGES FOR FENDI, KARL LAGERFELD AND CHANEL.

KARL LAGERFELD

2009

The hype and glory around Helmut Lang have been swelling for seasons, and now, **the cult has gone mainstream.**

—WWD 3.15.96

HELMUT LANG

2004

...the designer's message of understated elegance with an edge is quite clear. "Everything out there is either too mainstream or too elaborate. I am not trying to create fashion label pieces. I just want to create the right pieces in the right colors and shapes."

—HELMUT LANG; *WWD* 9.13.99

2001

2010

2003

EVERYONE IN FASHION KNOWS HIM AS A MASTER OF MODERNITY, one of the two or three most copied designers of the Nineties. The early rubber dresses, the techno fabrics, the stretchy Ts— all started on his runway....

—*WWD* 7.17.98

Buyers considered the
Lanvin collection this season
not only one of the
best ever displayed by that
house, but one of
the best ever
seen in Paris.

—*WWD* 4.1.15

1936

1936

Jeanne Lanvin is a name which means big business in the French Haute Couture....To have built up a business of such importance...
argues something of EXECUTIVE GENIUS, and this is the effect produced by meeting her....
She has the simple direct manner of people who do not have to pretend to be important.   —*WWD* 7.3.31

All the world
knows her
**delightful
period
frocks....**
—WWD 7.3.31

1936

1936

JEANNE LANVIN

RALPH LAUREN

The combination of
mythic possibility
and business brilliance
has made Lauren
**indisputably
the most
successful
designer in
the history
of American
fashion.**
— *WWD* 5.14.02

2009

RALPH LAUREN

> "What I stand for is **quality and timelessness.** The clothes are not about nostalgia, not about yesterday; they're about forever."
> —RALPH LAUREN; *WWD* 1.15.92

1989

> "I felt there was a
> **SERIOUS NEED FOR...
> TAILORING
> AND QUALITY**
> in the women's apparel field
> and that I could contribute
> something significant...."
> —RALPH LAUREN;
> *WWD* 11.8.72

2007

2009

1984

Ralph Lauren is
pure
American
Fantasy.

—*WWD* 4.24.78

2009

Mainbocher, the
great American
couturier, has
a unique
concept.
It is to make each of
his designs a
gold-edged security:
expensive at first,
but built to stay
at the peak of style
practically forever.

—WWD 4.22.56

MAINBOCHER

The Mainbocher opening
was given special
news interest by the fact
that the DUCHESS
OF WINDSOR, who is
still the number one lady
in the news, was a guest
of honor at his premiere.
Mainbocher has
consistently created
clothes for the beautifully
groomed duchess....

—WWD 10.28.37

1936

1947

1947

1942

1942

> "Don't let the fun of designing make you forget there is a war on. Make the most beautiful, functional dresses you know how.... **Simplicity more than ever before** in the whole of history of the world is the essence of being well dressed."
>
> —MAINBOCHER;
> *WWD* 2.28.45

Margiela obviously
wants his audience
to be as
**FASCINATED
WITH THE
PROCESS OF
CONSTRUCTION**
as he is.
—*WWD* 10.16.97

2006

MARTIN MARGIELA

IMAGES ON PAGES FOR HERMÈS AND MAISON MARTIN MARGIELA.

2007

Martin Margiela, the media-averse designer, has dueling reputations as a retail sell-through star and a journalist's migraine. He refuses to be photographed or interviewed face-to-face—he claims that **he wants the clothes to do the talking** and grab the spotlight, not his persona.

—*WWD* 9.13.99

2009

2007

2007   2010

Her own
wardrobe reflects
her adventurous
approach to
new ideas and,
on several occasions
to our knowledge,
it has aided and
abetted the adoption
of new fashions.
— WWD 11.14.40

1943

1941

1941

CLAIRE McCARDELL

The sashes, ties and strings that are her signature have been **the secret of making the Empire adjustable,** something that can be fitted properly.

—*WWD* 4.18.56

F201

1943

...McCartney has been credited with bringing new luster and buzz to the Paris-based house and attracting a new generation of customers with **her hip, cheeky approach to fashion.**
—*WWD* 2.28.01

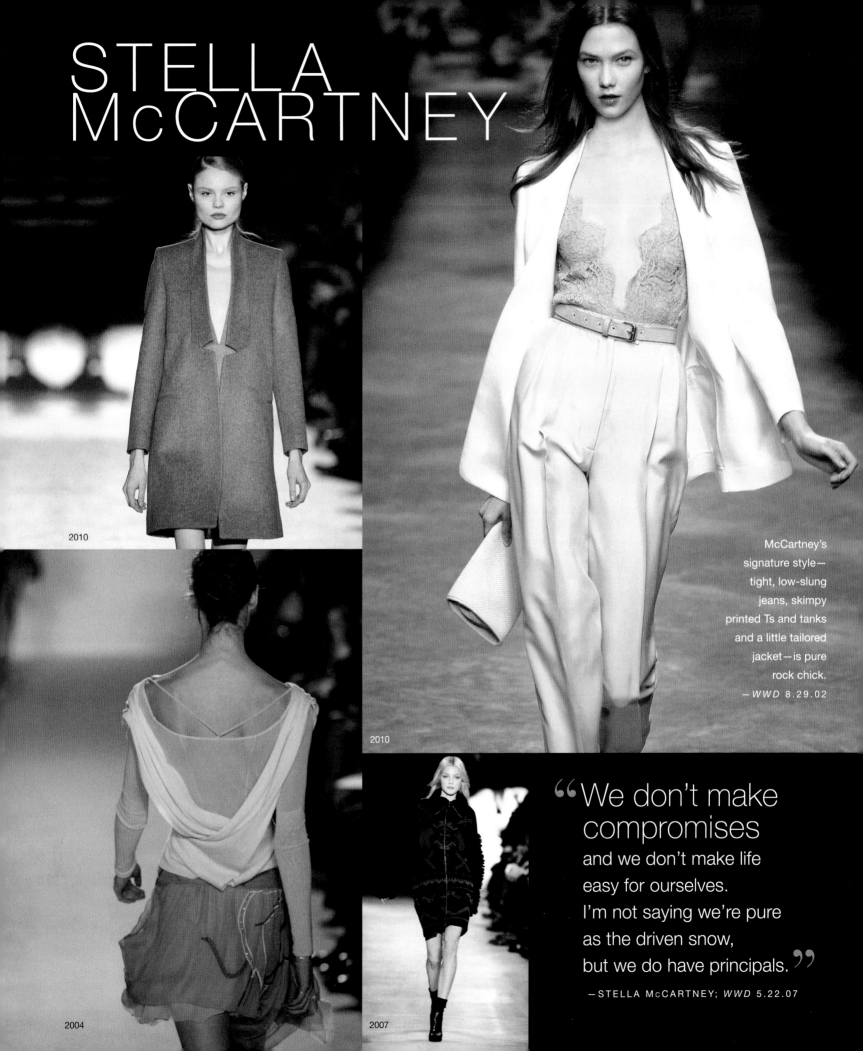

STELLA McCARTNEY

2010

2010

2004

2007

McCartney's signature style—tight, low-slung jeans, skimpy printed Ts and tanks and a little tailored jacket—is pure rock chick.
—*WWD* 8.29.02

"We don't make compromises and we don't make life easy for ourselves. I'm not saying we're pure as the driven snow, but we do have principals."
—STELLA McCARTNEY; *WWD* 5.22.07

2005

2004

Would that half of those [fashion shows] offered even the promise of **inciting the kind of passion McQueen typically triggers,** positive or negative; we might all have a lot less to whine about.

—*WWD* 3.5.07

2009   2003

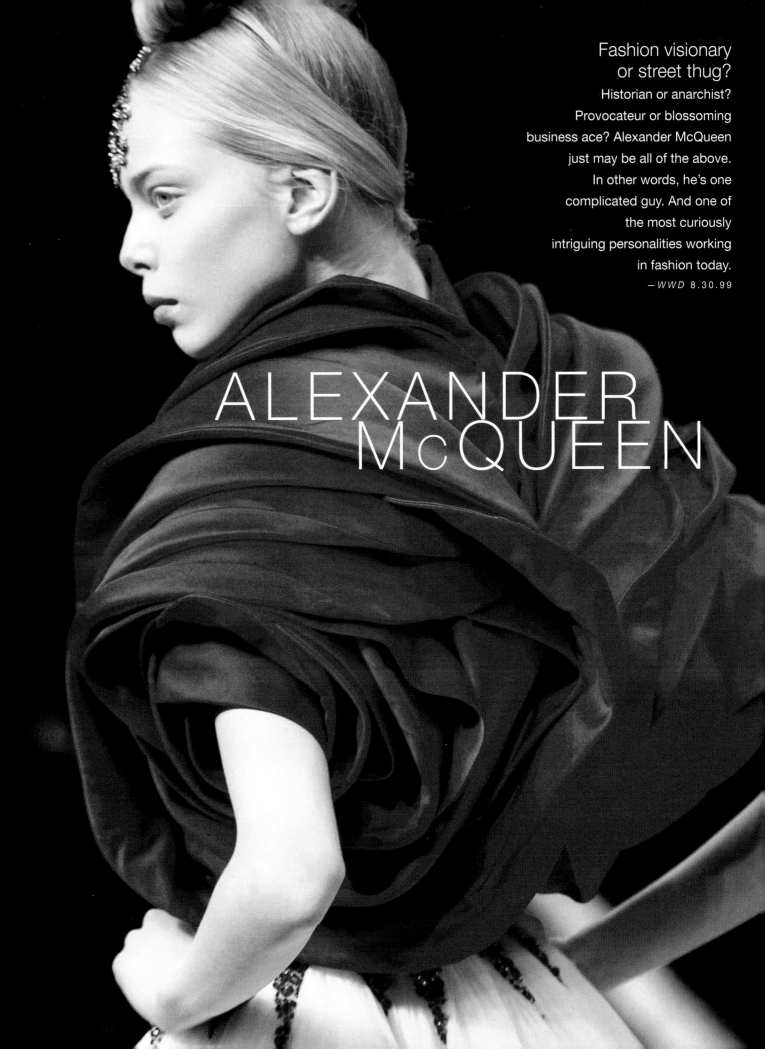

Fashion visionary
or street thug?
Historian or anarchist?
Provocateur or blossoming
business ace? Alexander McQueen
just may be all of the above.
In other words, he's one
complicated guy. And one of
the most curiously
intriguing personalities working
in fashion today.
—*WWD* 8.30.99

ALEXANDER McQUEEN

...the Missonis treat knits like paintings, with a personal palette and **a knowing eye for mixing plaids and stripes.**

— *WWD* 3.30.73

TAI & ROSITA MISSONI

1972

Striated space-dyed stripes and zig zags have always been synonymous with the name Missoni.

—WWD 10.14.74

1977

"There is a need for clothes that are easy to pack, easy to carry.... YOU ALSO NEED EXCITEMENT."

—ROSITA MISSONI;
WWD 10.17.75

1973

Mizrahi turned **his imaginative hand** to round-the-clock tartans that were among his greatest hits.

—*WWD* 4.17.89

1989

1991

2009

2010

He breathed enthusiasm and optimism and **IT WAS INFECTIOUS.**

—*WWD* 10.9.98

The new rage:
Isaac Mizrahi.
—*WWD* 4.18.88

ISAAC
MIZRAHI

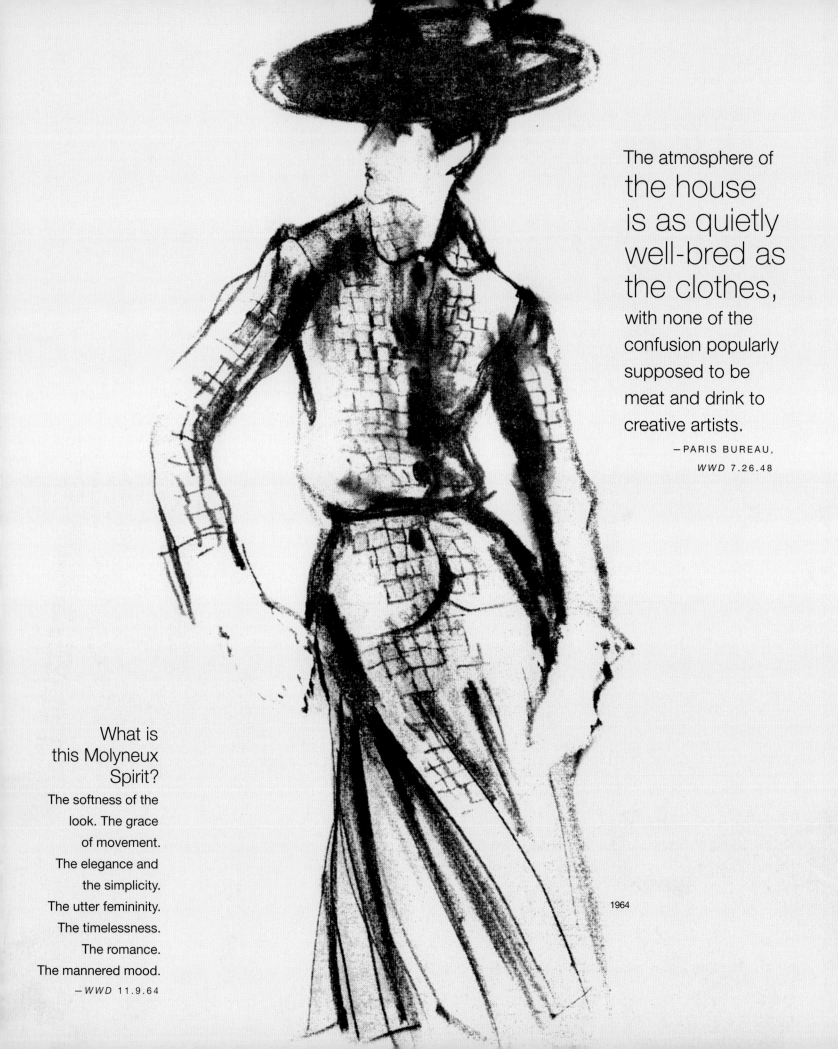

The atmosphere of **the house is as quietly well-bred as the clothes,** with none of the confusion popularly supposed to be meat and drink to creative artists.

—PARIS BUREAU,
WWD 7.26.48

What is
this Molyneux
Spirit?
The softness of the
look. The grace
of movement.
The elegance and
the simplicity.
The utter femininity.
The timelessness.
The romance.
The mannered mood.
—*WWD* 11.9.64

1964

1936

1946

1936

CLAUDE MONTANA

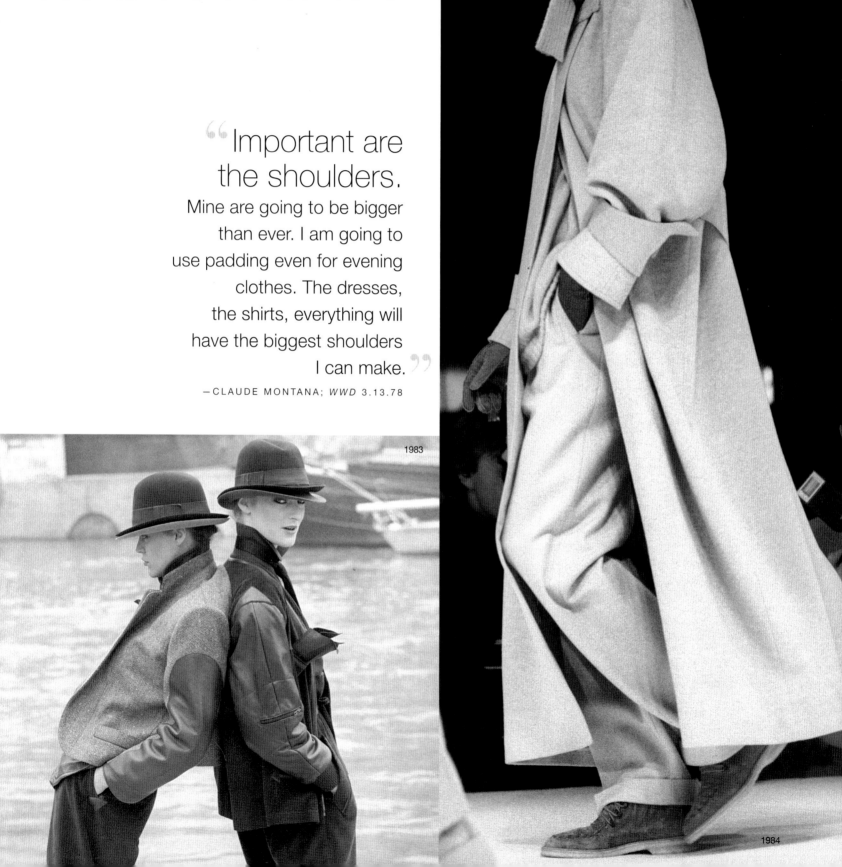

" Important are the shoulders. Mine are going to be bigger than ever. I am going to use padding even for evening clothes. The dresses, the shirts, everything will have the biggest shoulders I can make. "

—CLAUDE MONTANA; *WWD* 3.13.78

1983

1984

...the early concepts
were indeed quite extreme,
based on hard edged, attention-
getting interpretations of mannish,
locker-room fantasies—sailors,
Hell's Angels, football players, even
Wall Street bankers....

—WWD 5.18.84

1981

There's the Dauphin,
Claude Montana,
who dazzled the city
Saturday morning
with a perfectionist's
delight of a collection....

—WWD 3.26.84

WWD

WOMEN'S WEAR DAILY   VOL. 147 NO. 62
THURSDAY, MARCH 29, 1984   50 Cents

Montana: Fashion's New Dauphin

PARIS — Meet the
heir apparent to
the French fashion
throne. It's Claude Mon-
tana, who, in his recent
collection here, went
way beyond his custom-
ary theatrical clothes
into a new realm of very
sophisticated elegance.
Here, Dauphin Montana
brings his regal hand to
one of the season's fa-
vorite looks — the over-
scaled single-button
blazer in whipcord, over
a cashmere polo shirt.
For more on the
Dauphin's new clothes,
see pages 4 and 5.

1984

2002

"EVERY WOMAN
HAS A GODDESS
IN HER,"
Mugler once said.
"I LIKE TO
BRING HER OUT."
—THIERRY
MUGLER; *WWD*
1.21.03

THIERRY
MUGLER

1995

1992

1983

The Mugler image, he says, is about the **contradiction between being voluptuous and strict, modern and baroque.**

—*WWD* 9.21.93

Mugler:
Man of
the Hourglass.
While all of fashion
flirts with fit,
Thierry Mugler
wrote the book on
the subject.
—*WWD* 10.25.94

1995

1963

1963

1963

No other designer has ever quite caught up with the pristine beauty of the Norell black dress—

"Straight, simple, black"

is the rule of three for his new cocktail dresses.

—*WWD* 6.27.61

Norman Norell is the **PEERLESS CRAFTSMAN** of American fashion. —*WWD* 7.13.66

NORMAN NORELL

These are the Norell hallmarks:

The Impeccably-Cut Coat....The Paved

Sequin Dress....The Smoking Robe...

The Indispensible Suit....The Culotte

Pantsuit....The Jumper.... The Pantsuit....

The Chanel-Inspired suit....The Sailor

Look....The Chemise....The Big Coat....

— *WWD* 10.27.72

1973

...Owens has gained a cult following for his
rough-hewn, gothic designs.
—WWD 7.2.03

RICK
OWENS

...Owens tends to attract customers who prefer to be on the **FRINGES OF THINGS** and find out about his collection largely by word of mouth.

—*WWD* 10.23.07

2009

2005

2007

66 The informality is very California. The clothes have a glamorous feel, but in a punk-rock way that is intended to be effortless. Even if the pattern is complicated, the clothes are supposed to be thrown on and relaxed. 99

—RICK OWENS; *WWD* 8.18.98

2010

THAKOON
PANICHGUL

2010

2010

2009

2008

By now, Thakoon Panichgul has developed his own signature look, delving into the **land of geek versus chic** and always coming out on the right side.

—WWD 2.4.08

...lauded for his
soft, feminine designs and technical innovations.
—*WWD* 10.16.07

"Fashion is a commodity. The end result isn't to just get it covered in magazines or worn by celebrities. It's to have people go and buy the clothes and wear the clothes—that's fulfilling."
—THAKOON PANICHGUL;
WWD 2.5.05

2009

1936

1936

1936

Jean Patou
...one of the
**most
striking
personalities**
of the Paris
dressmaking world.

— *WWD* 1.8.32

1925

"I'm quite self-assured. I feel I don't need to show a lot to look sexy. Maybe I'm more casual, as well."
—PHOEBE PHILO;
WWD 10.5.01

PHOEBE PHILO

2010

IMAGES ON PAGES FOR CHLOÉ AND CÉLINE.

2010

She has quickly become
**one of fashion's
rising stars,**
acclaimed for a style that
deftly spans masculine
elements like trousers or
sweaters and gentler
fare such as light-as-air
dresses and frilly blouses.

— *WWD* 11.22.05

2006

2006

2007

" In the end, Saint Laurent was very easy to wear.
It was never contrived. You can wear a little dress and feel
very chic and Parisian because of the way you accessorize it or
because of its proportions. " —STEFANO PILATI; *WWD* 6.1.04

2007

2009

IMAGES ON PAGES FOR YVES SAINT LAURENT.

2009

Last season
felt like a breakout,
as if he had
finally arrived to
put his own
**mark of slick
sophistication**
on the house of
Yves Saint Laurent.
— *WWD* 10.5.07

STEFANO
PILATI

2010   2008

PAUL POIRET

Poiret's daring,
his innovations and
lack of regard for
accepted essentials both
of style and fabrics,
long ago made him a name….

— WWD 7.7.16

1925

1910

1911

1910

THIS COUTURIER FEATURES A VARIETY OF STYLE ELEMENTS like the 18th Century, the Etruscan, the Spanish and the Breton styles.
Of these, the Breton is expected to gain ascendancy for spring, according to reports from Paris. — *WWD* 11.24.15

ZAC POSEN

> " It's really important for us to make clothing that looks **beautiful, feminine and intelligent.** "
>
> —ZAC POSEN; *WWD* 5.13.03

2008

" I want to create a
global luxury lifestyle. "
—ZAC POSEN;
WWD 8.17.07

2010

2007

"The expectations from the press just
MAKE ME WORK HARDER AND
BE MORE CONCENTRATED."
—ZAC POSEN; *WWD* 6.2.03

2009   2007

2009

MIUCCIA PRADA

2009   2002

In many ways, Miuccia Prada
is in an unenviable position.
Her every move is supposed
to send shock waves 'round the
fashion world, each collection
expected to quicken the pulse
and alter the perspective of
everyone in the audience. It's
a burden born of
**EXCEPTIONAL TALENT
AND INFLUENCE,**
one only a very few designers
will ever know.

—WWD 10.8.97

2000   2005

In just a
few years,
Prada has
catapulted itself
from a little-known
upstart on the
Milan fashion
scene to a major
international
player.

—WWD 2.15.96

MIUCCIA PRADA

> "Glamour and elegance are all fine, but I'm really **working for things that make sense in our everyday lives.**"

—MIUCCIA PRADA; *WWD* 5.30.95

PROENZA SCHOULER

...the duo has developed one of the hottest names on the New York scene, winning acclaim for **sleek and intricate designs that nimbly straddle the tough-chic divide.**

—*WWD* 7.11.07

2011

2005

"WE'RE GROWING UP."
—LAZARO HERNANDEZ;
WWD 4.4.06

2010

2008

"It's a business, but we're much more interested in it as a craft."
—JACK McCOLLOUGH;
WWD 11.25.03

2007

Pattern and shape
are as important to
Emilo Pucci as the Arno is to
the Ponte Vecchio.
—*WWD* 1.17.69

1969

1966

202

EMILIO PUCCI

...the Italian designer has arrived at abstracts which are entirely in keeping with modern times. Colors are striking, featuring sea blues, grayed olive, lemon yellows, apricots, mauve and rose tinged wine.
—*WWD* 1.9.56

"Prints used to be staid, tame. I started the wild geometrical prints with wild colors."
—EMILIO PUCCI;
WWD 4.23.76

1964

1965

PACO RABANNE

...if there
is anyone who
thinks ahead
it is Paco.
— *WWD* 5.3.67

"PLEASE DON'T CALL ME A COUTURIER. I AM AN ARTISAN."
—PACO RABANNE; *WWD* 10.16.67

Plastics and pliers
are the two essentials
in Paco Rabanne's
brave new world of fashion....
—*WWD* 3.29.66

2001

"We wanted
to do something
small and
concentrated.
Something
bohemian and
sophisticated."

—KATE MULLEAVY;
WWD 2.3.05

2009

2009   2008   2007

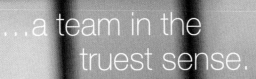

...a team in the
truest sense.

— WWD 5.29.07

RODARTE

Rodarte design duo
Kate and Laura Mulleavy
are a breath of fresh air.
Within the tight arc of
three seasons, the Mulleavy
sisters have won over
the fashion press with
the IRRESISTIBLE
JUXTAPOSITION
OF THEIR NERDY BUT
FASHION-OBSESSED
PERSONALITIES
and their exquisite, finely
detailed clothes.

— WWD 5.30.06

2008

NARCISO
RODRIGUEZ

" I want to see **women looking beautiful** again in a very glamorous way. "

—NARCISO RODRIGUEZ; *WWD* 10.8.96

2005

Rodriguez's core belief is that...

clothes should make an alluring canvas

from which a woman's personality can shine.

—*WWD* 9.30.99

2010   2003

Everybody knows
Sony Rykiel is
**A GENIUS WITH
SWEATERS.**
— *WWD* 4.17.73

SONIA
RYKIEL

2010

Above all
she designs
clothes
men will like.
Perhaps I should
not say it quite
so bluntly but that
is my real aim.

—SONIA RYKIEL;
WWD 9.29.66

2004

"I try to understand the
conversation between
the clothes and the body."

—SONIA RYKIEL; *WWD* 1.17.78

2001

2006   1973

1972

YVES
SAINT
LAURENT

There is only one Yves Saint Laurent and
there will never be another.

—WWD 7.28.88

1988

"My shape?...Very natural. Long and slim.
That is all I can tell you. I am faithful to myself." —YVES SAINT LAURENT: WWD 6.24.69

YVES SAINT LAURENT

"So they have crowned me king," sighs Yves Saint Laurent. "Look what happened to all the other kings in France."
— *WWD* 6.26.68

1965

1979

1976   1966

Jil Sander has charted
new territory in the
land of luxe, traveling
from a staunch
austerity into a world of
graceful,
cerebral chic.
— WWD 10.1.99

JIL SANDER

1996

"Minimal is a word
I don't put too much meaning
with....I work out so much
in the designing
that really the word
'pureness' is better."

—JIL SANDER;
WWD 5.17.95

1990   1996

SHRINKING
VIOLETS DON'T
INTEREST
JIL SANDER.
She makes clothes for
women who are
strong, confident and
extremely well-heeled.
—*WWD* 3.8.95

2004   1989

" I always loved the idea of layering. It started with Diana Vreeland when I was very young. I love the idea that, from time to time, a woman can change things around. "
—GIORGIO DI SANT' ANGELO; *WWD* 6.7.89

GIORGIO DI SANT' ANGELO

THE RENAISSANCE MAN of the jet age....
—*WWD* 10.16.68

1968

> "To be really chic is to choose something yourself which nobody has."
>
> —GIORGIO DI SANT'ANGELO;
>
> *WWD* 6.22.70

1976

1974

1971

"You're going to Mr. Scaasi's apartment?" asks the doorman. "You're in for a treat," he assures us.

— WWD 9.21.65

ARNOLD SCAASI

1984

Long before Christian Lacroix brought his pouf to Paris, **DEAR ARNOLD WAS POUFFING HIS PARK AVENUE PALS**....There's the ever-popular toadstool dress, the world's brightest bustle and enough sequins, embroidery, raffia, appliques, colored paillettes, bows and feathers to make Nouvelle Society Ladies swoon in delight. —*WWD* 3.5.87

1967

Among his private customers are many theatrical as well as social personalities. —*WWD* 6.10.63

1986

1973   1984

Success made Schiap
bolder and bolder....
"Away with the slouch,"
she cried, "and up with
the shoulders,"
which she padded.
She put the bust
back in its place,
the waist to normal and
lengthened skirts slightly.
The silhouette
of the Thirties
was born.

—PARIS BUREAU, *WWD* 12.22.66

ELSA
SCHIAPARELLI

1966

1945

1936

Even her ultra-simple black suits and dresses have belt or fastening, or use of fabric, that gives them originality. Button makers, costume jewelers, and accessory manufacturers generally owe her a debt of gratitude, for she has added to the importance of all these things.

—*WWD* 7.26.48

"I am eager to carry forward **the simple and pristine design....** There is a strong affinity between how I perceive my own design and the core values that the Jil Sander brand embraces."

—RAF SIMONS;
WWD 5.27.05

RAF SIMONS

2009

> "At the end of the day, it's the body that speaks: No matter what you cover it with, you can't ignore the body language. That was very much the intention...."
>
> —RAF SIMONS; *WWD* 5.27.08

2007

2008

2008

2006

2010

IMAGES ON PAGES FOR JIL SANDER.

WILLI SMITH

Willi Smith
believes
in comfort.
He also believes in
style. So far, the
30-year-old designer
has never had
to sacrifice one
for the other.
—*WWD 4.28.78*

1972

"My girls
move fast
and want
good looks
at a price."

—WILLI SMITH;
WWD 1.11.78

1973

The maestro of the mini
and keeper of the Sixties flame.... —WWD 4.3.85

1988

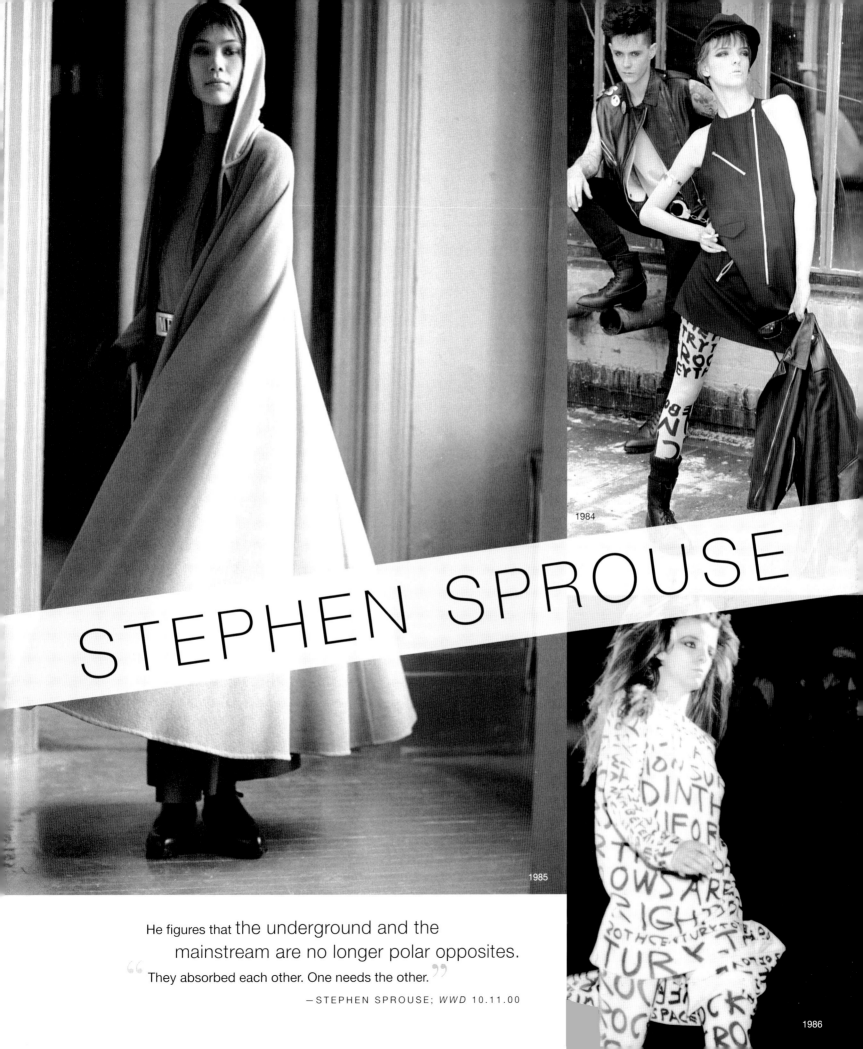

STEPHEN SPROUSE

1984

1985

1986

He figures that the underground and the mainstream are no longer polar opposites. They absorbed each other. One needs the other.

— STEPHEN SPROUSE; *WWD* 10.11.00

1993

She loves a kind of overt, hip fashion that manages to be both saucy and sweet, and she has a knack for combining the familiar and the frivolous in a way that makes perfect sense. —WWD 4.11.97

Sui is known for fun,
        tongue-in-cheek designs.
She makes liberal use of retro references and
        has a particular fascination with the Sixties and Seventies.

— *WWD* 8.28.95

2006

ANNA SUI

1994

"Real haute couture can be too couture.
**I LIKE TO MIX TRASH
AND CHIC.**"
—OLIVIER THEYSKENS; *WWD* 4.28.98

OLIVIER THEYSKENS

Olivier Theyskens,
formerly known
as the crown
prince of
glamorous
Goth....
The 26-year-old
Belgian...is also fully
fluent in the
stuff of refinement.

— WWD 3.10.03

2010

2009 · 2010

While he is clearly capable of chic, more often than not, Tisci is hailed as a Goth fashion hero. It's a description at which he doesn't bristle, but he prefers to label himself as part of a group of designers that mine the edgier, less sunny side of things.

—*WWD* 4.12.10

"I just really want to respect the past, but do Givenchy for 2005." And what are its hallmarks? Tisci threw out the words elegant, aristocratic, chic and French, but with a touch of irony or a "twist of craziness."
—RICARDO TISCI; *WWD* 7.6.05

RICCARDO TISCI

…his signature brew of **DARK ROMANTICISM** and Latin influences….
— *WWD* 1.20.09

IMAGES ON PAGES FOR GIVENCHY.

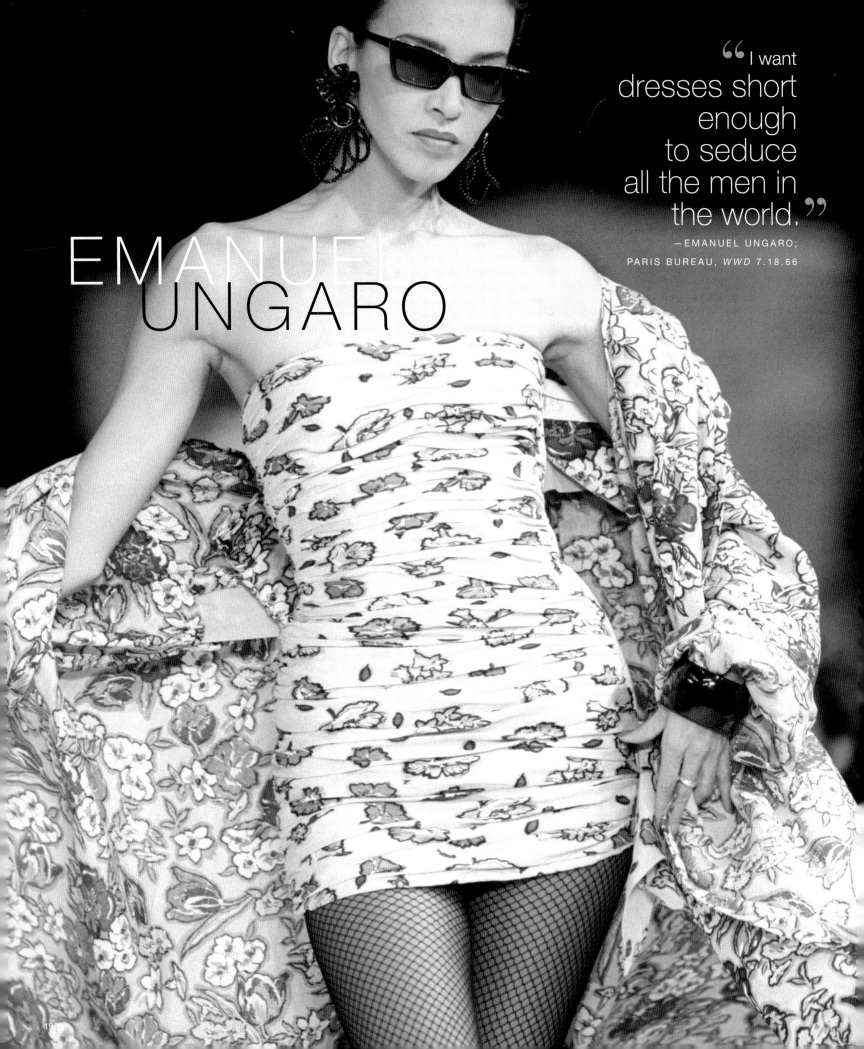

EMANUEL UNGARO

" I want
dresses short
enough
to seduce
all the men in
the world. "
—EMANUEL UNGARO;
PARIS BUREAU, *WWD* 7.18.66

1996

Even when she wears the pants, **UNGARO'S EXECUTIVE FLIRT IS ALL WOMAN.**

—*WWD* 3.26.8?

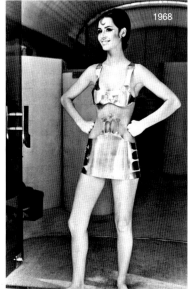

1988

1968

1995

" Who knows why
I started mixing prints.
It was an intuition. I started
[doing that] in 1968 and I was
killed by the fashion press for doing so.
I had the feeling,
though, that this was my style. "

—EMANUEL UNGARO;
WWD 1.16.90

"...I will be happy as long as one can say of my collection... it's chic, elegant, sophisticated."

—VALENTINO; *WWD* 9.12.67

VALENTINO

2010

Valentino is
Mr. Chic
of Italian fashion.

—*WWD* 7.22.77

1970

1968

2006

1973

When one particularly
sexy red dress appeared
on the runway
during a rehearsal, the
Chic exclaimed:
"IF A MAN DOESN'T
GO ABSOLUTELY
CRAZY OVER A WOMAN
IN THIS DRESS
it must be because she is a
monster." He had a point.

—*WWD* 7.19.78

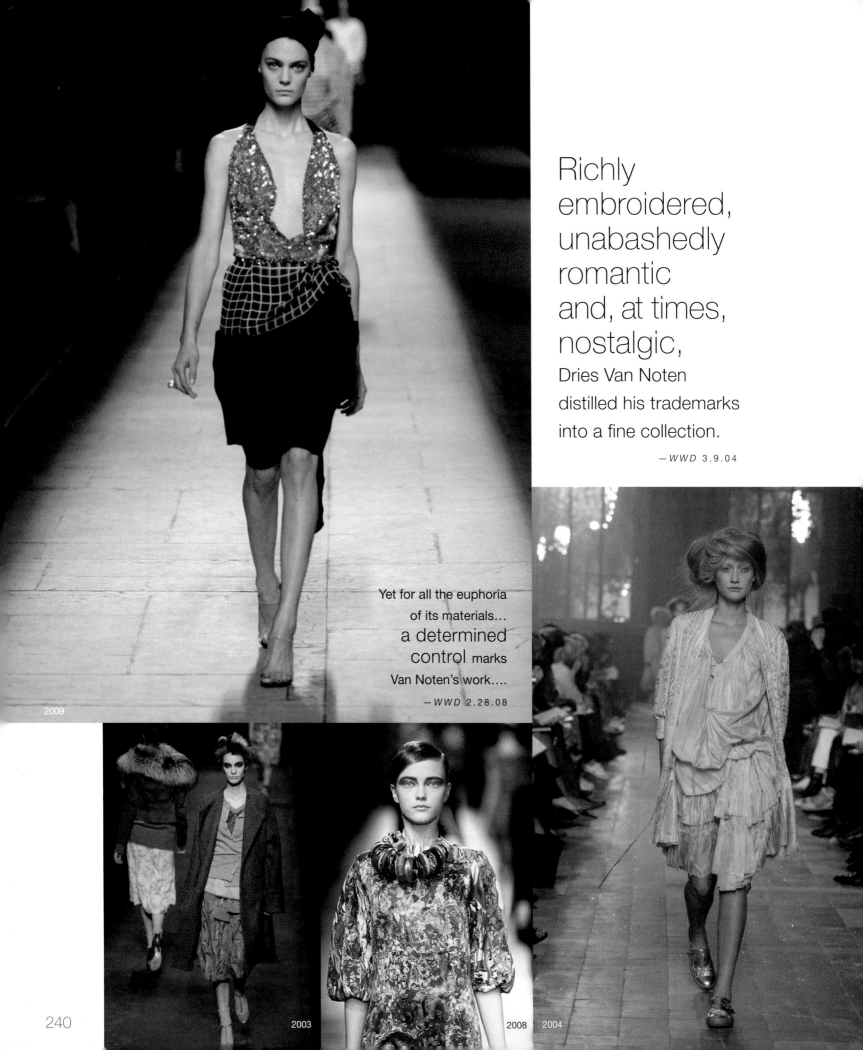

Richly
embroidered,
unabashedly
romantic
and, at times,
nostalgic,
Dries Van Noten
distilled his trademarks
into a fine collection.

— WWD 3.9.04

Yet for all the euphoria
of its materials...
a determined
control marks
Van Noten's work....

— WWD 2.28.08

2009

240

2003

2008

2004

...just the kind of
ETHNIC ROMANTICISM
Dries has always stood for....
— *WWD* 10.9.96

DRIES
VAN
NOTEN

2006

"I'M PROUD,
I'M PASSIONATE.
I'M A FIGHTER—
AND A SURVIVOR....
I feel great. I feel strong.
Life isn't easy for anyone,
but now I feel like
I can face it with strength."
—DONATELLA VERSACE;
WWD 10.8.04

2004

2006

2002

"I changed
the way
I want to see
women dressed.
I don't think they need
to turn heads at
all costs, but they can
attract with their
mannerisms, attitudes
or movements."
—DONATELLA VERSACE;
WWD 2.7.07

"A woman
has to be sensual,
not sexy,
which can be
aggressive or vulgar.
Sexy all
the way
is Eighties;
sensuality is
timeless."
— DONATELLA VERSACE;
WWD 5.23.02

DONATELLA VERSACE

GIANNI VERSACE

Gianni Versace
rocked fashion....
A master showman,
he was the force
behind a fashion
credo that was about
**glitz, glamour,
hype, youth,
sex and
lots of fun.**
And nobody did it
as genuinely as he did.

— WWD 7.16.97

1993

They've been described as clothes that make store hangers sizzle.... Whether you like them or not, they are clothes to be noticed in.... They are the stuff of Gianni Versace....
— *WWD* 3.15.90

1984   1993

The 27-year-old boy **WOWED BOTH MILAN AND FLORENCE**
last season with his graceful jersey dresses and subtly nostalgic evening clothes. — *WWD* 10.3.74

1990   1990   1990   1990   1990

MADELEINE VIONNET

Vionnet glorifies the
**feminine aspect
of fashion....**
—*WWD* 2.2.37

1961

In the 1920s, Vionnet first led fashion into body-conscious paths, with her **curve-conscious constructions** involving intricate bias cuts, masterly technique.

—*WWD* 10.16.61

1969

"I tried to make them look tall and slim. **BUT TO BE ELEGANT**…that's something else."

—MADELEINE VIONNET; *WWD* 4.21.69

> "Everybody talks about lifestyle but the truth of the matter is that **we are a lifestyle.** We make clothes for the last-minute date and the morning after."
> —DIANE VON FURSTENBERG;
> *WWD* 9.15.00

DIANE VON FURSTENBERG

2009

New renditions…still form the collection's core—dresses, tops, skirts that PYTs love—the girly factor sometimes tempered by graffiti or animal prints.

—WWD 2.12.02   2010

THE WRAP IS HER RESORT BASIC.

That's what Diane's business is built on—basic, easy-to-wear, sexy shirtdresses that sell. What makes Diane unique are her prints and her fit.

—WWD 9.17.73

1973

1973

WANG HASN'T COMPLETELY ABANDONED THOSE SUBVERSIVE ROOTS;
he's just filtered them in a slightly different (read: less tough and kohl-eyed sexy) way. — *WWD* 11.9.09

ALEXANDER WANG

Wang has a consistent vision and a strong sense of his customer, who's a little bit **GRITTY AND MOLTO STREET CHIC.**
—*WWD* 2.2.08

2010

2008

"I don't like things when they're **too perfect or put together.**"
—ALEXANDER WANG;
WWD 9.7.06

2009

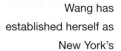

VERA WANG

2008

2008

2006

Wang has
established herself as
New York's
**EMPRESS OF
ARTSY CHIC....**
—*WWD* 2.7.08

..."Vera-isms" like tulle detailing,
roses and ruched belts—
"things that have become our signatures,"
in Wang's words....

—*WWD* 5.10.07

2009

"If I could transform people's perception of wedding gowns by making them **more modern, artistic, inventive or stylish,** then perhaps I could create a valuable, emotional franchise for the rest of their lives."

—VERA WANG; *WWD* 11.16.05

2010

VIVIENNE
WESTWOOD

Westwood says she started out
making Punk clothes
"to try to capture the sense
of rebellion
that was around London
at the time...." — WWD 12.22.82

1977

WWD
ACCESSORIES REPORT

Bottoms Up

Paris: Lights, Camera, Action!

PARIS — There's been plenty of cheekiness in fashion this season, but it took Vivienne Westwood to give new dimension to the derriere. And she did it in her exuberant fall show, the best of the ready-to-wear weekend. Here, Westwood's daringly shaped, Bubble Bum tweed and sheepskin suit, worn with platform shoes. For more on Paris, see pages 4 to 7 and 11.

PARIS — It was the moment Paris has been waiting for: Robert Altman finally stopped talking about his movie and started shooting it at Christian Lacroix's first show Sunday morning. You knew this wasn't going to be just any fashion show when a brawl broke out between a gang of crashers and security men at the entrance. It was getting positively violent — then all of a sudden, it stopped, and everybody was all smiles as the "Pret-a-Porter" cameras moved on to another staged scene.

The movie stars tried to look as normal as your average fashion victim as they paraded into the auditorium. Kim Basinger, playing a TV reporter, wore an iridescent Lacroix jacket appliqued with hearts. Chiara Mastroianni, as her assistant, sat beside her and read a book throughout the collection. Lauren Bacall, in an Armani pantsuit and an Armani-ized face, wore rubber-soled shoes — one beige, one blue. Sally Kellerman, as a Harper's Bazaar edi-

See PARIS, page 5

1994

2001

2003

2010

> "When you wear my clothes, you will be noticed."
> —VIVIENNE WESTWOOD;
> WWD 9.16.94

> "I have a way of cutting clothes that is VERY SEXY AND ACTION-PACKED."
> —VIVIENNE WESTWOOD;
> WWD 11.17.83

2006

2008

Sugar and spice,
that's what Jason
Wu's girls are made of.
— *WWD* 2.14.06

2010

"THE [FIRST LADY'S] DRESS HAD TO BE CLASSIC, but it had to say 'new'....It was about achieving that balance between the bold statement and also the feminine colors."

— JASON WU:
WWD 1.22.09

2010   2010

The Taiwan-born designer… has a knack for whipping retro-style pieces into thoroughly **modern looks for the contemporary power woman.**

—*WWD* 6.1.10

JASON WU

He designs for another kind of woman,
and an elusive one at that.
"She's living in my mind as a dream."…
For this phantom lady, Yamamoto says, he attempts
"to invent a sense of elegance
by making very constructed forms
in mannish styling."
—*WWD* 3.26.96

2003

YOHJI YAMAMOTO

Yamamoto is one of fashion's great creators:

ARTIST, INTELLECT AND TECHNICIAN

in one remarkable package. —*WWD* 10.4.05

2008

2010

Although Yamamoto has said his ideal customer is an older woman, the **CULT THAT BUYS HIS CLOTHES** with near-religious fervor is decidedly young.

— WWD 4.20.88

2003

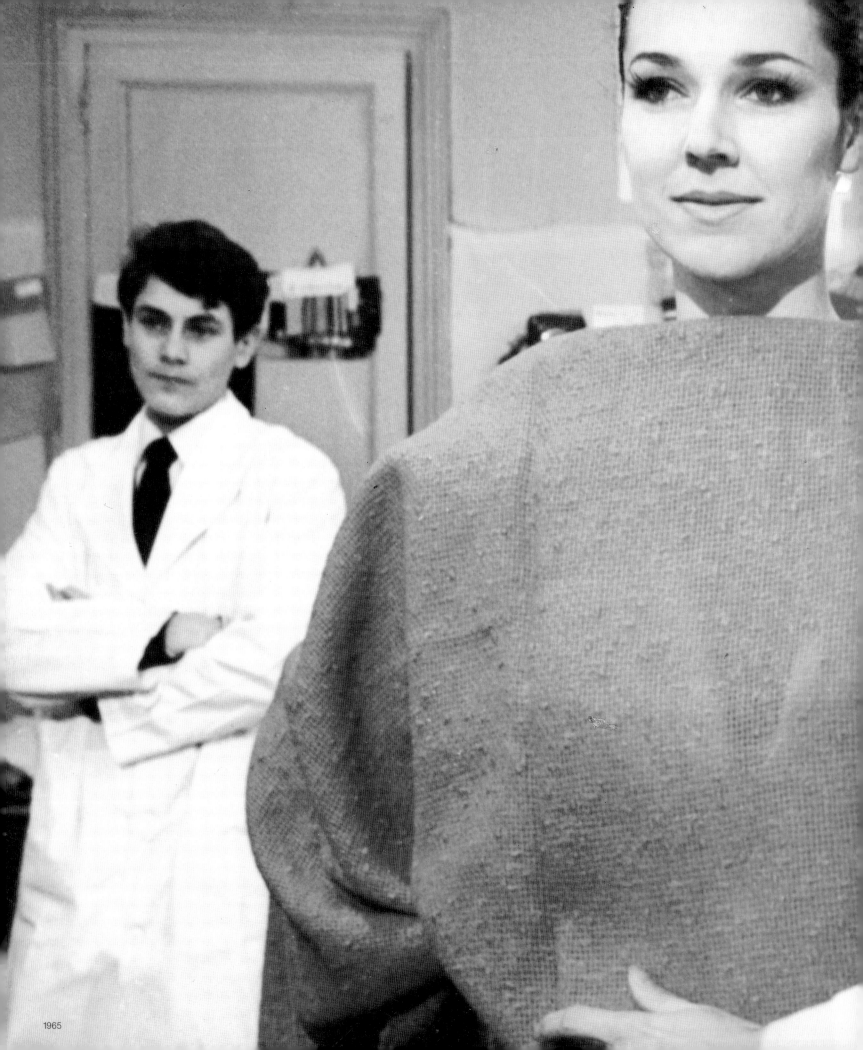

1965

FIRSTHAND

The following 30 interviews represent just a sampling of the voices that have spoken through the pages of *Women's Wear Daily* over the last hundred years. They also reflect the range of editorial styles the paper has embraced during that time.

LUCIEN LELONG

Lelong, in Style Communique, Expounds on Era of Sophisticated Simplicity

AUGUST 5, 1927

PARIS—Sophisticated simplicity is Lucien Lelong's slogan for the fall season. M. Lelong emphasizes that it is to be a season of simplicity in dress. With his showing of 273 models, which is about 25 less than exhibited during the corresponding season a year ago, he issued to the foreign correspondents and others, invited to his dress rehearsal on the evening prior to his general opening to trade buyers, a communiqué containing his opinions of the style trend for the coming season. The communiqué follows:

"If there is one trend in fashion today more noticeable than another, it is the trend toward simplicity. But, let me emphasize it—imaginative simplicity. We are in a decided reaction from the uninspired banality that has often passed for simplicity in previous seasons. Now we have simplicity of a different kind. One might call it an intricate simplicity or a sophisticated simplicity. The simplicity is only external and apparent, while an unusual and increasing complexity enters into the technical structure of the design.

"Such is to be the correct fashion in this dawning season, and, I make bold to predict, for many seasons to come."

A LAW OF FASHION

"Why am I so confident in this prophecy? Dress style seems to be such an accidental and uncontrolled thing that it would be perilous to attempt to chart its future course. And yet I believe that if a scholar's study were to be made of it through the ages, it would show that the appearance of dress is constantly responding to deep-rooted human instincts. There is a constant reaction of dress to environment, or such is my theory. I think these instincts and these reactions could be discovered. I believe it would be possible for us to codify, so to speak, the laws of fashion.

"It even seems to me that I can see one of these laws for myself. It is this: That dress style tends to react to the environment in which it is worn, but that reaction is rather an unexpected one. When life is simple, or quiet, or deficient in artificial excitement, dress tends to become florid and ornate, but when life and environment are highly sophisticated, then fashion seeks the simple.

"And with fashion in these trends go such intimate and personal objects as furniture and interior ornaments and decorations of all sorts."

EXCITEMENTS FOR SOCIETY

"On the face of it, this might seem to be a sort of compensation—the naive age seeking in flamboyant decoration the excitement which life withholds from it, and the complicated environmental reacting to the simple for sheer nervous relief. I maintain, however, that the truth is the exact contrary.

"It does not even have to be argued that the more complex life becomes the stronger are the excitements which society demands. Society grows jaded with naive pleasures. It demands ever a stronger stimulation. It turns constantly to more powerful sensations.

"And so, when society grows weary with one sort of a world, art strives to give it another and a headier one."

TODAY'S SOPHISTICATION

"All art is now pursuing the goal of simplicity—music, painting, sculptures, literature, the stage. But if you examine the finished works, you discover beneath the pure outer form an intricate technique which includes stern repression, the highest element in technique.

"It is complexity producing simplicity—the fillip to the spirit which the sated, sophisticated taste of today insists upon."

SIMPLICITY INEVITABLE

"And dress design is following this same instinctive movement. It offers now to the mundane modern woman, who is as carefully bred a product of civilization as an orchid or a camellia, that purity of design and form which alone can any longer impress her tutored senses.

"I do not argue that this law of correspondence about which I have been talking would necessarily have begotten the present silhouette itself—that, in other words, the present silhouette was inevitable, although I think it likely. But whatever the silhouette might have been, you can be sure that we would have been treating it in this same way—i.e., to give it a crafty simplicity. Dress fashion would have been bound to go along with the other arts in any event."

THE SALON CHANGES
"To show how seriously I am taking this argument and how strongly I am basing upon it my prevision of, and plans for, the future, I call your attention to the changes which I have made in this showroom since last winter. Where my stage used to be a recess in the wall I have now extended the platform well out into the salon itself.

"Why have I done this? Because in my opinion we are through with eye-stunning styles for a long time to come. Since the present simplicity is elaborated from a complex of technical components—cuts, fine details, and the like—it means that the model itself has to be brought close to the observer's eye in order to display its qualities. It takes a sharply focused scrutiny to detect the complexity of the design. At any distance the model gives the effect of being utterly simple."

ASYMMETRY AND HARMONY
"In addition to the basic trend toward the sophisticatedly simple, there are some important superficial movements in the fashion to be noted. It is, in the first place, to be a season of asymmetry. The symmetric and balanced dress no longer offers us anything new. Correct design is now design that is out of balance.

"But with this asymmetry comes a strong insistence upon harmony. In fact, what I call harmony has come to be an extremely important factor in good style this season. Color, length, and indeed the whole design must attain a certain 'rightness' which it is convenient to term harmony.

"I can best illustrate this by referring to the length of the skirt. Heretofore it has been possible to designate the correct skirt length in centimeters above the ground. It is not possible to do that this season. The proper skirt length now is that which harmonize with the individual figure wearing he gown. It depends upon the client herself. Too long a skirt and it is prehistoric; too short, and it is vulgar."

THE AFTERNOON ATMOSPHERE
"Then, too, this season is witnessing the beginnings of an increased formality in day attire over what has been the role for some time past. In other words, there is a certain coming back of the traditional afternoon atmosphere. We have been and still are in a morning atmosphere, so far as day fashion is concerned, due to the triumph of the sports dress—essentially a morning style. One sees sports models worn now to all but the most formal afternoon gatherings, a fact which offends some tastes here in Paris. But this season, at long last, there is a moderate feeling in the air for something more in the afternoon tradition.

"Whether this is the start of a transition or something fated for an early end it is too soon now to say. It is certain that for this season, at any rate, many smart women—the majority of them—will insist upon the sport style as usual. I believe, however, in real sports clothes for sportswomen, and have therefore included in this collection a number of afternoon gowns of more formal quality. Particularly the new feeling can be noted in some of my afternoon ensembles, which, while they have coats somewhat less formal than has been customary in the past, have dresses more habille, though, of course, simple."

A NEW ERA OF IMAGINATION
"One more important general point remains to be mentioned. With simplicity as the ideal in design, it might be thought that new dress creation would be deficient in imagination. The truth is exactly the contrary. We are just in the dawn of a new era of imagination in the making of dresses, and it is the quest of simplicity that brings it.

"The imagination now, however, is expressed in lines, cuts, and the choice and combinations of colors. These fields, together with the devices for gaining asymmetry in design offer an infinite scope for the play of the creative fancy. Not in my time has there been so much imagination put into dress as there is this season."

THE SILHOUETTE
"After such a detailed discussion of the season's trends there remains little to say of the silhouette in particular. As I mentioned above, the demands of harmony prevent any fixed rule of skirt length, and equally the asymmetrizing of the design by such devices as panels, flares, insertions, and the like makes it impossible to define the waistline strictly. There is no regular waistline.

"In short, dress is now adopting some of the most radical principles of composition evolved by advanced painting and sculptures."

LL BLUE AND DISSONANCES
"The exclusive character of my materials this season resides chiefly in their colors. I have adopted a special color of my own—a blue which I call LL Blue. I have this graded over the entire scale of shades, and it will be a distinctive fashion with e for the winter. But in addition to these the dyers have, following my specifications, produced for my exclusive use certain new and strikingly dissonancy color combinations.

"Taste in color may be educated therefore it constantly progresses. And so color combinations that even few years ago would have been regarded as a shocking clash now impose themselves upon taste as harmonious. These new combinations of mine carry the movement a step further. They can be called dissonant harmonies. They appear in new afternoon ensembles which have interested me during their creation, the gown and coast being in the dissonant shade and fur being used to effect the liaison."

FUR
"Fur itself is as much in favor as ever. I have used fox in all shades of brown and gray, a great deal of lynx, and also mink and ermine. Incidentally I am putting less fur at the bottoms of coats."

"Crepes, velvets and satins are the principal materials, and obviously they are more often plain than patterned, for the reason that plain weaves are better adapted to complex cutting. In sports models I am showing some handknitted tricots in modernistic designs. I remained faithful to lace during its eclipse. I was first to use it when it began to return, and now that it is in full favor once more I am as enthusiastic for it as ever.

"Below I append the list of weavers whose materials appear in this collection, acknowledging my perennial admiration of their genius and my personal appreciation of the inspiration their products always are to me:

"Silks: Messrs. Bianchini, Ferier; Coudurier-Fructus-Descher; Ducharne; Godde-Bedin; Pehel; Remond; and Veron & Lajoine.

"Wools: Messrs. Rodier and Meyer.

"Tricots: M. Lousteau."

EMBROIDERIES

"In embroideries I have favored the use of stones, both in embroideries themselves and in pendants. Some of the evening gowns have diamond buckles with diamonds slightly tinged with the colors of the gowns with which they harmonize.

"Finally let me add that nothing I have said is to be interpreted as meaning that I have gone to any extremes in these new movements and impulses. Just as I am against the usual and the banal, so am I also opposed to uncontrolled flights of fancy and extravagances of any sort committed in the name of originality."

—Paris Bureau, *Women's Wear Daily*

JACQUES FATH
Narrower Skirts Are Forecast for This Fall By Designer Jacques Fath on Visit Here

MARCH 30, 1948

Narrower skirts for fall, but width at the top in the form of back-swept capes and fitted jackets with peplums curved out over poufs and bows on tight-draped skirts.

A great liking for coral color and pale bronze.

Continued emphasis on a tiny waistline with softly-rounded shoulders, which use a bit of padding close to the neckline to achieve a pyramid silhouette.

For evening, lavish embroideries in cut steel, in semi-precious stones and sea shells.

That's the fashion news as seen by Jacques Fath, youngest big name designer of the Paris couture who came to town yesterday for a reception in his honor at Gimbel Brothers. M. Fath is 33 years old. His beautiful wife, Geneviere, to whom he has been married for ten years, is with him on this first visit to America.

"Better than even the most beautiful dress I ever hope to design is our son, Philipe, who is five years old," says Jacques, while Geneviere smiles happily in agreement. "He looks just like me, except to have his mother's lovely mouth," he explains. The Faths are both blond and handsome. Madame with brown eyes, he with pale hazel ones.

M. Fath opened his couture salon in 1937, to fulfill a dream he had since he was 14.

"At that time I say to Mama that I want to be a dressmaker, and she tells me I am very foolish boy," he recalls. "But from the time I am about 11, I have noticed that the clothes I think about, that I draw up here (tapping his forehead), are the ones that

designers show a few months from then. I open a fashion magazine, and there is the very dress I dreamed about three month ago! To become a designer became an obsession with me."

His grandmother, Caroline Fath, was dressmaker to the Empress Eugenie, while his grandfather was a painter, a pupil of Corot and an instructor at Beaux Arts. "So always, we have beauty and clothes consciousness where I was raised, and it is natural for me to want to make beautiful clothes for beautiful women, yes?" he says.

Even his Army career in World War II became involved with clothes designing. When his regiment was called up, he explains, "I am given pantaloons to fit a man 250 pounds!" Fath being a lean and lithe 160 pounds or so, it's easy to see why both he and the lovely Geneviere go into gales of laughter over the picture this recalls.

"I am cutting them down and sewing them up like the pantaloons pour cheval (horseback riding). The Capitaine asks me to do his so, and all the officers want the same thing. Soon I have a sewing machine, and even in Belgium, with the sounds of battle all around I am forced to go on stitching pantaloons on that machine! Is quite a war record, no?"

Monsieur and Madame Fath arrived in this country March 18, and have been in New York until their visit to Philadelphia. Present at the party in their honor yesterday were some of the women nominated as Philadelphia's ten best dressed in *The Sunday Bulletin* story of last December, along with a number of others prominent in local circles and social life.

"Since I have been in this country," said M. Fath, of this gathering, "I have not seen so many well dressed women."

Though he has brought no formal collection of his clothes with him, Madame Fath has 35 costumes designed by her husband and selected especially for their American visit. Purpose of the visit, he explains, is to learn more about the needs of American women and their clothes taste so that this collections may be created to appeal to them. He goes to Boston next, later to Texas, to Canada and perhaps to Mexico.

He's sponsoring for cocktail parties and for wear at crowded evening galas a new blistered nylon taffeta with a finish that's impervious to liquids, from champagne to just plain water.

"See, cocktail proof!" he demonstrates proudly, pouring the contents of a glass over a skirt and watching it roll away like the proverbial water off a duck's back "Practical, yes?"

—*Blanche Krause*

PIERRE BALMAIN

New York Stopover
with Pierre Balmain

OCTOBER 31, 1960

NEW YORK—Pierre Balmain stopped in New York last week for a brief and "private" visit. M. Balmain has just come from Toronto where he helped launch his new ready to wear at the T. Eaton Co.

He was overwhelmingly enthusiastic about the reception of his ready to wear at Eaton's. "We sold 12 models following the first showing"—and sees definite possibil-

ities of extending the operation through the Americas. "Yes, you could call it a kind of test," he said, adding that he thought it would prove feasible to produce the apparel in France and export it rather than manufacturing in the United States.

"We have a similar set-up in Australia... David Jones in Sydney has built a duplicate of my Paris salon in which to show the clothes," he beamed. The operation differs, he explained, because high customs duties, often 100 per cent, necessitate some local manufacture. "But the workmanship is excellent," he stressed.

Workmanship led M. Balmain to dismiss the subject of banning cheap copies of couture designs with a contemptuous wave of his expressive hands. "I have nothing to do with Seventh Avenue and Seventh Avenue has nothing to do with me...my clothes aren't 'vulgar' enough for Seventh Avenue."

He balances his lack of interest in the copying problem with complete confidence and delight in his private clientele, which "appreciates elegant, well-made clothes" and which has a loyalty he claims does not exist in the Americas. "Why, we can predict, fairly exactly, the number of coats, suits, dresses that our customers will buy each season...that is not possible here."

Elaborating his comments on loyalty, M. Balmain spreads his hands in horror at America's constant search for The New. He deplores the requirement of a "new" designer, a "new" name each season: "Designers that were called 'genius' last year or the year before are rarely heard of this year." He answers his critics who say he shows nothing new: "Of course, we introduce new ideas all the time...but they are subtle, not spectacular...we are not interested in the spectacular."

The Oriental influence can be found throughout the Balmain career and he admits that he has always been impressed with the simplicity and purity of line developed in the Far East. He did over 200 designs for the Queen of Thailand's recent world tour and bubbles with delight at the mere mention of her name. "She is so charming...unique among Orientals, you know, because she has a perfect figure for

Western clothes...most Orientals just do not have the correct proportions." Included in the royal wardrobe were five fur coats and several mink hats and M. Balmain is elvishly puzzled at she will do with them in hot, damp Thailand.

"In Thailand, the Queen does not wear a crown, but I insisted that she have one... so we borrowed one from one of the young princes...she was delighted and wore it all the time."

The little Siamese house he bought in a recent visit to Thailand is destined to become a beach house on Elba. "My first idea was to use an Italian pre-fab, but since the Siamese house is all marked, piece-by-piece, it is practically a pre-fab itself." Elba, of course, will be the design-headquarters of his newest venture—sportswear to be manufactured in Italy and marketed under the name "Elbalmain."

Italy is also the scene of his men's wear operation and M. Balmain makes his annual appearance at the opening of La Scala in Milano. "I wore a top hat there long before anyone else did...once my picture appeared on the front page, wearing a top hat...a very large picture...needless to say, I still wear the top hat, but so does everyone else now, so I no longer get a large picture on the front page." Having read that the opening of the Metropolitan Opera last Monday was more conservative and quiet than usual, M. Balmain was optimistic: "Perhaps, one day, it may even be elegant."

The Balmain plans? When he finishes collecting antiques—he has large and valuable collections of Galle and Tanagra—"I would like to build houses and design gardens...I was trained as an architect, you know, and would like, some day, to return to it in a small way...I am adding two wings to my house outside Paris and there is the house in Elba to be finished...and, of course, the little Siamese beach house...."

—*Women's Wear Daily*

"COCO" CHANEL
Conversations with Chanel

JULY 2, 1963

ON COUTURE:

"Couture is not just making sketches. Couture is architecture. It is proportion, the shape and length of the neck, the shape of the head, its proportion of the body. Couture is four centimeters here and five there. It is architecture.

"The designer who thinks he can do the sketches and put in a seam here and there and then leave for Spain the day after the collection is not being a couturier. You have to stay with it, to work out every detail yourself, to handle the fittings, school the mannequins, do the whole job.

"Fashion is an illusion. It is the colors of the cloth, the choice of mannequins, the setting. I try to present the least vulgarity possible under lights like those of a cathedral.

"Balenciaga is the only designer I admire. Courrèges sounds interesting but I don't know him. You say St. Laurent is staying small and not going into prêt a porter. Good. Cardin has talent but he makes too many shocks. I know all about Givenchy."

ON AMERICAN DESGINERS:

"There's no reason why the Americans can't produce a great couturier. When I opened there was one Spanish house and five Italian houses here among the French.

Nationality has nothing to do with it. As for Paris atmosphere, the writers and the painters talk about is all the time but a real writer can write in the elevator, on the street, or when his children are crying."

ON CUSTOMERS:

"There's this one and that one and the other one (she used the names) and they're all so famous and well dressed and they never pay their bills, never. Why shouldn't they pay when everyone else must? It's a form of stealing. And the princesses, some of them, they're the worst of the lot. When they write asking the price of something I give orders to set a price a little extravagant and then we never hear from them again."

ON HER COLLECTION:

"There will be changes but no shock. I don't believe in shock for shock's sake. A businessman doesn't demolish the company every fiscal year. The colors will be different this season, much much brighter and gayer and more exciting. Details will change. Some jackets will be longer, others short. You want different lengths to suit different women. But I love this look [pressing her hand against her shoulders, the upper arms, tightening the shoulders and bringing the upper jacket even closer, snugger to the body] and there will be even more of it."

ON DRESSES AND THE LITTLE BLACK DRESS:

"Some people think I make only suits. But look at this picture [*WWD*, June 18, Page 1] of Mme. Weisweiller. I can make a dress, too, you know, I live this dress. I have it upstairs myself. The colors are wonderful. Color is nearly everything. Yet there's a need for the black dress. What woman who does out often can afford to have a different dress every evening? Very few. But with a black dress you can wear it more than once."

ON BEAUTY:

"Anyone past the age of 20 who looks into the mirror to be pleased is a fool. You see the flaws, not the beauty. Beauty is charm, which has nothing to do with looks, and it's physical proportion, nothing too much, everything in balance."

ON MAISON CHANEL:

"Mihri Fenwick of *Marie-Claire* magazine is coming to work here. She will handle the press, eventually the salon, do a little bit of this, a little bit of that. She's a great friend of mine but she's not coming here because I want a friend. I want someone who can be a little tough, a little nasty, to help run things properly. This is a happy house and I don't want histories, just that everyone work hard and well. Mihri won't help with the designing. I do that myself along and I always will. Poor M. Tranchant [her homme d'affaires] is still ill and I need someone to help direct things."

ON AMERICA:

"They love me in America, or so I'm told, the way they love me here in the streets. The upper classes understand me and the lower classes, but the in-between don't and never will. Americans understand me and I like them. I am always meeting Americans in the Ritz elevator and the woman says she loves my clothes and her husband, standing a little behind, says mine are the only clothes he doesn't mind paying for.

"What problems he has, your President, the poor man. But he's young and strong and intelligent and that's what you need. Your whole country is young and alive and with a future. But the race problem, that is a great trouble for Kennedy, the poor boy."

ON FRANCE:

"This juke box age, and yet 4,000 people turned out for the mass for Bastien-Thiry (the executed, frustrated assassin of de Gaulle) and so there's hope for us yet. But there are too many bureaucrats."

ON SPACEWOMEN:

"It's not a publicity stunt. Women are different from men. Women are stronger in many ways, they live longer, they can work harder for longer periods. I think it is that men think too much and it kills them. Women are more primitive in their reactions and feelings and so they live longer."

ON MANNEQUINS:

"There are a few real professionals, mostly from the American agencies, but too many of them are bonnes a tout faire, worse than that, they are femmes de ménage."

ON EVENING DRESS:

"Courrèges is not entirely right [saying really elegant clothes can be worn around the clock without change]. There are times when you must wear a long dress—a Presidential ball, a gala at the theatre, and then only a long dress will do. But his point is interesting."

ON ACTRESSES:

"B. B. is money mad, Sophia Loren is a big peasant. Romy Schneider is fine. *Vogue* phoned me the other day about some clothes for photographing on Anouk Aimee. I find Anouk Aimee very gentille, very attractive."

ON FABRICS:

"I love to make the winter collection because then I can use these wonderful heavy Irish fabrics. Look at this suit, feel it, you don't get fabric like that in copies. I line up these wonderful Irish tweeds on two long tables and I walk up and down picking out what I want. Who can select fabrics from these little bits of samples? I found these Irish houses making tweeds for men's overcoats and I made them sell to me."

ON SPORT:

"I play golf, badly. I skied until five years ago when I broke my leg the second time and I quit. I don't swim and the sea is the only thing in life I fear [her favorite vacation spot is in Switzerland, as far from Europe's seas as you can get.] I love horse racing. I have two horses in training now. The better is a two-year-old I plan to race toward the end of the French season. I love animals but I won't have then around anymore. They are a bother and it's too sad when something happens to them. And they shouldn't let women bring dogs into restaurants. But I am very serious about the race horses and I love them. The brother of one of mine won the English Derby."

ON THE PROFUMO SCANDAL:

"It is sad for Macmillan who gave them so many good years and worked so hard for the British."

ON PRACTICAL CLOTHES:

"Look at this suit. It moves with the body when I move. It doesn't tug or pull. And look at the pockets, even a watch pocket in the skirt. Here is my handkerchief, here is my watch, there my key, here my money. You don't need to carry a bag." [Yet she carried a bag, a very small and very neat compartmented bag—the neatest bag this reporter had ever looked into.]

ON FASHION MAGAZINES:

"I prefer the newspapers. An hour after my collection I am going to call in all the photographers from the serious papers and let them take photos of the clothes. It's too much bother sending them out to the magazines, you have to send someone along with them, and they never come back on time.

[She mentioned a famous fashion editor.] "The most pretentious woman I ever met. How she was dressed! A man I knew came over to me and pointed her out at this party and he asked me, 'Coco, is that a madwoman?'"

ON WORK:

"I should really be well into the collection but I have to keep filling the orders. The American clients come too late but I must make the clothes they want. One woman this morning ordered 13 things when I should be working instead on the collection. To tell the truth, not one thing is made yet."

[She absent-mindedly pulled out of a pocket a bit of black knitting wool, looked at it, and replaced it in another pocket.]

"When I begin finding things like this in my pockets I know the collection is near."

—*James W. Brady*

VALENTINO

A 1965 Interview with Rome's Most Colorful Couturier

MARCH 17, 1965

"I adore being *simpatico* with everybody... and I want no rancor with anybody."

Valentino backs his words with talent and a driving desire to move ahead. In five years, the young, handsome Roman couturier (whose unused last name is Garavani) has come from a shaky beginning at 9 Via Condotti (some say the address is jinxed), where his early backers cast him adrift, to the crest of the Italian couture. When he had to close his first house, he swore to aim for the number-one couture spot in Italy...."I am an optimist...but also a great hardhead."

On couture and women: "When a couturier has found his style direction, he should follow it and not try to change. He still has freedom of colors, fabrics and embroideries. Women today want to have a suit they can put on two years from now...nothing is easier to lose than a client who finds the things she buys go out of style too rapidly. In the first place, a woman should dress up...but has lost the habit. Necessarily, her wardrobe should not be too big. It is enough to have two good morning outfits, some three-piece ensembles and a suit or cocktail dress. Boutique articles such as sweaters and skirts I do not want to consider. The things that really make a woman elegant are the accessories...many and expensive. A good suit rarely loses its fashion, but a pair of shoes or a handbag soon lose their freshness. It is things like these that must be renewed continually.

"Women of today have a duty to be *soignée*. They should be well made up, absolutely wear lipstick—I detest women without lipstick—and be well coiffured, not running around with dangling straight as if they just finished a home shampoo. In this

regard, American women can give advice to the Italians. But while an American woman is perfectly neat from morning to evening, she is not so *soignée* as Europeans and rarely combines her accessories correctly. Italian women are vain, but after a time, they seem to get bored...and I think their attitudes today are a kind of reverse snobbery. They run around from morning to night in sweaters and skirts, which, in my opinion, are for the country, *never* for the city.

"In my home, I am something of a meticulous old maid...and hate disorder. Often, when I'm in bed reading Mickey Mouse, which is my favorite reading material, I get up to make sure everything is in order in the house."

—Adriana Grassi

GIORGIO DI SANT'ANGELO
Di Sant'Angelo's Head
OCTOBER 16, 1968

Giorgio di Sant'Angelo's head is in everything...from rtw and accessories to hairpieces and furs.

The Renaissance man of the jet age studied with Picasso on a scholarship, was an architect in Europe and is now making bigger grooves since he won his first Coty award this year for his imaginative accessory designs.

He has expanded his operation, is doing his own rtw align with accessories. He just signed a contract to do furs for Chambers-Sherwin, purse accessories for Whiting Davis...is still doing scarfs for Sally Gee, gloves for Crescendoe. He'll soon do a movie with Veruschka...he'll act, design the clothes and the scenery. It will be filmed in January by an Italian movie company.

Giorgio settles in the chrome and black leather chair. His new sterile office is comfortably cluttered with mementos. On the desk, antique miniature frames contain photos of his family. He's wearing a blue velvet Edwardian suit—"I designed everything myself from tie to buckled shoes." His fingers are ringed ornately...are moving all the time as he talks about his world of fashion.

"I don't consider myself a designer. I do a little bit of everything. Just to design clothes is not interesting. It's to create a new total look...a new idea. I design accessory clothes...put-together clothes.

"Never one dress but things to combine, like sportswear 24 hours a day. Imaginative clothes, I detest anything that is a status symbol, that is chic or proper. I dislike the ballgown...the tea gown with the placement of the pin just so.

"I like women to look imaginative. Costume jewelry is best when it really looks fake. My clothes are sensual. They have to have sexual attraction."

He would like to change fashion simply. "The futuristic mood and space suits are out. The simplest way...with layers is the easiest. I have worked in that concept with my wrap-around idea for day and evening. I see nylon jersey as the fabric of the future. Placement of color relating to construction is my important message."

Giorgio digs the Seventh Avenue establishment. "S. A. created the fashions of the world. It's filled with the greatest designers. They work side by side, from the president down to the little assistant.

"If you gave them the best fabrics, the five best tailors and seamstresses like in Paris, imagine what they could do. In Paris it works the other way around. They copy what is done in the United States the year before. St. Laurent has imagination...picks up good ideas...produces a look that is less couture.

"Clothes should be less expensive than they are. I wish I could produce my clothes inexpensively. Who has money today to spend $1,000 on an outfit? There is no necessity for them to be that expensive... or overdone. My clothes cost $100 to $200 and to me that is still too expensive."

He thinks Rudi Gernreich is the best designer in America. "He has done basics and changed the look." He also mentions Galanos...and the Grand Old Master— "We have to respect him...he is an old man. He has done a great job. I used to love Courrèges but he hasn't done anything in the past five years."

He claims, "I was the first to work with plastic jewelry before Paco Rabanne. I did the first square-fingered glove for Crecendoe and introduced hardware on gloves that contributed to the youth market for gloves."

Giorgio also says he was first to put the zip into gloves with a non-irritating industrial zipper. To his credit also...colored Dynel hairpieces for Reed Meredith.

After living in the U. S. for three years, Giorgio says he wouldn't move back to Europe or any other part of the world. "New York is the greatest city. It's the center of art...it's where everything is happening...an opening every night, people to meet...places to go. I love it here."

During the summer he went to Europe (backed by a small couture house) to investigate the potential of opening a European market for his accessories to be produced in the States and sold in Europe. "But when we went to the different manufacturers they already had tear sheets of my work from the magazines and were knocking them off."

On fashion: "Fashion is happening on the streets. Fashion is to transport what you have in your mind. Most designers pick it up in the street and make it official. Nothing has happened in fashion since the 20s. Furniture designs, music, art, painting was great. But since then nothing...until now.

"There is a complete revolution all the way around. In music, the arts, painting, sculpture. Designers are very involved with life. My inspiration comes from my friends...the people I surround myself with...like Veruschka, who is like a sister to me."

On citypants: "American women invented sportswear…invented pants. Besides they have been around for 100 years. Some of those chi-chi ladies would wear them. I like the way most American women dress. Even in the Midwest, when they are corny they are corny all the way."

On nudity: "I think baring some of the body is good but what St. Laurent is doing I don't like. How many women can go without a bra today? Nudity with a certain mysteriousness is sensuous. Plain nudity doesn't do a thing. I was the first to walk around with my shirt open to my pants.

On drugs: "I was born stoned. Maybe the kids today have to discover themselves with drugs, but not me. I don't use any. I had my problems when I was a youngster. I took a sleeping cure in Switzerland… for 15 days I was asleep. They feed you intravenously. I had to do it for complete relaxation.

"When I woke up I felt as though I was reborn. My parents do it every year. Of course, it can't be done in America. It is illegal here but it was very good. Marijuana is all right for anyone who needs some acceleration, but I don't need any."

—*Margaret Mazzaraco*

YVES SAINT LAURENT
ON THE YVES OF THE REVOLUTION

JUNE 15, 1970

PARIS.—Yves Saint Laurent is at a crossroads in his life.

His next couture collection which he will present in July may be the most important of his career. And Yves knows it.

With Yves Saint Laurent, one always expects much. But one never expects what one should expect. And maybe it is because Yves has spoiled us. He has lead us to expect a new shape, a new mood, a new length, a new woman every six months and he's been doing it with stunning regularity for the past ten years.

Now Yves is ahead of himself and he is ahead of us.

"All that—a new shape, a new length—is false now. For me, fashion today is much more a state of spirit…and image…colors. Above all, fashion is work. The only thing that matters to me is my work. Now, my work pleases me."

"All around us, the Establishment is crumbling. In this context, what meaning does fashion have except as work?"

These are the clues to Yves' new thinking and he's frank to admit it has caused him a lot of anguish. But the relaxed, smiling man, curled up in the corner of his brown leather sofa, has worked his way through the anguish—"or at least I've learned to live with it," he smiles.

For a man who, after all, makes his living designing and selling clothes, he says he'd be perfectly happy to see every woman in the world in the same dress. "A uniform for day and a uniform for night," he says. "Like Chinese women. In this way, women will rediscover their personality."

It is, in essence, the Chanel approach to fashion. Yves has always loved and admired Chanel. Now, he is coming to approach fashion more and more the Chanel way. Evolution rather than revolution.

Yves grins: "Don't get me wrong. I'm not talking politics."

But he knows that there is a revolution in the air and he knows that clothes are a big part of it.

"Hippie," he says, "is more than a way of dressing. It's a spirit which fills young people. I don't know any young people who are not hippies in their spirit. This is what it is all about. When the revolution comes, it will come from the young people."

For the first time, the youngest of the couturiers is putting himself a little bit aside from the whole youth movement. At 33, Yves seems to consider himself as more a participating onlooker.

"These young people who are making the revolution have no program. They just want to destroy and then see what happens. Before, revolutionaries always destroyed an existing society to replace it with something else. There was always another plan.

"It's an irreversible conflict of the generations."

Out of this conflict, Yves sees the fashion lesson.

"It's always like this in fashion and you can see it in the young people of today. Every 25 years the body changes…the gestures change. There is a new body emerging—slim and long. Girls who are now 14 will grow old in a different way than the woman who is now 35 or even 25.

"Of course there are exceptions but I'm speaking of the mass of women. The woman who thinks she is in fashion because she puts on a long skirt is a total masquerade."

He sees the revolution as the consumer society pushed to its limits. "Look at all that advertising—you must buy these shoes to go with this bag to go with that belt. Such advertising takes people for imbeciles. The results? The young don't shop in the big stores anymore."

He talks about the gala in the Rue du Faubourg St. Honore organized by many of the luxury merchants along the street. There was a parade of Cadillacs, Rolls Royces, Bentleys, high fashion mannequins, horse drawn carriages. The luxurious works.

"And afterward everyone danced in the streets. How can anyone dance in the streets when there are riots in the streets," Yves asks indignantly. Because of his Rive Gauche Boutique on the Faubourg, he was asked to participate but he refused. "It's a disgrace. Those days are over."

Yves is very aware as he sits in his beautiful apartment on the Place Vauban that he is not one of life's "have nots" but he knows he's worked for what he has and as he says: "Either one gives up everything or else one lives one's life just up to the moment. The drama is that there are so many stupid rich people. Luxury—so few know how to use it and make it respectable."

Yves is just back from a holiday in Brittany and looks as tanned as if he had been in Morocco.

"I love Brittany," he says. "The air is so healthy and I was so tired when I went there…too tired, really to go to Morocco. In Brittany, you almost have the impression that you are in another country. Ireland, perhaps. It's so wild."

He discovered an abandoned chateau near Concarno which had belonged to Prince Yousopof. "It looked almost as if Louis of Bavaria had built it. I loved it so much I wanted to buy it but it was too expensive. But I haven't given up. The will be other chateaux."

He talks about his new apartment on rue de Babylon which he just signed for the day before. "The rooms are just as big as the rooms in a chateau."

The new apartment which Yves will move into in the fall, spreads over two floors and opens to an enormous garden. "The only noise," Yves says, "is the sound of tennis balls from a neighborhood court.'

Then, all of a sudden, he looks around the objet-filled rooms of his Place Vauban home and says: "I am sad to leave this place because of the view." (The apartment looks out over Les Invalides.)

"And besides, " says Yves, "I'll have to learn new gestures for the new apartment. I know where everything is here…where I can turn." He points to a small end table and says: "I'm always knocking that over."

The room is heavy with the smell of incense, rich and musky, as the Hofbourg Chapel after High Mass. On Yves' favorite cobra-legged table, an enormous bouquet of white peonies.

If you ask him what he has been doing lately, he grins and says: "Nothing. Even lulu is locked up. She is being punished."

He's been rereading Proust. "It's my bedside book. I read it every time I go to the country but I've never finished it because I don't ever want to be finished with it."

Another Yves' enthusiasm: *Women in Love*.

"I saw it the first day it opened. That girl was marvelous—the one with the bangs.

And the sets…the little details. I want to go back again and again. It was a very real picture for me. Did you know the décor was done by Luciana, a girl who used to be a mannequin for me. She was a mannequin just for the experience of it. She was great."

He's been to see the Matisse exhibit twice "but the second time, I found it too beautiful. Think how Picasso was involved with his times. How his work reflects what is happening around him and the world. Matisse was so uninfluenced by his time. From 1905 on, he was always the same—the painter of eternal happiness. He never evolved. As a body of work, he is very egotistical."

This spring, Yves started to take yoga lessons from Mme. Raga, the most famous yoga teacher in Paris. "But I could never get the breathing straight," he laughs. "It was too much of a discipline. It called for too much will power and I'd rather put my will power into something else."

"It appears that yoga is the secret of happiness. I guess I'll have to find my happiness somewhere else."

If you ask him to define happiness he chuckles: "I've run after it in so many ways. It's a runaway thing."

And then he jokes about being kidnapped. His eyes behind those dark rimmed glasses grow enormous and he says: "The program of the left is to carry off the boss."

Hazel, his new chihuahua, is growing impatient…leaps from her master's lap and gives the fire screen and energetic lick.

Yves stretches that long frame and says:

"When I'm inspired, I only have to work an hour a day. Even half an hour is enough. I used to be able to talk about my work. To say 'pink this season'…or 'long this season.' I just can't talk about what I'm doing any more. It is something that touches at my humanity very deeply."

Then he bounds from the sofa and says:

"My pen has been very agile this season."

—*Claude de Leusse and Patricia McColl*

DIANE VON FURSTENBERG

EYE VIEW: *Diane Means Business*

JUNE 14, 1973

NEW YORK—Princess Diane von Furstenberg is a jet-setter. Everybody knows that. What they don't know is that some of that jetting is from Lord & Taylor's in Atlanta to Rae Phillips' specialty store in Shaker Heights to I. Magnin's in Los Angeles, and that her flights take off at 6:30 a.m. The princess does that traveling to promote her dress business, so even if she weren't a princess by marriage and in the jet set, she'd qualify for an airline's million-milers club.

"Yesterday morning I got up at 5:30 a.m. to go to Washington. I was so tired. I said, 'I'm young. Why am I spending the best years of my life like this?' But I know why. It's because I love my business," she tells *WWD*.

Born in Belgium, she has the glamour that monied Europeans cultivate, but she is softer and prettier than she appears in most pictures. She tells *WWD* about projecting for increases and how her dresses hang, but despite the SA lingo, overtones of the privileged life are clearly there.

The phone rings, "Hello," she says. "No, Egon isn't here. He went to Brazil for a few days." The call for her husband out of the way, she goes back to business.

Diane von Furstenberg, Ltd., will sell $5 million worth of simple shirtdresses this year, she estimates. That's a tenfold increase over last year. "Last year I sold 35 stores. This year it's about 700, and everybody is buying more than they did last year," she explained, adding that her Italian production plant could fill the quantum jump in orders because she had projected for them.

"The success of my business is that customers like my dresses and come back for more. The dresses got to be known," she explains.

In spectacular fashion, Diane became known as well. She and her husband, Egon, heir to a German title and the Fiat fortune, were on the New York social scene. *Town & Country* launched them as trendy couple of the moment by putting a semi-nude photo of them on the cover. Next came a sensational *New York* magazine piece about their married life. Then *Newsweek* picked up a picture of her at a Dallas party wearing an almost-frontless dress.

Such wide press coverage would make any SA designer drool on his piece goods, but Diane makes a mezzo e mezzo hand gesture about the value of her personal publicity.

"People may come to stores to see me because of it, but that doesn't sell dress," she comments. That is like a politician saying, "Crowds may turn out to shake my hand, but that doesn't mean they'll vote for me." Their initial interest helps matters though.

"Undoubtedly, her personal appearance with her clothes is one of the keys to her success. Stores buy quantities when she goes out to promote," Bill Blass observed. He was the one who sent Diane and her clothes to Bloomingdale's, which launched her. Blass continued, "When Diane told me she wanted to be in this business, I realized she was dead-on serious. I knew she had personal flair and the desire to succeed."

It was Blass who introduced Diane to Rose Wells, who was then a vice-president of Bloomingdale's.

"I told her the dresses had good bodies but that she had to do them in smaller prints than what she showed me and that she should sell them for under $80." Ms. Wells said.

Bloomingdale's buyer Elaine Monroe said, "We've done very well with Diane.

She's smart and knows how to promote. Plus, there's the combination of the right price, the right fabrics for the American way of life, and her timing. She's done it all herself."

Her first business steps were tiny ones, Diane explains. "Before I was married, I started working on the dresses with a friend in Italy. When I came to the U.S. to visit Egon, I showed some of the things to people here. Diana Vreeland, who was then editor of *Vogue*, told me to go into manufacturing rather than open a boutique. After I married, I worked from my apartment. I even did the invoicing myself. I showed at the Carlton and then I took a small office uptown. I was afraid to come down to SA. I was young and inexperienced, and I was afraid the sharks down there would eat me up."

But the clothes didn't sell. Charles C. Bassine, now chairman of the executive committee of Arlen Realty and Development Corp., sent her to John Pomerantz, president of Leslie Fay, Inc., for advice.

"I told her to get a sales manager, to move downtown, to keep on importing and to keep her look," Pomerantz recalled. "I haven't said six words to her since."

Diane took every bit of his advice, and the sharks haven't gotten her yet. Her showroom is at 530 Seventh Ave., but she doesn't mix with SA. "I have no idea of what happens on SA. I take a taxi to my office each morning. We were here a year on April 1. I wear jeans like today because I help ship the clothes and so I can't do any selling myself. Sometimes I hear the salespeople here say, 'Oh, Diane's never here. She's always traveling around Europe.' Then I go out and serve the buyers coffee, and they don't recognize me. I don't even wear make-up," she tells *WWD*, "but I did today for the photos.

"I'm usually in by 10 and leave at 3," she says. "I love coming here. It's like coming home to my parents. That article in *New York* wasn't completely fair, but I said, 'What the hell, it didn't hurt me.' But the people here were hurt.

"The people in the stores were hurt, too. They are always so nice to me and they make me feel welcome. No one has ever been hostile to me because of what

they may have read. One only gets hostility from friends. Hey—I never realized that til this moment.

"There's no glamour to all this. I arrive at stores early in the morning and the elevator man says, 'Who are you?' and I have to explain why I'm there. But it's all worth it. I want to do everything myself. I'm not trying to fool anyone like those designers who franchise. Of course, I don't pretend I do original things. Dresses aren't creations. Since a dress was a dress, it had two sleeves and one skirt. I pick prints, choose colors and style the dresses last. St. Laurent, Halston and Ungaro, to a certain extent, are the designers who influence me."

After some fervid hairbrushing for the camera, she goes on, "I just try to make comfortable shirtdresses. I'm pro-women, and I want them to look nice. Most designers want women to look like fools." Her eyes narrow. "I can't think of a dress without it being a shirtdress. I don't know what will happen if styles change, but I know fabric is very important."

Diane von Furstenberg is not a woman to limit herself. She's preparing a cosmetics line for the fall. "I think this business is going to be huge. Some people envy me and I'm afraid of that, but I still think this business is going to be huge. I was thinking of going into children's wear, but there aren't that many hours. If there were time, I'd love to make real jewelry. I love stones; they're cold and feel good." She clenches a handful of imaginary rocks.

"The thing is, I want to do everything myself. I don't think designers who franchise are doing the right thing." She rules out the possibility she might merge her firm with her husband's men's wear house.

For now, the thing to do is make the most of her dress business. "I may open an office in Italy, so I could sell Japan, Canada and Italy," she says. It's not that simple, according to most U.S. dress manufacturers. The princess says they're right. "Europe is not as well organized as the U.S. When a store there says yes, it doesn't necessarily mean yes. Only a European can understand them."

All right, she's got everything. What makes a glamor girl decide it's worth it when she wakes up at 5:30 a.m., eyes puffy with sleep, to fly to Cleveland?

"The two things I created myself are my two children and my business," she answers. "I think of myself as a mother and a businesswoman. Getting money from a father or a husband isn't the same as making it on your own. Now I could get two bags, put one child in one, the other child in the second, pick them up and take off. I'm free to go anywhere. That's how I know my choice is staying where I am."

—*Kathleen Brady*

CALVIN KLEIN
An Anti-Materialist Turns 30 and Waits to Go Co-Op

JANUARY 30, 1973

Calvin Klein moves restlessly on the U-shaped brown suede sofa in the starkly lit modern Upper East Side apartment he shares with his wife, Jayne, their 6-year-old daughter, Marci, and a huge sheepdog named Snoopy.

"My image is that I'm young, eager and kind of sensitive," explains Calvin.... "But I've just had a very traumatic birthday—I turned 30.

"Five years ago, I knew exactly what I wanted—to have my own coat and suit business. I did it with my school friend, Barry Schwartz, and his $10,000. We've surpassed all our expectations. We are constantly refusing takeover offers from public companies. Now the big question

we face is just how far do we want to expand."

"We retail coats and suits from about $140 to $160. Last year our volume was $4 million; this year we expect it to be $4.5 to $5 million."

At present, expansion plans include taking over the 11th floor at 205 West 39th St. vacated by Dan Millstein—Calvin's first employer when he graduated from the Fashion Institute of Technology—for showroom and offices; the present fourth-floor quarters will be used as a cutting room.

"Negotiating with Dan to take over his showroom when his company went out of business was one of the hardest things I've ever done. When I first called him about taking over his space, Dan didn't want to talk to me and our relationship got so bad that I finally had to leave everything to Barry."

Ironically, Calvin believes that a major reason for his own company's success is that so many coat and suit manufacturers have disappeared from the scene.

"We have very little competition, and that's what makes it easy for us. So many people today say there is no coat business. My God, there's plenty of it around. I wouldn't mind a little more competition—it makes me work better."

Calvin and Barry went into the "contemporary" price range in 1967, he says, because he saw a void in the market. "There has always been a couture level of clothes, which I always thought was kind of dead. The level beneath couture interested me—clothes that are good looking but also young...clothes that Jayne and her friends would wear."

Calvin met Jayne, who is 10 months younger than he, when they were both students at F.I.T. "And we'd lived most of our lives in the same Bronx neighborhood, so it was practically a girl-marries-boy-next-door-story.

"Jayne is constantly in my mind when I design. She is our kind of customer; she grew out of wearing junior clothes five or six years ago. She wanted something better. But she certainly wouldn't buy clothes on a couture level. They're too old and too expensive for her.

"Our kind of customer just doesn't believe in spending that kind of money on

clothes. They're not that important to her. She'll spend it on travel or decorating, but not on clothes.

"She likes to look 'today,' but she doesn't want to spend all day worrying about what she will wear at night. She's very secure about herself and her clothes."

The Kleins have moved four times since their marriage eight years ago, the most recent move from Forest Hills, where their favorite night out was hearing a rock concert at the Forest Hills Music Festival.

They've been in their present apartment for 18 months and have had it extensively decorated by John Stedila, a young decorator whose work they saw in a magazine.

"We moved here because we knew the building would probably go co-op," says Calvin, who is still waiting for it to happen. To get an apartment the size they wanted, the living room was expanded by knocking down a wall and "adding on" a bedroom and bath (now a wet bar) from the next apartment. "We've spent a lot of money fixing it up. Jayne keeps kidding me that the moment it's completely finished I'll want to move.

"I probably will. My only real hobby is studying the Sunday *New York Times* real-estate section. I think I must know the apartment market as well as any agent. We go apartment-looking even now. And if we found something we like better, I'd think nothing of leaving here—even after all we've gone through in decorating it."

But Calvin reckons that his real major hang-up is that he "eats, sleeps and drinks the fashion business...It's really true that if you're going to be successful you have to work at it hard. I'm completely disorganized about everything except my own business.

"We travel a lot, but I don't consider I've had a real vacation in five years. Wherever we are, when I walk down the street my eyes are on something that someone else is wearing.

"My job is my hobby as well as my work. At night when I'm home I'll sit down to relax, then maybe I'll do 100 sketches.

"I should exercise—some mornings my back tells me, just bending over to brush my teeth. But I just don't have the patience. Two years ago I joined a gym....I was so exhausted the evening I went that

I took a cab from 39th to 34th St. I paid the $200, but I never went back."

Calvin is in the office by 8 each morning and leaves about 7. "Until this summer I worked six days a week...then we rented a house in Amagansett and started going there weekends.

"In the beginning it was seven days a week in the shop—and often 24 hours a day. Barry and I would ship until 3 in the morning and then sleep on the convertible sofa in the showroom.

"There isn't any job in the place I haven't done—and I'm really proud of it."

Now Calvin and Jayne send Marci to Dalton. ("When I pick her up at a friend's after a party," says Jayne, "I'm the only mother—everybody else is a maid.") They've also replaced Calvin's stolen Jaguar with a Mercedes and are looking for land to build a house in Easthampton, but he insists he has no status symbols: "There is not any one thing I own that would upset me greatly if I lost it. I've started collecting some things—old lithographs, posters. But I don't intend to keep them the rest of my life. I want to constantly change things. If I had everything I wanted, it would be a bore."

As for today's mood in fashion, Calvin says his favorite French couturier is Yves St. Laurent because "he is the only one who's in touch with young people today."

On this side of the Atlantic, he says, "When I was at school I loved the things Tiffeau did, and today I think Chester Weinberg is one of the most talented designers. He is one of the few couture-level designers doing younger clothes.

"But there are really no leaders in fashion today. No one really can dictate what fashion will be from season to season. It's not good or bad—it's just what's happening.

"The customer doesn't care how talented or friendly a designers is....If his clothes don't work for her, she won't buy them.

"You get the message when you're in a store and a woman tells you she's shortening your coat because she doesn't think the length is right for her."

Calvin believes that many stores are underplaying the customer.

"The styles that sell best in our collection sell equally as well in New York, Chicago and Denver. It makes no difference. Maybe years ago what sold in New York one season would sell in the Midwest the following year. But television has changed all that."

Calvin sees big changes taking place in retailing in the '70s.

"Most people I know tend to shop in specialty stores because they find the kind of merchandise—sportswear, day clothes and evening wear—that they like best. And they keep going back to that store.

"If department stores are going to keep up with the times they will have to change their coat, suit and dress departments to 'resource departments.' Buyers will shop resources rather than markets. Everything I have to offer—coat or dress—should be sold in the same department and bought by the same buyers. If I put two good dresses in a collection and they're bought by the dress department, they get lost. But if they are sold along with my others clothes, they get snapped up."

But Jayne has the last word.

"Barry sums up Calvin's attitude to business this way—'he's the easiest man in the world to get along with, as along as he gets exactly what he wants.'"

—*Elsa Klensch*

MADELEINE VIONNET

Paris Eye: Vitality and Vionnet

JANUARY 29, 1974

"They're on the right track," said Madeleine Vionnet when she learned that New York designers were calling her the season's new inspiration. "I can only compliment them. As for myself, I've never done what's in fashion and never been inspired by anything outside my own head.

"Actually I've never done fashions. I did harmonies, things that were pretty together. They resembled nothing I'd seen."

Madeleine Vionnet will be 98 in June. She is pale, lucid and placid. Everything she did, as she explain it, seems to have been so simply appropriate that her things need little explanation beyond their having been done. Her motives were uncomplicated: she liked beautiful things and had

to earn a living. Her likes and her need predestined her career from the age of 12 when she was apprenticed as a seamstress to the wife of the sheriff of her home town, Aubervillers, outside Paris.

Later, she worked for dressmakers in Paris, trying to stay close to the Gare de Nord. "My father would come home to meet me when the train arrived at the La Corneuve station. I was afraid to walk home in the dark."

At 20, Ms. Vionnet went to London to work for Kate Reilly, a stylish Dover St. dressmaker. She returned to France to work for Callot and later Doucet. In 1912 she founded the house of Vionnet, which stayed open until 1938.

"What happened in 1938, Solange" she asked her nurse. "Oh yes, the war. The war was why I closed down. And then, after all, I was quite old. I couldn't go on forever. I hadn't the strength."

The Philips appliance company now occupies the townhouse of the Ave. Montair where she had her salons.

Ms. Vionnet explained her career in the house with the air of being asked the obvious: "When I had a beautiful body to dress, it was a pleasure. And I did my best to arrange the others. I dressed all those who wanted to come to me. I never advertised or ran after customers. I dressed them in my style. Women from all milieux, providing they had the money to pay. All the queens. The Queen of Belgium, the Queen of Spain, The Queen of Romania."

Ms. Vionnet was the first designer in modern history to work on the bias. She and Paul Poiret, her contemporary, took women out of corsets. But Ms. Vionnet's bias dresses increased the intimacy between the dress and the body even further. Her evening dresses, kept in a state of tension by the cut that went against the weave, clung to the body and caressed it with each movement.

Her explanation for why she chose the bias. "Everyone else was doing straight cut. I had to find some other way that would be my own way."

Ms. Vionnet was aware of what everyone else in her trade was doing, but none of them were her friends. She was married and divorced before she was 20, and in her own description loved to spend her time "behind my own walls."

"I detested going out."

About Chanel, Ms. Vionnet says "she had a good business."

About Poiret, with whom she disputed the distinction of being the first worker at Doucet to get the mannequins to take off their corsets, she says: "He and I had our house the same time and we often had the same customers. I did 'very lady-like' things and he went way overboard."

Ms. Vionnet still lives in the townhouse she bought in 1929. The original furniture she assembled is still there, although showing some signs of age. In recent years, she has moved her bed into a corner of the living room, rather than expend herself on the stairs.

"Those parchment walls," she pointed out, "it took the skin of a sheep for each of the squares. It would be impossible to do that today, the cost would be prohibitive."

The cost of luxury, Ms. Vionnet maintained, has driven down contemporary taste. No one now, can create, as she did, "without a thought about cost," those dresses that depended on the most subtle and complicated sewing and cutting. "It all began with the laws that brought in all those social security payments and minimum wages," she lamented. "Real couture became too expensive.

"People became content with half-measures.

"In all the arts we've become content with half, with mediocrity. If an artist has a lot of talent and can wait to be covered with glory, that's all right, but if he can't wait, he's likely to do something easy and commercial. He works to eat."

—G.Y. Dryansky

HUBERT DE GIVENCHY

Givenchy: Easing into Slimmer Shapes

JANUARY 31, 1975

PARIS—Movie-star handsome. Six feet six inches tall. As elegant in blue jeans and bare feet as he is in black tie. An escort for elegant women—Bunny Mellon, Capucine, Audrey Hepburn.

At 48, Hubert James Marcel Taffin de Givenchy is perhaps the last of the "grand" couturiers. Grand in his life style, grand in his concept of the couture.

His Paris apartment is a mini-museum of modern art. In the entry, an enormous Arp and a Picasso. On the terrace, a Calder. In the dining room, two Nicholas de Staels, a Matisse and a Braque.

He commutes to his country house near Paris—it has a swimming pool, of course—in a blue Mercedes 220 SL and has just bought property in the French Alps near Megeve. His two dogs, a whippet and a basset—Candy and Lippe—stay home when he works.

Givenchy has owned his couture house since 1952, seven years after he began his fashion career at the age of 18 in the house of Lucien Lelong.

That was just after World War II and, as Givenchy says: "Ever since, the couture has been on the downslope. If only a few of us are to remain, we must do our very best. If I have a role in life, it is to keep up this profession as long as I can. If the couture ever stops, it will never exist again."

When preparing collections, he arrives at this couture house by 7 a.m. and usually remains until well after 7 p.m.

Asked about creating luxury clothes in today's troubled economic and political climate, he replies. "Every epoch has its

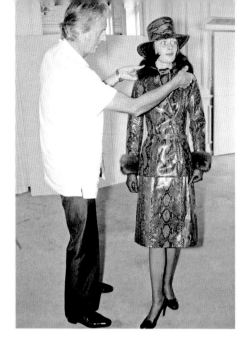

recessions, it brakes my enthusiasm. And once you lose your enthusiasm for your work, everything goes.

"In my case, I have 170 workers depending on me. If I am not enthusiastic, how can I hope they will be? It is an even greater risk for all of us to try and create in these difficult times and that is why we must try even harder. You can't stop life from happening. I am not a defeatist."

Givenchy, who was born in the north of France, belongs to the minor French aristocracy. He is the complete patriot, "I am not basically a political person, but if you are a citizen of a country, then you must do your duty. We have the chance in France to have a marvelous country and we had good luck in our last presidential elections. But the French are never content because they are spoiled and always want more."

During the 1968 student revolts, Givenchy demonstrated for Charles de Gaulle. "We had closed the house because we were afraid of incidents. The workers had all gone home. I turned on the radio and heard the general's appeal. I'd never done anything like that before, but all of a sudden I left the house and walked up the Champs Elysees. To be there as a presence. It was an unforgettable experience. One must have the courage to show one's opinions."

Now he leaves politics to the professionals and concentrates on his first love—couture, "I am crazy about this profession. I have wanted to have my own couture house since I was a child. The biggest happiness I know is to arrive here early in the morning. To listen to the Portuguese cleaning women sing. To be alone in my studio with my beautiful fabrics. To hear the workers arriving, the phone starting to ring. For me, it is like a heart beating. My day always ends too soon. I'd never change my profession for anything in the world."

—Patricia McColl

HALSTON
A Seventies Icon
Talks About Work, Rumors
and the Revelry of Studio 54

OCTOBER 30, 1978

It is early for Halston, 46, to be home. "I am never here before 8," he says, as the rain begins to beat and the lightning crackles outside. "And if I have friends in for dinner, it's usually about 10:20 or 11." Slightly eery, empty, isn't it—being alone in this place? "No, its terrific," he answers in his hard-to-place, WASP-y accent. "I might have a friend over, or several. People sort of find their place here—Liza [Minnelli] on the floor, Bianca [Jagger] on that chair over there, Martha [Graham] right here, Andy [Warhol] comes a lot."

At which point the phone rings: a young socialite friend, Catherine Guinness. Halston greets her in his most melting voice and says, "Yes, I'm having a few friends over and then to Studio."

"Studio," he calls it (Studio 54); as do, one supposes, the die-hard habitués. "It's

a democracy," he says, when asked about his fervent attachment to the place. "You see a David Bowie there, Liza, unemployed actors. And it generates energy." Does he dance? "I never dance," he answers almost primly.

"No one bothers me there," he says; he can escape his image. "I have a lot of different public images, but very few people know who I am and what makes me tick. People don't know me. I'm rather cozy. I'm a fair guy."

He hints it is the climate of SA that has fabricated his intimidating image. "You have the terrible problem of jealousy in the fashion industry, and from a lot of designers, too.

"There is this constant jealousy," he complains, slowly sipping his drink. "You're taller, you're older, you're younger....

"Or you're more successful. I've always been successful on different levels. From the moment I started in fashion, success liked me, and I like it. I've never had lean times. I was ambitious and I wanted to do things. You see, you hear the craziest things about everyone—but I'm just a person like everyone else." A slight pause. "Well, not like everyone else. There's more publicity, more picture-taking. That's sort of the hardship part sometimes. Everyone knows who I am; but I don't know who they are.

"You're only as good as the people you dress," the Halston motto goes. "I happen to like women who do things."

He dismisses the thought that he has any "power" over these Ladies; but who can deny the vatic aura of those wardrobe-planning caucuses, or the devotion that they evoke among his following? At his suggestion, mannequins will shear their locks to Punk length (Connie Cook and Pat Cleveland one day, recently); Lee Radziwill and steely Katherine Graham will bow to his council; Mary Lasker will come to him for stately caftans, and Liz Taylor will deny herself Palm Beach-y get-ups, in favor of his bias chiffons and satins. "You can only *suggest*," he says, with a knowing smile.

Discreet or outré, he knows what They want, and is adroit at handling both, nimbly walking the tightrope between Miss America conservatism and High Style theatricality. "I've done some mad things in my day,

darling," he says, with a glimmer. "Some of the most extravagant hats there were." His signature pillbox for Jacqueline Kennedy—discreet, elegant and utterly serviceable—has somehow obliterated the other end of his spectrum (the wild, feathered extravaganza for Maya Plisetskaya in Avedon's '66 photo, for instance). In the Seventies, it is his public image that swings between the two poles: Dressed in a banker-ish pinstriped suit, he will wow the crowd at a Girl Scouts of America meeting (as he did this past spring when he redesigned their uniforms); two nights later, he will set the cameras clicking at "Studio" with a wild-eyed and skimpily clad starlet.

How he manages to do all of this—run the Empire, keep up the night life and the workaholic pace—has prompted speculation…drugs being one of them.

His reaction to this is unflustered and biting. "I put on dark glasses and everyone thinks I'm the number-one-coke-head of the city," he retorts. "Everyone gossips about everyone else." And then, vehemently: "You can't take drugs and work, to keep up my pace. Everything it gives you it takes up." He attributes his energy, instead, to "a lot of vitamins. And I eat less than I used to. Fish instead of meat. I think eating less is in, eating more is out.

"I love gossip and hearsay, but I hear I've done so many raunchy things it's unbelievable." He mentions a party he gave—"a costume thing"—this past July for the employees of Studio 54. "And then I read about it in the columns the next day, and one said I wore a one-shouldered dress, and the other said an off-the-shoulder dress. Whereas," he teases, "no one knows what I wore except the people who were there." But he cannot resist admitting, when pressed, "A black cashmere body stocking."

—Francesca Stanfill

GIORGIO ARMANI
The Blazer's Edge

MAY 16, 1978

MILAN—"When I was young, I studied medicine because I wanted to be a country doctor. Since I didn't like studying so much, I gave it up. But the idea of being a simple country doctor was my dream," says 42-year-old Giorgio Armani, at the top of the big league of Milan fashion talent today.

And like a simple country doctor's Armani's manner and personality are devoid of affectation. There are no-stereotyped fashion house-head mannerisms. There is no long, anxious and exhausting tension-filled wait to see him. He strides in with his bulldog, Gigi. Assistants and public relations officials are left working in unending, linking rooms in his palazzo with intact frescoes dating from 1680.

The voice is bass, and baby-blue eyes and patrician gray hair highlight the short, solid, almost Greek-discus thrower physique.

Since he speaks no English and the reporter no Italian, he uses French to go through explanations of the profusion of modern, easy, relaxed furnishings in such a baroque building. The furniture, he feels, creates the feeling of clean and modern duality. "And I would not put fuss with frescoes," he says.

The air of calmness, a sense of a smooth operation, begins at the top with Armani himself. At Giorgio Armani, there's a high-intensity feeling of attention to technique. The designer is concerned with perfecting technique in his designs as well as the selling of the clothes and the organization of the work force that surrounds him. Although his favorite word when talking fashion is allure, he gives the same feeling of confidence you would appreciate upon consultation with a new dentist.

Armani didn't just bounce into his spot in fashion. After dropping medicine, he became an assistant buyer of men's clothing for a big Italian department store. After that, he worked at Cerutti for eight years as a designer. There's no doubt that Armani's inventive ways with blazers for men and women is based on his Cerutti years. Between Cerutti and the start of his own firm three years ago, he freelanced for many Italian factories.

For over a year, he's been called everything from the "King of the Blazer" to "Milan's St. Laurent." This season, his military touches are nothing more than that: refined touches to update his favorite blazers and over-blazers, with skirts or pants.

Armani clothing is a favorite because it looks easy to wear, it's investment clothing and it's quality. Currently, a blazer in a New York store is about $450. "Simply a question of customs and entry taxes. In Europe, the same jacket cost around $300," says Armani.

There's a consistent streak of non-color colorings in the Armani world.Taupe shows up in his own suede jeans and American suede bucks. The same shade's was custom-sprayed on his Jaguar. His house is full of taupe shadings. And his bedroom in his apartment is deep taupe.

"I like basically no colors, sharp blacks. When I do a collection, my favorite part of the work is the research of the colors and the fabrics. The cut comes second."

In the palazzo, there's one room just for fabric appointments, which is unusual. Most fashion houses meet the fabric vendors on the same grounds where the assistants work, and fabrics are banked up in any free corner. The only crowded space is the showroom where racks of fall and winter clothes spill out into adjoining hallways. As you pass by, the bigger shoulders protrude on the hangers and perforated suede epaulets on some jackets give an illusion of exaggerating the point while staying completely in line with a narrowed-down look.

How did Armani manage his big-shoulder approach?

"It's very simple. Shoulders and lapels are different, but the detail is not something a woman can't wear. Bigger shoulders give more allure and are more feminine. It's less casual, but more elegant. "When I thought of doing the big square shoulder, I asked myself, 'What's it worth?' I build my reputation on making clothes that are very salable and very wearable, commercial if you want. And I don't just do runway looks in the collection. Everything is shown and shipped just as you see in the show. Nothing is changed.

"That sudden retro style of exaggeration in Paris is amusing, but I think it difficult to sell and to wear. For Hollywood-style 1950, you have to be tall, thin and extremely beautiful. Everyone isn't.

"Hollywood glamour 1950 isn't my idea of modern. But I do find that in Paris there are designers who can take the value of retro style and build up an elegant collection. And then there are others who only exaggerate without creating balance. It's important to me to think of the business of selling and buying and clothes that women will wear in actual, today life.

"As for the big spencer look in Paris, how can some people do that when it's already been done? I like the shape of a spencer for women. It gives allure. But it's not new. And it's a little retro for my taste," says Armani.

Kenzo is the one Paris name Armani is curious about, but it is Yves St. Laurent who heads his list of favorite "creators." "I like St. Laurent because he's always in a state of high grace. And if he's made a mistake, there's still something. His way of mixing colors is fantastic. Kenzo is very amusing and genius. I also find Karl Lagerfeld very, very strong, but it seems difficult to wear. I think a woman must put herself in a mood of thinking she's like Lagerfeld to wear his clothes. But if I were a woman of wealth and had to decide between wearing a Geoffrey Beene or a Lagerfeld, it would certainly be Lagerfeld."

When thinking about America, he's pro its obsession with youth and its easy sporty elegance. "What I don't like is when American men try to dress in a very elegant way because they don't know how. Americans that you normally see on the street look ridiculous when they try to wear a navy pinstriped suit with a satin tie. But American men have a certain innate elegance when they wear sportswear.

"American women follow fashion and thus they are quiet, elegant, today. I find the idea of American elegance more international in feeling than what is considered Italian elegance on a broad scale. What is always shocking is that American women, even if they are not young, become so in the way they put themselves together.

"The feeling of youth is so much more amusing in America. It's more ironic than in Italy. In American, the sports clothes (athletic gear) have details, a feeling for colors. When Italians do sportswear, it's too serious. They even make uniforms look overdone," states Armani, who did his version of "elegant military" with feminine fabrics such as satin, taffeta and soft washed leather. "What I like are American Army uniforms. They are the most beautiful in the world. They are simple yet they have interesting details and shape."

Totally apart from Armani's easy, relaxed and modern elegance that could look good on Barbara Walters, Barbara Streisand or Empress Bokassa is the world of evening clothes. Armani has no drop-dead entrance clothes. "The life of ball-gowns and ballroom clothes is completely finished all over the world. And for evening clothes, there are plenty of creators who do that very, very well. For the moment this problem of dress-up in the evening is a bit difficult for me.

"My eveningwear is amusing, modern and easy. A woman can wear the same satin trenchcoat to work and to a party. I have low gold leather boots with a gold leather shearing jacket over a gold Klimt-inspired-print silk dress. It's the choice of fabrics and the mix of modern shapes which make evening special in my collection. And I will continue this feeling for the moment although I could do princess taffetas like Kenzo if I wanted."

Only steps away from the fashion house is Armani's small, natural and taupe-toned bachelor flat. The architecture of the building is Baroque Mussolini, which is common throughout Milan in big buildings built after the last war. Armani's livingroom has box-shaped side chairs and a large rice silk sofa from a shop in Milan called Mister Luna.

He apologizes for the art that is not hung on the polyurethaned walls. "If you go to Capri for even two days, you have to hide valuable things in Milan. People will somehow get in and take the whole apartment away," states Armani, who leaves his gold shaving brush out only because he thinks a burglar would think it fake.

If Armani entertains, it's bound to be simple and without fanfare.

"Among fashion people there exists a certain coldness. And I must say, in Milan we tend not to mix just like in Paris. I don't have a worldly social life. I usually have dinners in restaurants or with friends at home. In Milan, we don't have distractions like Studio 54, good theater or a lot of films. It's a great city for working 11 months nonstop and then having one month for holiday.

"In life, there are things I might need. And one is that I lack a great deal of time for private life. I love tennis, and I hardly have time. Perhaps I lack a true family, a wife and children. But I've made the choice to be a bachelor. I'm very egotistical, especially about my work. A wife and children would simply distract me from my work.

"Time to learn more about the world from the past as well as the present is something I dream of. I would like to know other parts of the world through the spirit of the people, not as a tourist. That takes a lot of time."

Does Armani want a fashion empire? "Yes. I hope to have a perfume one day, but then I don't dream of writing books. If I wrote a book like some of the designers who always talk about it, then I would be a writer, not a designer. I dream of perfecting my work as a fashion creator. I also want to teach others to work better around me—this is my ultimate goal.

"My tastes are simple in life. I was born into a simple family, and I have worked very hard to have things like a pure gold shaving brush among other things. My success hasn't changed me. And you don't see things like 17th, 18th, or 19th Century antiques or art in my house because it's not me. As I wasn't born an aristocrat, it's useless to try to become one through fashion. I don't want to be too distant from my roots. It's only important to be modern in my work, and honest."

—*André Leon Talley*

KARL LAGERFELD
The Kaiser Shares a Few Pointed Opinions and Remembers the Early Days

MARCH 2, 1978

"I'm nothing but a streetwalker. And I say that because it is nearly impossible to be so busy always promoting one's product. Streetwalking is the way things are done in modern life. One must always push in personal appearances, social promotion," says Karl Lagerfeld of his overall fashion work which includes Chloé—one of the most successful of the new perfumes on the market in the last two years.

"At the age of one, I gave my first commercial smile, for the advertising of my father's business," adds Lagerfeld (a real German baron) while sitting erect on his state bed in his formal 18th-century receiving room. Lagerfeld is the prime heir to the German Glue Klee fortune, Europe's equivalent of Carnation condensed milk. As a young boy of a privileged family, Lagerfeld has early visions of his fashion career, which led him to Paris in 1952. In 1954, he won the International Wool Competition first prize for designing a coat. The same year, Yves Saint Laurent designed a dress and won first place in that division of the competition.

Long before Paris, Lagerfeld was already freaked out on fashion. "When I was four, I asked my mother for a valet for my birthday. I wanted my clothes prepared

so I could wear anything I wanted at any time of the day. I was a clothes freak. And I was mad for dressing differently at least four times a day. At 10, I was always in hats, high collars and neckties. I never played with other children. I read books and did drawings night and day.

"At five, I started my French lessons with a teacher who was one of the 56 war refugees that lived in our country castle outside Hamburg after World War II. I made early preparations for coming to France."

Designer for Chloé for 14 years, Lagerfeld today has 30 licensees in Japan (half under the name Chloé, the other signed Lagerfeld); 20 licensees in Germany, as well as the Eve Stillman lingerie in the U.S. He has just signed licenses for sunglasses and a porcelain china collection for the German company Hutschenreuter.

Lagerfeld's influence is widespread, although it often remains unspoken of. He started his kind of layering in '69, unconstructed silk dresses in '72, unfinished hemlines in '74 and in '77, a return to the use of lace on cotton tulle. Designing freelance for Fendi for the last 12 years, Lagerfeld has turned furs inside out, upside down and the fur industry around with his innovations. The Paris Chloé boutique is often visited by SA designers and manufacturers who buy his dresses and jackets to copy.

"I have no opinions whatsoever about my influence. Who cares? What is important is what I will do, not what I did in the past." Although Lagerfeld claims not to think of past collections, he is constantly barking to intimates how he did spencers for Chloé last October, before Yves Saint Laurent showed them for couture in January this year.

"It's the most flattering thing in the business to be copied. What really makes me laugh is Chantal Thomass using the lace-embroidered cotton tulle I first designed for Foster Willi St. Gall last year. Since she buys a fabric later, she can sell her dresses at half the price of a Chloé.

"My work with Fendi only really started to move six years ago. I finally got the sisters to see how we could really change the shapes and treatments of fur.

"The world changes, youth changes, your skin on your face changes," adds the 39-year-old Lagerfeld. "I advocate change. What I do is create change seen through my view of the world around me. What I hate are designers who make the same old jacket or sweater differently season after season and call it their personality, their evolution, their style. When I hear I'm called an 'intellectual designer,' I hate that. What is the worst is a fashion designer who talks all the time of his or her creativity, what they are now, how they evolve. Just do it and shut up."

Lagerfeld can't stop talking about his new mood at Chloé for fall–winter '78.

"People who make clothes should avoid at all cost the idea that because Paris is in a difficult mood, fashion must be severe and serious. During the war, fashion in Paris was unbelievably amusing. In the streets, it was always the same dark suit on women with the most eccentric hats ever. Women often wore hats that looked like wedding cakes."

Lagerfeld will show whimsy, tongue-in-cheek elevator-attendant hats with chin straps in everything from red patent to black suede with day and evening clothes. He is also thinking of piling up junk jewels he calls "theater jewels" due to the state proportions. On a day suit, he will pin brooches with paste stones the size of golf balls.

"Accessories should be funny. Humor is vital, and I always make accessories that amuse me. They also aid in playing down the bourgeois aspect of the dresses.

"Women can't wear real jewelry anywhere these days. The funniest thing to do is to make a joke out of the whole concept of wearing jewels.

"When I show tennis shoes with evening dresses, big hats with tulle veils or when Donna Jordan wore rhinestones in my shows with sports clothes, everybody is quick to say it is bad taste. They also make racist remarks about my being German, but I don't care. They criticize what I later see as trends.

"As for clothes, I don't like words like modern or classic for my next collection. My mood is Oskar Schlemme because his shapes, curves and angles as a member of the Bauhaus have always been my favorites. I am still working on a new technique for a volume I want that stands just lightly away from my body. Oversoft and unconstructed shapes will not work. I am treating silk, velvet and satin in something I know as 'bouti,' which is like double-faced quilted material what is weightless."

Between fitting sessions, sample-fabric meetings and licensee conferences, Lagerfeld still finds time for his fetish—the 18th century in France.

His new apartment, with restored wood paneling from the destroyed Palais Royal in the Tuileries, is replete with antiques. Each window is draped to the floor in $100-a-yard taffeta de ninon curtains. Besides the seven rooms, Lagerfeld has three rooms behind the kitchen that are full of books divided by subjects. His marble bathroom is flanked on both sides of the entrance by floor-to-ceiling wood shelves full of his "night table" reading.

Another passion is antique auctions, where Lagerfeld will buy everything from a vintage Mme. Grès jersey and cape and give it to Paloma Picasso, to a Louis XVI bed for his mother's apartments in the same flat.

"I am always gambling at auctions," says Lagerfeld, who spent $4,000 last week on a gilded Louis XV canapé attributed to Tilliard. The chair's estimated value is $100,000. Lagerfeld's taste for auctions is so developed that he will rise at 5 a.m. on a Sunday to be chauffeured to the Belgium border to attend an auction of entire paneled rooms in old estates. He also often sits out entire afternoons in the airless and smelly Palais D'Orsay auction rooms nervously waiting to bid.

As for Club Sept, Lagerfeld never goes there. Last night, the big opening of the Sept au Palace, Lagerfeld planned to go to the movies with a friend. "Social life is nothing in Paris. There are no great houses, imaginative parties or wonderful hostesses. I have dinners with friends or stay home reading or working," continues Lagerfeld, who eats at least three times a week at La Coupole with Anouk Aimee, Paloma Picasso and her gang or Anna Piaggi, when she is in town.

If Lagerfeld suddenly stopped making dresses, what would he do? "If I listen to my fortune teller, I'll become a movie producer. I would make very sophisticated but mean, mean, bitchy Marx Brothers–type comedies. They would be mean, but in a light way."

March 12, the date of French elections, used to be a constant subject on Lagerfeld's tongue until last week, when he decided he had had enough of all the polls, publicity and front-page stories of the candidates. "As for the elections and the fear of socialism, my favorite definition of socialism is when the late Candy Darling said: 'I want everybody to live on Park Avenue.' As for the possible crisis, I can't vote as I am a guest of France. I must say I feel like people must have felt before July 14 in France in 1789, sitting on this bed and dressed this way.

"The day we begin to pay 90 percent income taxes, life will not be very glamorous. I will then rent rooms here because all I have is beautiful beds. And instead of spending $200 a night for dinner with friends in bistros, it will be spaghetti at home.

"There is a turning point in France. But I see a big room with lots of doors and no keyholes. Where is the door to the new world, the new hope? I prefer to imagine the world from my windows rather than see the often unpleasant reality."

— *André Leon Talley*

RALPH LAUREN
Ralph Lauren: Restless and Reaching

DECEMBER 11, 1978

EAST HAMPTON, N.Y.—Ralph Lauren settles lovingly into the black cockpit of his Porsche Turbo Carrera.

Clearly a favorite toy, the car was customer-made to his specifications: Darth Vader black, without a gleam of steel or chrome to break its sleek lines. Lauren loves it. The car definitely has presence. It matches his sunglasses, his bicycle and the new luggage collection he designed to go with it.

In the soft, chill gray of the afternoon, the Porsche lurks like a submarine in the driveway of Lauren's rambling beach house here. Rented by the Laurens year-round for the last four years, the house, with

its casual furniture and backyard vista of dunes and sea, is their weekend retreat.

Here, Lauren is just plain "Daddy" to his small sons, Andrew and David, and to his 4-year-old daughter, Dylan. The three, bundled up against the sea breezes, have just finished playing ball with him on the lawn.

But it's Saturday, there are chores to do, and batteries conk out even on the man who made the hacking jacket great. Ralph has to go to a nearby garage to arrange a tow for the dead Land Rover in the driveway.

The Porsche noses slowly out of the compound, but once it hits an open stretch of toad, Lauren opens it up. It whines like a 747 on takeoff.

"Listen to this sound—it's fabulous," he yells. The whine goes into a roar, and the quiet East Hampton countryside goes by in a blur.

"Speed—fast—it's very exhilarating. I don't know if it gets my tension out or what—but it gets my head somewhere else. You really have to be finely tuned, you've got to make all the moments count," he announces with the kind of gusto usually reserved for beer commercials.

He could easily fit into one of those commercials. At 39, Ralph Lauren is in very good shape, physically and financially. Silver-haired and green-eyed, he jogs every morning, and his tight-fitting T-shirt and worn jeans mold the results. Slightly rugged, extremely confident and moderately macho, he wears a got-it-made aura like a label.

It's an attractive label. Enough people bought it last year to being sales of Lauren products to $75 million at wholesale—a figure that's expected to crack $100 million by 1980.

But the man behind the label ("I never knew what a designer really was—I thought designers lived on a cloud and sort of draped things around") admits he easily might have chosen a different path.

Raised in the northern Bronx, the son of a painter of decorative furnishings effects such as faux bois, Lauren grew up in, as he says, "an Ivy League period" that colored his dreams and later influenced his designs.

"I wanted to be a basketball player, but I wasn't tall enough. When I was growing up, I loved movies and I loved a certain style—the kind that goes with a tweedy, rugged horsey atmosphere. I don't know if the things that inspired me ever existed. I loved Fred Astaire, the Duke of Windsor—they were my inspiration. I wanted to be a teacher at one time. I never thought of money—I thought of loving what I did. Teaching was away from business. I never loved the business world per se. I never loved fashion. I just had style as a kid."

He did, according to Calvin Klein, who grew up in the same neighborhood. "I'm younger than Ralph, so we weren't friends, but I remember seeing him around the neighborhood," says Calvin. "He always had a sense of style in the way he dressed. He wore Army clothes—he would mix them with tweeds and always looked terrific. He had a sense of his own, so that, in the neighborhood we both grew up in, he stood out more than anyone else."

He still does. As the Porsche slinks through the village on the way home, young girls stop and point. Despite his protestation that, "My life is very quiet and very private—I like to be a little out of things," Lauren makes it hard not to notice him, a characteristic that has marked his career.

Armed with a business degree from City College, Ralph got a job selling men's ties. It was the eve of the widetie, and he saw it coming. His company didn't. "I had ideas and they really didn't want to listen to me" he recalls. Another company did, however, and Lauren began designing ties. Polo was born and Lauren was launched.

The early days were not always easy, though, "I designed the ties, backed them and delivered them on Saturdays in a bomber jacket. A lot of store wanted me to make them narrower, but I wouldn't change, because I believed in what I did and stuck with it," he remembers proudly.

"I've built everything I've built on my own terms, everything I've gotten. I've never had to rationalize anything," he emphasizes.

"My success is just a real feeling of self and self-confidence. It gives you a feeling of accomplishment, a special confidence that you can do more than you ever thought you could do. One of the things I'm very proud of is that I've never done anything that I don't want to do.

"I think one of the important things to me is that I do what I believe in, on a level that's the best I can do. Take it or leave it—not in a cocky way—I've made my own statement."

There are those who differ with Ralph's assessment of himself—"egomaniac" being one of the more common adjectives that comes up. To that, Ralph answers, "Having a strong ego is healthy. Believing in yourself and believing that you can do something is not being an egomaniac. Someone saying that is someone who really doesn't know me."

Back in the beach house's long, beamed living room, Ralph lights a fire and settles down on a leather couch beside the person who probably knows him best.

Ricky Lauren is a warm, vibrant woman with long, blondish brown hair, candid blue eyes and small, delicate features that are pointed up by the heavy turtleneck of the navy fisherman's sweater she is wearing.

A former teacher, she has been married to Ralph for 14 years. "Ricky was going to college, teaching at night and working for an eye doctor during the afternoon. I met her at the eye doctor—six months later we were married," Ralph recalls.

Since then, he says, she has been a lot of the inspiration behind his work, "She's the kind of girl who can look good in anything; elegant and chic and rugged and outdoorsy—that's the kind of girl I

design for. She's not a fashion girl—she's more active than fashion-conscious. Ricky is involved with me and the kids. She's not phony in any way. If I've been married for 14 years, you know why."

What, then, about the occasional rumors of indiscretions on Ralph's part? "People can say anything they want. Ricky doesn't have too much competition—it's not as if I have a dog at home and no one sees her," Lauren snaps back. "When I'm away, what Ricky is worrying about is not whom I'm with, but how I am."

Ricky agrees, insisting her only worries are for Ralph's "health and his mental stability."

"I wish he'd take it easy, have fun and not take it too seriously, because it's a serious business," she says over a mug of coffee, passing around rich brownies (made by his mother) and fresh apple pie (made by her mother).

And Ricky Lauren is not shy about saying what she thinks. While aware there are problems that beset the wives of many famous men ("I'm supposed to be off somewhere in the woods. I had children and could have stuck my head in the sand"), she claims she hasn't had any.

"If I ever feel left out, it's my own problem," she says in a low, forthright voice. "Sometimes I wish I were a little more involved in the technical parts of the business. I wish I could be more helpful, but my hands are tied. I am very, very critical of his shows because he likes that. Somebody has to be honest," she says with a grin.

Ricky also has strong opinions on what she—and other women like her—are doing right now.

"From my point of view, a woman having children—that's a career. I am also working and this is the work I do. Some women feel they're no good unless they DO something.

"It's very nice to be in my position. It's like a fairy tale—at night, dressing up—but it's lovely to know I can come home to a very solid foundation. I think that's what keeps Ralph sane, too."

Ralph agrees, noting that when the family is out here at the beach, they enjoy staying home. "We're taking the option of doing what we really want to do. I love

coming home and being home. This is not boring or fake. This is a great house with all the things we like—tennis, the ocean.

"I get movies every weekend and cartoons for the kids. When I come here, I really like to relax. I love movies, I've always been inspired by movies, acting, directing—not that I've done it yet, but I'd like to in the near future."

Ralph is dead serious. After he was quoted recently about his desire to be an actor, agents called to encourage him, he says.

"I wanted to know why—I want to do something that's quality and not for the wrong reasons." So, he told them, "If you don't really think I've really got it, if you think that I'm on a giant ego trip, tell me—I've got other things to do."

He says they told him he'd be terrific, that he could play any kind of role. Ralph thinks he can, too. He already has some of the marking on natural actor, enhanced by sheer exposure to the show biz aspect of SA and his own role as a merchandiser. Like many an actor, he instinctively knows how to move and how, at a click of a camera, to show himself to advantage.

As Stuart Kreisler, a longtime friend and president of the Kreisler Group of which Lauren is a part, points out, "The areas for which Ralph has a tremendous talent are presentation and the way he's exposed."

So, why not? "First of all, you can't be afraid to fall or fail," says Ralph. "A lot of people can do more than they think they can. I know if I go into a movie, I'll probably get shot down. But if I don't and think I can do it, then, I'll get shot down by myself."

What roles would he like to play? Lauren thinks a moment, then grins. "I don't think it matters as long as I ride a horse," he jokes, admitting he wouldn't mind playing a cowboy. In fact, he's been brushing up on his equestrian technique at a nearby stable.

"I was going to say God, in *The Ten Commandments*," teases Ricky. "One of the interesting things the agents said was that I can look many different ways—I can look Ivy League one way or very rugged like cowboy," says Ralph. But, he adds, "I relate to people who are my size, like Humphrey Bogart or Al Pacino."

Why does he think he can do it? "I've never gone to acting school or fashion school, so it's all come out of myself. I started in the men's business and then went into shorts and suits and the whole wardrobe, which was unusual. Then I went into the women's wear business, which was really unheard of, so I'm very proud of that. I found my own route," he says simply.

"I can do anything I want. That is a fabulous feeling. And I'm young enough to do anything I want to do—and THAT is a great feeling. I don't think I could ask for anything else."

—*Lisa Anderson*

PIERRE CARDIN
Cardin, the Empire

FEBRUARY 26, 1979

PARIS—You could probably find some Pierre Cardin gadget among the walkabout aborigines in Australia as well as in any local American drugstore. In Indonesia, a Pierre Cardin label might be fake, but that doesn't stop people from buying it. Pierre Cardin, (who happens to be the official spokesman for a group of European and American businesses against international commercial counterfeiting), is fighting a long battle to gain what may be $5 million lost in fake Cardin goods. Such is the strength of his name.

In 1977, Cardin's 350 licensees did $250 million in sales and grew to 395 in number at retail by the end of the year. "The sales increase went up 15 percent in '78, and those figures don't include the perfume," adds Cardin, referring to the only franchise not under his supervision. According to well-informed industry sources, Cardin perfume shipped approximately $21 million to $23 million. Men's wear manufactured in the U.S.A.—the only separate figure Cardin will quote—brought in $2 million in '77.

With 300 factories and nearly 140,000 people working in the Cardin licensee empire in 40 countries including China and the Soviet Union, Pierre Cardin at 55 could be called the commercial fashion king.

His name is on entire bathrooms, cigaret lighters, bicycles, electric razors,

fruit juices, sofas, rugs, lamps, dolls and telephones. "We no longer have Cardin chocolates because they were too expensive," adds Cardin while sitting in his headquarters in Paris, "but we do have chocolates in the Maxim's deluxe grocery stores." In addition, the new Paris Maxim's chain of deluxe groceries carries Cardin-designed crockery, cutlery, linens.

Soon corporations will be able to fly for $2,300,000 in American Aviation jets with stripes and decor designed by Cardin. In the early Eighties, there will be Cardin-designed Cadillacs. There is an endless list of the usual fashion products. Besides his pret-couture ("exact copies of the couture sold in Paris boutiques and in Japan with prices falling between deluxe ready-to-wear and couture"), Cardin's rtw is sold in 500 boutiques for men and women. He recently showed a collection of over 200 styles to be sold only in Arab countries.

With the largest empire of any designer, one could say Cardin is probably the richest. Cardin will only say about his personal wealth: "My wealth is less than you can imagine and more than you think."

He says that the only thing that interests him is the press. "It transmits the image of one's 'griffe' (fashion name). I have always given a great importance to journalists and the media. I make four or five trips a year around the world just to do radio, television and interviews. I love it passionately.

"When I make a collection, I think of the press, not the clients. If the press accepts

my collection, automatically the clientele will accept it.

"And unlike other couturiers, I will say that I read a bad review of my work. It is painful for me. I am sensitive."

Cardin may not digest properly bad press from his various shows, but he has a gargantuan appetite for anything printed about him. He can show you press books for every country and nearly every product. From his recent trip to China, his office has already filed two enormous and weighty black books with clippings from countries including Japan and India.

Cardin's penchant for publicity paid off most handsomely when his already-planned trip to China found him entering the country just as the trade doors opened. Cardin returned to a front-page story in *Le Figaro*, several pages in *Paris Match* and a *New York Times* story saying he had said in Paris that "the Chinese Government had named him as a consultant to its textile-trade agency. Under the agreement with Peking, Mr. Cardin will advise the Chinese on how to style their textile products to make them more marketable in the West."

However, a high Chinese official responsible for this area reports no deal has been made and doubts there will be one. And Cardin now says, "Nothing has been realized, finalized or decided. I don't want to talk too much before anything happens.

"There are 100 million people in China who have lived for decades without any exposure to the West," he says. "I think they are ready to evolve. They have incredible facilities for exportation of fashion. I visited numerous silk, leather and cashmere sweater factories and the factories where they make my rugs. Chinese textiles will yield positive growth between that country and the West."

Cardin intends to export Chinese clothing to France and other points on the globe.

It's as if Cardin is one of those Napoleonic types who speak to destiny.

Nothing can shake him from his unique spot in the fashion world. He carries himself with a hauteur. His carriage is always noble, except when he slouches into huge, comfortable sofas. With expressive eyes, always a calm smile and bold military gestures of the hands, Cardin propagates Cardinology.

"At seven years of age, I dreamed of being a couturier without knowing what it meant exactly. I knew then I wanted to drape, construct and create shape," says the man who came from a poor Venetian family and started by working in a clothing shop in Vichy, France.

"After the war, I worked at the number-one houses when they were number one. When Paquin was number one, I worked there. I made all the costumes and masks by hand for Marais in Cocteau's film *Beauty and the Beast.* I worked at Shiaparelli for one month. Then I went to Dior in `47 where I learned my craft perfectly.

"I am a technician. And I have a solid base thanks to Dior. I can drape easily, and I have a complete knowledge of cut, bias, making a buttonhole, making patterns. For me, fabric is nearly secondary. I believe first in shape, architecture, the geometry of a dress.

"My base is me. You can never say my collections look like somebody else's. They are never chic Thirties, Forties, Fifties, Nazi, Captain Molyneaux, Marilyn Monroe or this Jacques Fath mood that has descended upon Paris now."

Cardin's couture showings still have certain elements of moon-walking types clad in vinyl-trimmed tubular constructions. Hats look like saucers with roses. But he also constructs caps and coats with incredible three-dimensional form. For couture twice a year, Cardin prefers to show his designs for men, women and children at the same time.

Cardin was the first to show an rtw collection in Paris, in 1959. "My first rtw, I showed in a theater. All the big French newspapers hated it. Rtw is for me a modification of the creativity released in couture. Each season, my democratic rtw is sold to buyers even before the season gets in full swing. I have never shown another rtw since the first.

"It seems the Paris productions in this field are so extravagant and extraordinary today. They have music and models for shows that are seen literally nowhere else in the world. The models are nearly stars themselves. I see no interest in making this music-hall, circus atmosphere to end up selling commercially blouses, skirts, pullovers and jackets that differ very little from season to season.

"Couture is different. The clients have big spending budgets for big fantasy and often dresses they will wear only once. I would like to know if all those incredible dreams you see on such extraordinary models in Paris rtw ever reach the customer through the stores."

Rtw or high fashion, who does Cardin admire? "Only Balenciaga, Schiaparelli, M. Christian Dior and Courrèges. Each had his or her own authenticity. Balenciaga was a great creator. Schiaparelli gave women a chic that was typical of supreme modernity for her time. Courrèges really created a coup in fashion when he first became independent. And M. Dior was always following his own path.

"As far as I'm concerned, Chanel never influenced fashion one bit. She made things with good taste, very simple and easy to wear. One suit in her entire career is not sufficient. One has the impression she created a million things by repeating one formula for a little suit."

Cardin has 12 technicians in his design studio for fashion. For his 395 licensees, Cardin directs through Paris his contractors, factories and his directors in each country. Is quality control important to him? Does he design every single Cardin product?

"It's not enough to just sell my name. I pursue the quality of Peirre Cardin. That is my life, and I'm proud of what I do. I need it to be very well made. Here, we don't just make things for another licensee deal. It's a creation. I supervise. I have directors in every country where the products are made. If a sofa prototype has been made in Italy, they bring it to me for final approval or I go there. For the Cadillac car, I have design assistants who are completely supervising my details for the painting of the prototype. I designed the car. Like in everything I touch, I am my own patron, my own designer.

"Industry creates quality upon demand. Obviously, if one prints a deluxe art book, it's on a different level from a paperback. I have my `griffe'; I want it to be respected."

Cardin's Evolution shops, which opened in Milan, Paris, London and Buenos Aires last year, carry numbered series of furniture in the neo-deco style designed by Cardin, Mazon, Pacos and Prevost. "These designs are like artworks and are shown for prestige. Yes, they can be ordered (in large numbers) upon request, but most are designed in numbers of 10."

The private life of Pierre Cardin is complex, hidden in quiet pasttimes. Never flashy, his sporting life consists of frequent nightcrawling in Paris. To relax, he could do anything from taking a quiet stroll in the flea market on Sunday to buying a prestigious and much desired building on Place Francois 1er in the heart of Paris couture-land. Valentino, Inc. wanted this building and quietly negotiated for nearly a year; Cardin swept it into his empire in a day.

Cardin doesn't drive a luxury limousine, but he loves to madly beat red lights at night. His first large apartment, which he first occupied 20 years ago, is a sprawling first-floor flat filled with a mix of antiques on Quai Anatole France. Although Cardin's sister now lives in this apartment, which he still owns (Cardin lives in a five-floor apartment on Rue Elysees), he uses its glass-enclosed marble winter garden for most of his big, formal entertaining. This is where Cardin built a little stage and introduced Jeanne Moreau and Mireille Mathieu, before he bought the theater Espace Cardin for $30 million near the American embassy in Paris.

It is there, at Espace Cardin, that you'll see him at a Fashion Pack–filled event: concerts, his own fashion spectacles. And upcoming is an exhibition of American Indian art organized with the help of Marlon Brando.

"I'm very happy living alone and working," says Cardin. "I make most trips for my work and not for my personal enjoyment, but I love it. I do get tired often, but I snap back quickly.

"Twenty years ago, I dreamed of life and industry on the moon. Today, I expect nothing of the future. Things come in life one after the other."

—*André Leon Talley*

BILL BLASS
Heart of Blass

JUNE 24, 1982

NEW YORK—None of his friends in Fort Wayne, Ind., could understand why 8-year-old William Ralph Blass chose to draw the things he did. While other children presented sweetly acceptable sketches of houses and pets, little Bill came up with detailed renderings of cocktail shakers, Manhattan penthouses, men in dinner jackets and women in white fox coats.

That this child in the dead center of middle-class middle America at the height of the Great Depression should create a fantasy world straight out Cole Porter or Ernst Lubitsch seems today uncannily prescient. Bill Blass celebrated his 60th birthday on Tuesday as a man who represents the quintessence of urban sophistication to millions of people. He lives in a penthouse on East 57th Street, he wears a dinner jacket with more ease than any man in town and designs for—and often is seen in the company of—just the sort of women who would have worn white fox had they lived 50 years ago. As one fellow designer puts it, "He's the last of the movie stars."

Blass himself doesn't perceive the metamorphosis from home-town Indiana boy to millionaire designer and bon vivant

as surprising. "I don't think coming from Indiana has much to do with anything." He says in an even, low-pitched voice that suggests a gentrified Clark Gable with a touch of an English accent. "Norell came from Noblesville, Ind.; Cole Porter, Mainbocher, Hoagy Carmichael—they all came from the Midwest. They had a sense of what they wanted to do; that helps more than anything, I think I know I did when I left Fort Wayne."

That confidence has sustained Blass very nicely. Success didn't come early to him, but when it did, it came in torrents. Today he stands as the sole head of an empire that encompasses 35 licenses bearing the Bill Blass label—everything from chocolates to hosiery—and takes in about $200 million, with a personal income for Blass of an estimated $3 million. He is the owner of four floors in 550 Seventh Ave. His lavish, only-for-the-affluent ready-to-wear line—while a comparatively minor source of Blass' income—has given him stellar visibility, showing up on everyone from Jackie O to Nancy Reagan, from Farrah Fawcett to Claudette Colbert. They are clothes with their own distinctive nimbus, a compound of snob appeal and an amusing sense of the sheer joy of dressing up.

"The ultimate role of clothes is to please the individual," says Blass, "not to keep one warm or cool. Nothing gives people a greater sense of pleasure than knowing they look better in what they have on than anything else." Another Blass dictum: "You can't take fashion seriously. Those who do are a bloody bore."

This sybaritic philosophy of dress was shaped, in large part, in the flickering half-dark of Fort Wayne's movie theaters on Saturday afternoons in the Thirties, while an enchanted Blass digested endless images from the films "portraying a very sophisticated way of life—the type Kay Francis starred in."

"Never underestimate the great power of films during those years; for 15 cents, it was a great escape," says Blass. "Every Saturday afternoon with Garbo, Dietrich, Lombard dressed to the nines. My God, think of those clothes. Movies really gave me my background in fashion."

The son of a hardware store owner who committed suicide when Blass was 5, Blass says he had decided to become a designer by the time he was 6 or 7. "Fashion has a glamour; a kind of excitement that had nothing to do with the environment I was in," says Blass. "I seemed to be passing time, just waiting." He went through the perfunctory motions of the life expected of him—joining the high school football team, sketching for the school paper—and began selling sketches of dresses to SA by the time he was 15, for $25 or $30 apiece. He graduated from high school and took a train straight to the place he'd always intended to go, New York.

"I remember friends of the family asking why I wasn't going to the art school in Chicago. That's not at all what I was looking for. If you're going to pursue something, you have to be in New York. Somewhere around Pittsburgh, I had some doubts, but never after that."

In fact, Blass' slow 40-year ascendency to his present status seems to have been remarkable free of doubts or regrets. As he takes inventory of the various phases of his career—his first job as a sketcher at 19, a detour of 3½ years with the Army in World War II, gradual stages of apprenticeship at the firms of Anna Miller and Maurice Rentner—he says the only thing he wishes he'd done differently was to have worked for a couture house in Paris early on ("I wish I'd learned more of my craft from that standpoint").

"A lot of what happened to me had to do with luck, but an awful lot with patience—sitting back, accepting what comes your way and digesting it. There are a lot of designers younger than myself who are no longer visible because they didn't have that. Patience is a boring word, God knows, to apply to a career, but if you strive too aggressively, it's somehow not as satisfactory as the things you wait for. If you want anything badly enough, you get it, in time."

Being a designer on SA in the Forties and Fifties provided an exacting test of patience. "At that time, designers were kept very much in the back room, almost something to be ashamed of. The minute a collection was over, we were encouraged to take long holidays, which gave the manufacturer a chance to totally change the collection." But even when Blass was working with this shadowy profile for other people, he insisted on being allowed to diversify himself. "I put the pressure on to get them to allow me to do things like children's clothes. Once you were classified on SA, it was virtually impossible to get out of. I had a hell of an argument at the time I went into men's wear, when I was with Rentner. My partners took a dim view; they said, 'How can you spread yourself that thin?' But there just wasn't enough to do between 9 and 5." At Maurice Rentner, where Blass had worked since the firm merged with Anna Miller, he became increasing visible, swiftly amassing a heady following of socialites and celebrities, many of whom remain his customers. In 1970, he acquired complete control of the company from his partners Eugene Lewin and Herman Seigenfeld and the ever-expanding empire of Bill Blass, Ltd., began to assume its powerful form.

Blass says he's found many more pleasures than pains in taking sole command of his operations. "When I had a partner, I had to discuss everything. It always seemed to me after I had my control, things were much easier." A designer who travels extensively to promote his collection, and to feel out the sartorial interests of women in various parts of the country, Blass says that what he misses most is time. "On the other hand, I can't imagine taking a holiday and sitting on an island, as I used to in Havana. The business part—which wasn't easy to learn—has become almost as fascinating as the creative end of it—the juggling, the maneuvering."

Still, Blass hardly has been the stern, work-obsessed Calvinist at any point in this life. In half of Blass' dream when he came to Manhattan was to become a successful designer, the other—and probably equally potent—half was to inhabit the world he saw in movies as a child. From the beginning, he seems to have slid into that world with suave facility into a part for which he had been privately into a part for which he had been privately rehearsing all his life.

"I knew a few people when I came here," he says casually. Whoever they were, they must have provided smooth conduits to cafe society. Blass recalls his youth in New York as a blur of evenings spent at a series of clubs whose names he reels off like memorized poetry. "There were night clubs of every description. I'd go to the Stork Club or Morocco, Le Roux, 1-2-3, the Bombay Room . . . Society then was built on being out and being seen. These people may have had marvelous homes in the country, or marvelous apartments, but no one seemed to be in them. I often wonder how in the hell I was able to afford it."

His social propinquity—in both New York and Paris, where he'd go to see the couture showings in the Fifties—gave Blass a chance to observe the type of woman who eventually would become his customer and to formulate his notions of American style. He remembers watching Gloria Vanderbilt, currently one of his favorite social partners, and C.Z. Guest at the Ritz Hotel in Paris.

"It was years ago, when Dior ruled the fashion world with the tailleur and those hats. Well, Gloria would show up with her long hair, a white shirt, gray flannel pants and a sable coat; and C.Z. would be in a twin sweater set, tweed skirt and flat shoes—both of them looking like a million bucks. There were the French women, extraordinary in their big hats and padded hips, and two American women who were better dressed than the overly jeweled, overly dressed Parisians."

Blass' admiration for the American woman of style has been more than reciprocated. He remains the most sought-after escort of society's grandes dames. "Bill Blass is all things," purrs Pat Buckley. "First and foremost he's a gent, with innate charm—and fun, amusing, well-read, intelligent, filled with sex appeal and a very, very good friend."

Asked to account for his popularity, Blass offers jovially, "Maybe it's because I have two dinner jackets." He does say he possesses a prodigious, and genuine, interest in and curiosity about people—"All of us are shy, but if you're really interested, then that's less of a problem"—and adds, appropriately enough, that the only career other than designer he could have envisioned for himself is that of a diplomat. "It's his interest that makes him what he is," confirms Diana Vreeland. "He has a great relish for people and the charm of this life. This is a big, rich country, and Bill Blass looks it right in the face."

Also key to the Blass charm is an impeccable code of manners. "I think good manners are incredibly important," says Blass. "Also rewarding. If you employ good manners, people respond in kind." Accordingly, Blass says the men who influenced him most in his early life were Serge Obolensky and Reed Vreeland—"two men who stood out because they always made one feel very welcome, interested in what one was doing. Reed Vreeland had the best manners I've ever seen."

While close friends of Blass are quick to praise his gentlemanly deportment, dry Noel Coward-ish wit and silver-tipped matinee-idol good looks, they say the most profound source of his appeal lies in something more substantial—a deep kindliness, compassion and instinctive generosity with people.

"One thing that impresses me enormously about Bill is his generosity with himself with people in all facets of life," says Missy Bancroft, a long-time friend of Blass, who is the godfather or her three children. "It can be his chauffeur, or the people who work for him. He really cares and asks about them and their family. When I had my children, Bill was always at the hospital. If there was any chance any one of them was in trouble, he'd go out of his way to spend time with them. He doesn't go away without calling to say where he is and when he's coming back."

"With all he has to do, he always finds time to give up an evening that might not be important to him, but is important to me," agrees designer Mollie Parnis, who's known Blass for 25 years. "Through the good and bad times, he was always there when I needed him."

Parnis notes that Blass is one of the few designers she knows whose success has aroused minimal resentment on SA. "I've never known anyone who wasn't rooting for him. You hear about other designers, 'Oh, he walks over dead bodies.' I've never heard that said about Bill."

Adds fellow designer and close friend Oscar de la Renta, "in a profession where we all have such egos, I think he's fabulously unselfish. I think for him friendship comes before anything."

Asked how he's changed with success, Blass' friends of long standing say that—in the tradition of all good movie stars—he really hasn't. "He's simply more," booms Diana Vreeland. "He's still that combination of big-town sophisticate and small-town boy," says Gerry Stutz. Offers Francoise de la Renta, "If anything, he's appreciating life more than he ever did. He looks it. When I see him, I see a happy man. There's a serenity about him now."

Blass is inclined to agree with this last judgment. "I suppose I was very definitely depressed about 10 years ago—it has to do with one's personal life, with one's assessment of oneself. But the last four or five years I've been fairly content. I think a lot of it has to do with being alone more."

His greatest pleasures, today, come in being with small groups of friends—preferably people he's known a long time— reading as many as five books a week, collecting the dizzyingly eclectic range of prints, antiques and bibelots that fill his penthouse apartment and, most important, spending time in the 18th-century country house in New Preston, Conn., with his two beloved golden retrievers, Kate and Brutus.

"It's the tranquility, the quiet time in my life. When I'm outside reading, and the dogs are in the pool, it gives me a sense of peace. It's the necessary balance if one sees a lot of people. I'm in bed at 9 and up at 6."

If there are bêtes noirs lurking in the corners of Blass' life, he takes pains to conceal them. Though a man who is never without a cigarette in his hand is sure to have his anxieties, friends of Blass say they never see him depressed or moody." I find blowing up, losing your temper, showing you're upset is a part of oneself that shouldn't be publicly exposed. If one is bothered, one should walk around one's apartment at 3 in the morning. That's partly the army—it taught me discipline, also to accept the situation I was in and make the best of it."

On the subject of his future, Blass says, "I think it's unlikely I'd retire; I don't think that's ever the answer. Here again, I don't try to predict—either the pleasures or the disappointments."

Asked how he'd describe himself at 60 to someone who never had known him, Blass—who habitually substitutes "one" for "I"—is unusually discomfited.

"I'd say he's 40ish," he begins with a chuckle.

Pause.

"First of all I wouldn't describe myself." Pause.

"If I was applying for a job, you mean? He laughs at this.

This is succeeded by a longer pause and a slow drag on his Carlton cigaret.

"God," says Blass, exhaling smoke. "Who knows?"

—*Ben Brantley*

REI KAWAKUBO
A Reflection on Beauty, From a Designer of Few Words

MARCH 1, 1983

What is beautiful is beautiful. And there are things in culture and tradition you can't be blind to." Not surprisingly, Rei Kawakubo identifies the most explicit sources of inspiration as "the varied kinds of fabric I've seen in my lifetime—often something quite distant from clothing. A piece of paper, for example, or carpeting."

For fall, the unlikely cue for fabric comes from "Something way back in my childhood—a crumpled kind of cardboard I used to play with."

Kawakubo shuns collective labels. "I'm not very happy to be classified as another Japanese designer. There is no one

characteristic that all Japanese designers have. Each is an individual, with individual tastes....

"Here the women are working, they're on their own and they buy their clothes with money they've earned themselves. In Japan, when a woman gets married, she seems to conform to a certain way of dressing appropriate to a married woman and mother. She considers the social situation, and other people's opinions....

"Women tend to say it's hard if you're a woman. But if you know you really want to do it—that you have to—then it's not difficult. It follows its own course."

—*Ben Brantley*

PERRY ELLIS
In an Interview Just a Month Before He Died, the Designer Talks About Some of Life's Curve Balls

APRIL 9, 1986

The past two years have brought great change to Perry Ellis's life, not all of it good. But now the designer feels it is time to look ahead.

On Jan. 2, his close friend and business associate, Laughlin M. Barker, president of Perry Ellis International, died after a long illness. His death, associates say, left Ellis deeply depressed.

"It's been a difficult time for me," says Ellis. "Laughlin was an extraordinary man, and I loved him. We worked together

24 hours a day, and he brought genius and humor to this business. We were together five years, and there was never an argument or a disagreement."

Sad though he still is, Ellis looks much better. He's just returned from a trip to Los Angeles, where he visited his infant daughter, Tyler Alexandra Gallagher Ellis, and her mother, Barbara Gallagher.

He is also looking to the future. Since he began designing in 1978, much of his time has been spent in the pursuit of a successful fashion career. Today, however, he wants to allow more time for personal pursuits.

"Life can be more than just a full-time job," says Ellis, who turned 46 in March. "The heart and soul of the company is still very much here, and it's changed. I used to do such wild looks, and now I want to be more serious about life and the quality of my life....

"We all change and evolve, thank God. I think I know where my customer is. I look at my work now and it's still the same spirit, but it has matured."

Ellis runs an unusual studio in which his employees are free to express themselves creatively. They are even allowed time off to indulge in other interests. For example, Jed Krascella, vice president of design for the collection and longtime employee, has been pursuing an acting career and will take time off this summer to study theater in England.

"The qualities of life are not the same today in terms of taking time for reading, for being quiet, for being away at the ocean and for being with my daughter, who has added enormously to my life. I'm maturing and the business is maturing.

"I feel I can do a lot of things and take advantage of life. My little girl is an enormous pleasure and joy to me. I never realized how important a child is, how they can make you laugh. Oh God, it's wonderful."

—Susan Alai

CHRISTIAN LACROIX
An "Overnight Sensation" Talks About the Long Way Up

FEBRUARY 25, 1986

According to Lacroix family folklore, back in the Fifties, grandfather Lacroix gathered all his grandchildren to ask what they wanted to be when they grew up. "One said he wanted to be a doctor," recounts Christian Lacroix, "and when it was my turn, I supposedly shouted out, 'Christian Dior.'"

Lacroix, 34, laughingly tells the story to prove that, like most overnight successes, he didn't arrive overnight. Nevertheless, after the designer presented a bright and wickedly young spring couture collection for the house of Patou recently, Paris erupted in stunned delight. Everyone forgot that Lacroix has been doing Patou's couture since 1981. And even though the front rows were still lacking the all-star presence of the leading couture customers, a youthful contingent of fashionable fans collapsed in ecstasy over the designer's neon pompon-covered bermuda shorts, the short and wild baby-doll silhouettes and his Dali-esque handpainted ballgowns that transformed into minidresses with the snap of a detachable skirt.

Fashion pros and groupies in their austere black-on-black fashion uniforms suddenly were rhapsodizing about the joys of wearing behemoth straw hats trimmed in tropical flowers à la Lacroix.

One of the dresses was featured as front page news in *Le Figaro* the day after the show.

All this uproar is exactly what the house of Patou wants. It stopped making its own ready-to-wear line three yeas ago and actively is seeking a new licensing agreement for rtw with an outside company.

The fuss has not yet pierced the meticulously preserved splendor of the Art Deco Patou headquarters at 7 Rue St. Florentin, founded in 1919. Here, an inexperienced, unknown Christian Lacroix arrived four years ago to take up residence in the couture atelier.

"The house was like a sleeping beauty when I arrived," he says. His game plan: "We did not want to do the haute couture of the others. We had to find another way for the Eighties.

"We wanted to show that haute couture was still alive, that it could be new. I think all the designers in couture are going in the same direction—very simple, very austere. I felt I wanted to do something different and more...baroque." He emphasizes the last word with a mischievous smile. "Haute couture must be a little operatic, in my opinion. For many years, the couturiers have been following rtw. I think we've got to rediscover the exuberance of haute couture. I want to be followed."

While many of his most ardent fans are the young and very social Parisians such as Pia de Brantes, 25, who wears a Patou creation practically "every time I go out at night." Lacroix has developed a very loyal clientele, often the impressed mothers of those PYTs. "It's not a matter of age," the designer says. "One of my first clients at Patou was 70, and she always chose something with the strongest, most dramatic lines."

Will he ever forsake the company that launched him and design under his own name? "Oh, perhaps someday, but not for a while," says Lacroix modestly. "This sort of idea is on every designer's mind. But there is a lot more I want to do here. We have not finished yet."

—Anne Bogart

GIANNI VERSACE
A Reflection on Pride, Honesty and Women

MARCH 15, 1990

They've been described as clothes that make store hangers sizzle, skirts so short they could double as belts and body-sculpting dresses you can't sit down in. Strut goddess Cher wears them, aerobics queen Jane Fonda sports them and night creature Grace Jones flaunts them.

Whether you like them or not, they are clothes to be noticed in, and they are hot. They are the stuff of Gianni Versace, the Italian designer who every season jolts the fashion press into a world of female body worship via the high-voltage show with a capital S.

"Sexy is honesty," says Versace, who claims he is sick of people referring to his clothes as sexy. "I think directness is sexy, saying what you think, being who you are, not being hypocritical. Sexiness is part of life!

"Why be ashamed? Look at the animals! They are not ashamed. But people are always made to feel guilty. I don't understand all this guilt stuff. I am a Catholic, but I refuse the hypocrisy of the Catholic Church. I am against things that go against nature."

Nobody can accuse Versace of being dishonest, indirect or, for that matter, boring. What motivates this 44-year-old designer to continuously find new ways to bare navels, thighs, backs and other parts of the female anatomy?

"I *adore* women, I *love* women," answers Versace matter-of-factly, relaxing in his sumptuous apartment above his atelier in his palazzo on the Via Sant'Andrea. "As Chanel said, many designers are gay and many designers don't like women. Chanel maybe was right, I don't know. I adore women. But designers, most of them, seem to hate women by the clothes they do."

The topic of androgynous clothing makes Versace become suddenly outraged. "A lot of designers seem to think women want to be transvestites, that they don't have the courage to be women. But I think that women must be women!

"That is clear, underlined, that is the direction for the Nineties. No one has the courage to say that letting women be women is chic. But I ask, 'Is it chic to make women into transvestites?' That is *not* chic....

"Donatella controls me in a lot of ways," Versace confides. "We talk all the time. Last night, I was in the kitchen, and she was in the bathroom, and we are on the phone talking about two dresses that we wanted to cut from the collection. We always check things out with each other. If she doesn't like a sketch I have done, I will usually cancel it. We are more than brother and sister; we are like good friends. I think the fact that we come from a simple family in the south that was very strong, has helped a lot....

"I love the body," he continues. "When I was very young, in my mother's atelier, I always saw women in lingerie and other wonderful things, and I would make fantasies. They sometimes would call my mother from school and say, 'Your baby is a maniac'....

"I love pearls," he says. "To me, they are class and elegance. But elegance has to be updated, and for that reason, I put it with the wild. The mixture of pearls and leopard makes it modern. I believe in contrasts. Like right now, we are in a 17th-century room, and there is an airplane flying overhead. That is the contrast of life today."

For the Nineties, his message is one of "freedom, freedom, freedom," Versace says.

"The message is to let your womanhood show and be proud of it. Equality does not come in being like men. Be proud of being women, but understand men without having to let the masculine part come out. I understand that the Eighties were useful to women because they grew a lot and gained what they wanted. But now is a time of reflection for women."

Versace adds that he, too, is now more liberated: "It took me my whole life, 44 years, to be as I am now—free. I never put my face down or am ashamed. The only joy I have is my work and my life, and I must play until I die...."

—Glynis Costin

JOHN GALLIANO
Galliano the Great

OCTOBER 11, 1993

PARIS—He was the talk of Paris all weekend. After a season-long absence, British designer John Galliano came back with a vengeance in a collection filled with directional jackets, fresh bias-cut dresses and the only new kilts anyone's seen in the last fifteen years.

The collection was inspired by a fairy tale that Galliano made up himself, and in many ways Galliano's career is equally fantastic.

He is, as the fashion press has long proclaimed one of the most talented designers around, with a creative,

artisanal know-how that has captured the attention of many, including the Chambre Syndicale, which made him a member this year.

Another admirer is Karl Lagerfeld, who once commented, "Though he doesn't know that names of the things he is doing, [Galliano] could do something because he has a feeling for couture and craftsmanship."

The designer has even won society ladies like Beatrice de Rothschild and Sao Schlumberger. He was out partying with them one night recently at Paris's China Club and The Casbah, where they took in some Egyptian belly-dancing.

Fun, whimsical, a dreamer—call him what you will. The 32-year-old, Gibraltar-born designer is the one who, in past collections, has turned his girls into en-chanting marauders, Napoleon's Josephine and even Blanche DuBois, cutting layers of fabric on the bias in what has become a Galliano signature.

But you need only take a look at his own fanciful exterior to realize that the boy has plenty of imagination. He balances a gargantuan black, fur-lined nylon hat on his head (he claims that he hasn't taken it off since he received it from fellow bleached-blond Jean Paul Gaultier), sports a pencil-thin moustache with an identical line down his chin, rock-a-billy sideburns, an ac-cidentally ripped, Union-Jack jacket (which he says, he's been wearing for weeks), aviator sunglasses, inside-out sports socks and unlaced Doc Martens with the tongues flipped out.

And this is the man who is proclaiming death to deconstruction this season. "I'm tired of the throwaway look," he says. "I find the destroyed clothes very negative. Some of them are incredibly elegant, like when Margiela does it, but I see more of a positive future—a return to noble fabrics. Women have been shortchanged for quite long enough now. We should return to things that mean a bit more."

To Galliano, the new message is about "technique and elegance." The designer confesses to an obsession with the great old couturiers ("If there's an exhibition, I'm the first one with my head under a skirt"), and says he seeks

to modernize their techniques in his own designs.

"People in my generation are getting less and less educated about the fit of clothes," he says with concern. "The age of Gap is great for some, but to appreciate a well-cut jacket is something that perhaps you can only experience if you go to a flea market. There, you can find a wonderful bias-cut dress.

"And this season," he announces, "I've designed a very positive collection—in cut, color and construction."

All this doesn't seem too out of the ordinary for Galliano, who has been turning out "tailored clothes with a twist," as he once described them, since his London debut eight years ago. That was with a collection created for this gradua-tion from St. Martins College of Art and Design. It was then, thanks to the keen eye of Joan Burstein of Browns, that Galliano became a name to be reck-oned with. Since then, however, he has become a somewhat on-again-off-again designer, having had a series of financial backers, including Danish entrepreneur Peder Bertelsen.

"It was partly my fault," admits the designer. "Maybe I didn't surround myself with the right people, powerful people to guide me forward. It's taken me a long time to get production and business sorted out."

Now, with an apartment in the Marais and his trusty, long-time British assistants by his side, Galliano is under the wing of Amor. The hip "fashion house" operated by new backer Fayal Amor also consists of Amor's own pret-a-porter label, as well as Plein Sud and Aquagirl. "There's no con-tract between us," claims the Moroccan-born Amor. "We gave him all this because I said to myself, 'It's impossible for a guy like John to disappear.'"

And, though simple generosity is a rare quality in the fashion jungle, Amor insists that "I just decided to help him. We have different paths—he doesn't care what he sells and doesn't sell, he just wants to touch people with his creations. He's the most talented at what he does.

"I'm no Bernard Arnault," adds Amor. "You have to invent another system for

a creator like John, kind of like Alaïa did at the beginning." And so, Amor is help-ing Galliano find a group of investors.

As for Friday's collection, Galliano says, "There's always a character who inspires me. This season, she's made up several people. We like to know how she moves, how she talks, does she live by electricity or candlelight, what perfume she wears, who she wrote to—generally build up a painting of her."

Meet Princess Lucrecia, Galliano's imaginary Russian beauty, whose life reads like "Anna Karenina Escapes Russia."

"She's got very pale skin—you can almost see the blue veins on her fore-head. She has badly henna-ed hair and dirt under her fingernails from garden-ing. She's a very sensuous woman, in complete control of her own destiny," recounts her master. "As we get nearer to the collection date, everyone knows who she is—what time she wakes up, where she hung out last night. You know her so well—I know it sounds bizarre but the spirit will kind of tell you how to put the clothes together."

Galliano swathes his Russian princess in lace camisoles paired with big crino-lines and layered, embroidered overskirts down to the floor or in *Arsenic and Old Lace*–inspired jackets with micro-mini kilts of lace, embroidery and a dash of tartan, along with Stephen Jone's dainty tricorn hats and Manolo Blahnik spats.

"What we show on the runway is an invitation," says the designer. "I'm not a dictator. I don't tell people what to wear." He does, however, give free advice.

"If I were an art student, I'd be on the third floor of La Samaritaine in the chil-dren's department, buying up kilts," he recommends. As he sees it, "If the kid can go out and do his own John Galliano, now that would be wicked."

—*Heidi Lender*

TOMMY HILFIGER

Crossing Over: Hilfiger Charts His Course in Women's Wear

MARCH 6, 1996

Tommy Hilfiger is determined to get women back into department stores this fall. "There are customers between the ages of 18 and 50 who shop in malls, but are drawn into specialty stores. They've been turned off by the department stores. The merchandise hasn't excited them," said Hilfiger, who hopes to change all that when he unveils his new women's casual-wear and jeans lines.

He believes these better-priced collections are just the antidote for a depressed women's sportswear business. "I think the demise of the business in department stores gives me a better opportunity to capitalize on the situation," said Hilfiger, who expects to do $100 million in wholesale volume with the women's lines in their first year.

"We think the opportunity in women's is much larger than men's," said Hilfiger.

Some 25 percent of the business will be fashion that is "Mod, hip and fresh.

"It's to keep my design team inspired," said Hilfiger. "We'll set trends in that area. We can take Mod and make it more fun. We take trends and make them important to the fashion world."

Part of Hilfiger's success in men's wear has been his ability to dress a range of people from 15-year-old high school students to 60-year-old golfers. He's also become the designer of choice for such rappers as Salt-N-Pepa, Snoop Doggy-Dogg and TLC.

"I think it had to do with the fact that we pushed certain buttons within the music world," said Hilfiger. "Rock and rap stars started wearing my clothes. We dress a lot of athletes and actors on *Beverly Hills 90210.* These people send a message of what is hip and what is allowed."

While Hilfiger acknowledged that few men's wear designers have been able to successfully cross over to women's apparel, he believes he's got a great chance to succeed.

"The stores kept saying, 'Do what you do for men for women,'" said Hilfiger, explaining why he went for a better-priced casualwear line, and not a pricy designer collection. "It's not exactly men for women. We have to have a certain amount of femininity to it."

—*Lisa Lockwood*

HELMUT LANG

Helmut Tells Why New York Is His Kind of Town

MARCH 11, 1998

"I feel very at home here," Helmut Lang said, discussing the permanent shift of his business headquarters to New York, after 15 years in his native Vienna.

Lang said having his design studios and headquarters in Austria had long been a creative advantage. "It's not a place where fashion is an issue," he said, dressed in an unobtrusive gray cashmere V-neck sweater and dark trousers. "It has no distractions." But logistically, "We reached a point where it started to get really complicated" he said, describing the challenge of running a fast-growing international business from Vienna when the focus of activity was often elsewhere, including manufacturing in Italy and staging runway shows in Paris and New York.

"New York is, in many terms—and not only fashion terms—the most important place to be, the most urban place to be," he said. "It adds a very interesting dimension to the European education I've gone through, because the U.S. is quite different. I have a lot of friends here," he added, "So it made sense businesswise, personally and emotionally...."

"I'm not looking for a huge organization," Lang said, revealing a business style tinged with the same conviction and rigor that defines his minimalist clothing. "We work with a small group of people. That has been an advantage in the past."

Asked if he had ambitions to license his name into any other product categories, he replied: "I think we have everything."

"The main policy of our house is to have one strong clothing line and one trademark, which could mean that the jeans one day get absorbed in a very big main collection," he said. "The name can carry from basics up to luxury items. For me, that's a modern concept of clothes that one collection combines basic as well as luxury, hand-finished products. That's the way people dress today....

"For products that have a day-to-day use, distribution can be very large," he said, referring to jeans and underwear particularly. "For products that are very special, the distribution has to be very small.

"I'm kind of interested, after a certain while, in establishing denim as a real basic business, but still in the spirit of our house," he said. "The most important thing will always be the product and the freedom of design, and then we take it from there....

"The copying problem doesn't start with the runway shows, but begins with fabric and production companies," he stated. "That's not an issue. I couldn't say only

American designers find inspiration in my collections. That wouldn't be fair."

Asked about how he copes with the pressure of being a fashion leader, "It has never tortured me," he said. "I always do exactly the thing I want to do for the next collection. I always do what I think is right for the next season.

"In the end, we want people who wear our clothes to look good," he said. "At the end of the road, that's something you shouldn't lose sight of."

—Miles Socha

ALEXANDER McQUEEN

The Alexander Method

AUGUST 30, 1999

LONDON—Fashion visionary or street thug? Historian or anarchist? Provocateur or blossoming business ace? Alexander McQueen just may be all of the above. In other words, he's one complicated guy.

And one of the most curiously intriguing personalities working in fashion today. In a world of spin, McQueen presents something of an oddity. He refuses to be spun, a street-smart Sammy Davis, Jr., whose "I've-gotta-be-me" mind-set runs deep—and sometimes dangerous.

For all his bravado, and that's plenty, in moments of candor McQueen exposes intricate layers of insecurities. Not about his talent; never about that. Complete confidence fuels the creative aspects of his work. But he's far less certain of how he fits into the fashion hype machine.

With his sometimes out-there clothes and theatrical presentations, he provides plenty of editorial juice, yet he is extremely press-wary. And he puts to rest the notion that, in our technological age, the world is one great big global village: His journey from freewheeling London to haute Paris and the house of Givenchy has been rough at times, a short underwater train ride, maybe, but a world away from the comforts and securities of home. "I'm not this enfant terrible, or whatever it is—stupid word," McQueen says. "I'm not like that at all, but sometimes I act like that."

Next month, McQueen will try out his act on a new stage, when he shows his Alexander McQueen collection in New York rather than his hometown of London, where the show has been the main event for some time. It promises to be the hottest ticket of the spring season.

For months fashion types have been atwitter about reports—probably true, but unconfirmed—that he will not present in Manhattan, but a bridge or tunnel away, perhaps Long Island City or Staten Island.

Forcing people off the hallowed Isle of Manhattan—that's about the most audacious a move in fashion since the demise of the corset. But then, McQueen has a set of you-know-what to spare. Just the shift to New York took nerve. To many people, McQueen is London Fashion Week; without him, uncertainty hovers over its future.

McQueen views the move as a matter of pragmatism. "The people who should see the clothes should see the clothes." he says, referring to a number of top American editors who don't make the trip to London.

And he hasn't made many wrong moves yet. One could argue that not editing all your expletives or your temper in front of journalists is a mistake, as his rough-and-tumble demeanor has garnered him his share of bad press. Yet despite the blackguard persona, McQueen cares a great deal what people say about him, and when he feels wronged, is utterly unforgiving.

Press woes aside, however, he was one of the youngest high-profile design appointees

of the past few years, just 27 when he took the reins at LVMH's Givenchy nearly three years ago. And he already boasted a remarkable resume: He had started showing in London almost immediately after graduating from St. Martin's, getting rave reviews for his Savile Row technique and his brilliant showmanship.

Now, McQueen loves to flaunt his business acumen along with his creative gifts, and he takes serious exception to the idea that his work is not commercial.

"I think the word 'commercialism' has got this gray cloud over it, but I don't think it's a bad word," he says. "You can have spontaneity in commercialism. I've always been a business person, but it's just that the way I do my business is different from most."

Of course, the concept of commercial is relative. McQueen's signature shows have been wild theatrical extravaganzas with provocative themes and often eerie titles—"The Highland Rape," "The Hunger," "Dante"—fashion's equivalent of the psychological thriller, intense, complicated, dark.

And in the watch-out-George-Lucas category, his special effects have ranged from fire and rain to a giant aerosol can splattering Shalom Harlow with green paint. He even described his last show, inspired by a snow globe and featuring a finale on ice skates a la Sonja Henie, as "a winter wonderland, with a sinister side."

By now, McQueen's story is the stuff of legend, in fashion circles and in London, where he is a star. When one of the city's famously engaging taxi drivers learned a passenger was in town to interview the designer, he launched into an informed discussion of McQueen, his background and his dual design responsibilities. But then, McQueen—or Lee, as his friends call him—is one of their own, the youngest of six children born to a taxi driver and his genealogist wife.

Certainly in class-obsessed England, the background makes for good dish, even though in reality, few designers working today were to the manor born. McQueen himself thinks it sets him apart.

"I've never fit into Paris," he says. "I can't get into that superstar lifestyle, I just can't. I think I've tried to mingle. I've been out to dinner with John [Galliano]; I've had dinner with Madonna. But it's just not my world. We just don't fit properly."

Nor is fashion his only interest. McQueen is something of a media-age Renaissance man. Last year, he directed a music video for Björk and guest-edited an issue of *Dazed & Confused.* For some time he's toyed with doing a book, and he may work with photographer Nick Knight on a project for the French Ministry of Culture's millennium extravaganza in Avignon.

But fashion comes first, and McQueen is determined to make a success at Givenchy, where the challenge has been huge. He succeeded, not Hubert de Givenchy, but John Galliano, who served an interim season before moving on to Dior, so there was a certain schizophrenia in the minds of retailers, not to mention the Givenchy staff.

But more significantly, save for the enduring aura of Audrey Hepburn, the house had no real fashion image at all. Hubert had settled comfortably into the knitted-suit world of silver-coiffed madames who had left fashion concerns behind a long time ago. For McQueen, retaining the client base was never the issue; those ladies would be moving on soon enough, and not to another label. Instead, his mandate was to find a new identity for the house, and along with it, a new, younger client.

Despite reports of internal skirmishes, the LVMH brass seems more than pleased with his work. When the *New York Times Magazine* ran a feature on Bernard Arnault last summer, much speculation swirled around the fact that McQueen was the only designer photographed with him. And last month, Arnault was quoted as calling McQueen "the most capable of creating new ideas."

By McQueen's lights, however, the revolution has barely begun. When he signed with the house in 1996, he was vehement that a full-blown turnaround would take time.

"People aren't going to get wonderful things overnight," he said then. "I don't expect everyone to love what I do right away. I'm not going to be intimidated." So far, he has experimented: less theater,

more theater, relaxation of the famous McQueen peaked shoulder, incorporation of more knits and sportswear with the suits. Even going the logo route presents its challenges: As he says wryly, "The 'G'—think it's taken."

McQueen readily admits that he hasn't yet hit on the perfect new Givenchy look. To this end, he met with American retailers in July for input. Now, he says, his goal is to develop a signature with the modernity of Jil Sander, but sexy: "That would be brilliant." Nevertheless, the line has come a long way. "I've not done a bad job in bringing up the profile of a company people had only know for Audrey Hepburn," he says, stressing that design is only one element of success. "We all have to work toward a goal, and we need to understand what that goal is. We need a consistent image, from the clothes to the advertising to the stores. I'm doing my best to make it work."

The various LVMH appointments reaped all sorts of press, not the least of which was busybody speculation about a Brit tiff between McQueen and Galliano. Not so, says Lee. "John sent me flowers once before the ready-to-wear," he recalls. "It was really sweet, and I phoned him up and he said, 'Good luck.' In some ways we've both been used, not by LVMH, but by the international fashion people as a story link. Actually we're both very good designers, and we know what we're doing." As for the primary philosophical difference between the two, "John's a hopeless romantic and I've become a hopeless realist, but you need both in the world."

Odd as it may seem, McQueen is also something of a traditionalist, not only in terms of technical skill—but in his views on the role of fashion in society. He takes a sensible approach to couture: "This is not about news, it's about the woman who wants a dress for a wedding or a bar mitzvah," and he notes with dark humor that "we probably have more clients for the couture than the ready-to-wear."

McQueen, however, thinks fashion should hold a mirror to the times, in all its realities. His boldest argument came in a photo shoot ne conceived for his *Dazed & Confused* issue last September. The now-famous piece, photographed by

Knight and styled by Katie England, featured people with severe physical disabilities wearing clothes that had been custom-made by a number of designers. (Later, he cast one, Aimee Mullins, a para-Olympian and aspiring model whose legs had been amputated below the knees due to a birth defect, in his spring show.)

"The concept was that fashion should reach everybody," McQueen says. Individualism—it's a major theme of McQueen's conversation, especially regarding gay culture. He is outraged by what he sees as self-induced stereotypes. "Gay people—I don't think they promote my life very well," he says. "I'm careful about what sort of partner I choose, because I'm not into the usual gay sex thing and the fairies and the clubs and all that."

On the conservative side, Lee?

"Yes, I am. I had one boyfriend that really screwed my head up with gay culture and really took me through some of the seediest places in my life. It's not me. I'm very romantic, very caring and very loyal, and this sort of gay idealism, it's something that I'm not a part of and something that I don't want any connection with. I won't be any type of stereotype. I feel gay society's worst mistake is stereotyping itself. They don't even realize they're doing it. I mean, fashion queens are the worst, or if you don't fit that bill, are you a bloody Mary, a muscle Mary, one of them queens that pumps up and then gets mad when people say you take too many steroids? Well, honey, you do! Yeah, there's so many stereotypes, the leather queen—you know, it's like, it makes me sick.

"I just don't like being labeled," he says. "At the end of the day you're an individual. Maybe I'm bitter. Maybe I'm the one who's not normal, because I can't handle the situation in my life."

McQueen has been trying to work it all out in therapy for years. "I think it's good for everyone. I don't think anyone's life has been that easy."

But he brushes off the suggestions that he may not be totally comfortable with his sexual orientation. "I've been openly gay since I started work," he says. "But I have a very thick family connection...."

The family issue. Like many young adults who are perhaps not quite free of adolescent rebellion, McQueen wears the badge of his roots with both pride and resentment. He can still summon a pout when relating how artistic careers were discouraged with gusto in his family, but just as quickly, he can turn almost mushy with remembrance.

"In a working-class family in London, you have to bring the money in, and artistic routes were never the means to that end. But I put my foot down...I thought, 'I'm not gonna do that. I'm not gonna get married, live in a two-up, two-down and be a bloody black cab driver.'"

After a job in Milan with Romeo Gigli, McQueen returned to London and moved back home with Mum and Dad to attend St. Martins. Once, he and his father got into an argument when the elder McQueen suggested he whip up some pants to sell on Roman Road, a market in London's East End.

"He wanted me to run up a few pairs of trousers and try and sell 'em down the road...to get a stall, a market stall!"

Relating the story gets him worked up. "All he saw was the bad side of the situation: You don't have money for 18 months!...Well, I'm still very close with my mum and dad....It's not easy." He then defends his parents' perspective. "You look at their backgrounds. They were brought up in a part of East London called Stepney during World War II. My dad was beaten a lot by his father and his mother; my grandfather was a drunk. Beaten, so was the rest of his brothers and sisters, I mean, there was 12 of them. So you know, just trying to put food on the plate for 12 kids during wartime is not easy."

Lest sentiment get the better of him, however, McQueen can enjoy a laugh at his family's expense. "Two brothers and three sisters, and my mother said. 'You were the only one planned.' I said, 'How can you plan the sixth kid? Did you just get up for a cup of tea and....'"

McQueen is equally irreverent in discussing "coming out" to his parents. "I mean, my mum cried, of course, but I think she thought it was her duty to cry. I think she thought, she's got two other sons and three daughters, she can afford it."

Of course, there were clues early on, especially in the turn his athleticism took. He earned a brown belt in judo and like his sister, took to swimming. But unlike his sister, he went for synchronized swimming.

"I was the only boy out of 40 girls. And my mum was so embarrassed, she couldn't watch me. I had to wear a grass skirt and go around in a circle." It was, he notes, his first—but not his last—exposure to the rustle of raffia.

McQueen generally operates within a protective cocoon, an insular, understanding world in which work and friendship commingle. "It's a nice bunch of people. We're close-knit, and we keep that guarded," he says. Sometimes they vacation together. While planning the New York show this year cut into holiday time, last year, his entire staff spent a week in Majorca. "Janet's baby came, it was lots of fun." McQueen says. "They call me Poof Daddy."

In addition to his full-time employees, "the team" includes England, Janet Fischgrund, former head of PR who now consults on special projects, and Sam Gainsbury, who produces the shows. Working together is second nature. By all accounts, McQueen acts on an impulse, swiftly and with precision, both when he hires and when he makes creative decisions.

"When he first asked me to work with him," England recalls, "He didn't really know my work. He just liked the way I looked, he thought I'd bring something to it."

The same snap judgments apply to calling the shots at work. "He has these lightning reactions," says Knight, with whom he frequently collaborates. "He's very, very, very swift and very quick."

"He's really easy, really straightforward to work with," says Gainsbury. "I mean, he's no angel, he's sometimes difficult. But everything is black and white with Lee. He likes something or he doesn't, whereas the rest of us might waffle. It's instant, it's a gut reaction always with him."

McQueen admits to an overly sensitive streak, but refuses to characterize it as a flaw. "I'm also overly romantic. What people think is aggression is passion for what I believe." Yet he acknowledges that years of living under the volatile guise of

the enfant terrible have worn him down to utter frustration. "Because," McQueen states his case, "I'm actually a nice guy."

—*Bridget Foley*

SONIA RYKIEL
Q&A with Sonia Rykiel
OCTOBER 1, 2008

PARIS—As she celebrates the 40th anniversary of the house she founded in 1968, Sonia Rykiel, a beacon of St. Germain's arty style, is hardly ready to call it quits.

In an hour-long interview, Rykiel, in a green marabou vest draped over a flowing black ensemble, stressed that la mode remains the grand passion of her life. Though she's suffering from bad knees, the red-haired designer is in fine fettle and ready to start the next chapter of her legacy.

It's one that involves the family. Her daughter, Nathalie Rykiel, is the house president and an important confidante in business and style. Rykiel's granddaughter Lola, a dancer who lives in New York, is also involved now in promoting the house though Rykiel said she doesn't want to force her hand: "She has to decide if this is what she wants to do herself."

Rykiel has brought fresh creative blood into the studio, too, underscoring a desire to keep the house in step with a younger generation. Earlier this year she promoted Gabrielle Greiss to oversee women's ready-to-wear.

Seated in her apartment across the street from her shop, Rykiel explained her decision to share the creative reins after years of working alone, reminisced about her early days and forecasts the future.

WWD: How did you start in fashion?

SONIA RYKIEL: I didn't have a métier. I was supposed to be a mother, like my mother, who didn't work. I had two children—Nathalie and Jean-Philippe. My husband had a boutique called Laura. I wanted a maternity dress and I couldn't find anything I liked. Everything was abominable. So I made one. Then I made a pullover. *Elle* put it on the cover. Then *WWD* elected me the queen of knitwear.

WWD: How did you work at first?

S.R.: I made clothes spontaneously. When it rained, for example, I designed a trenchcoat. When it was cold, I did a coat. I followed my instincts. It was fantastic for someone who knew absolutely nothing about fashion.

WWD: So you didn't always want to be a designer?

S.R.: Not at all. I could have been a writer—which I am. I could have been an actress—which I am, because you can't do this métier without being an actress. I could have been a sculptor or an artist.

WWD: But you were always interested in style?

S.R.: Not really. I was raised in a very bourgeois family. We always talked about politics or art or paintings. Artistic things. I had an uncle who was a painter. He taught me how to see beautiful things. How the mix of yellow and blue makes green. It's my baggage.

WWD: Success came relatively fast?

S.R.: Very fast. As I said, I didn't know anything. Since I didn't know anything, I did everything I wanted. I didn't listen to anyone. I was so violent, so authoritarian, only listening to what I wanted and myself. People loved me or hated me. Those who loved me, loved me a lot. The others, I didn't bother with them very much.

WWD: Your designs were always linked to St. Germain and the Left Bank.

S.R.: Maybe. I don't think I'm a designer for St. Germain. I think of myself as a designer for women everywhere. I'm more interested in a certain ethic for women, a certain sculpture for women, a certain attitude. Women who interest me are politicians or writers. Women who love life, who love to eat, who love children. That's what interests me. Where is the woman of St. Germain in that? She belongs there because that's the culture of St. Germain. It's a question of appetite. The women of St. Germain are voracious. They love literature, cinema, to look at the vitrines, to shop for antiques.

WWD: That's the type of woman you like to dress?

S.R.: I've never been interested in dressing one woman. What's interested me was to have a philosophy. It hasn't been important to put a woman in a blue dress. I wanted to dress women who wanted to look at themselves. To stand out. To be women who were not part of the crowd. A woman who fights and advances.

WWD: That brings up the late Sixties, when you started. It was a time of social upheaval, especially for women. Do you think women have come out of that era with more liberty now?

S.R.: Not really. I think women today don't have an attitude of liberty. There are so few women today who look at themselves truthfully in the mirror, during a day, a week, a month, a year, to know what they need to show and what they need to hide. Women learn to cook and read, and they work. They don't learn how to dress. They are always with a saleswoman in the store whom they ask what they should wear. I don't believe in that at all. Women should look at themselves and decide for themselves what color or length they should wear.

WWD: You suggest that they find their own personality through clothes?

S.R.: Yes. I wrote a book on the subject when I started urging women to learn how to find their own fashion. Not to follow the dictates of Saint Laurent or Rykiel or any other designer. It's very important.

WWD: You've never been interested in following rules.

S.R.: I never went to fashion school. That's why I sewed things inside out and did superpositions. I did everything people told me I couldn't do. People said making clothes inside out was not proper. I disagreed because clothes that are inside out are as beautiful as a cathedral. There's symbolism in putting on a sweater inside out. One says that if one puts on a sweater on inside out, one will receive a gift. I played with that.

WWD: Do you find that fashion has changed?

S.R.: It's completely different from when I started. Fashion today is another story. You have to understand it. Swallow it and digest it. Today I don't invent in the same way. We don't live in the same way. With all of the computers, it has changed the way we design and cut. It's incredible. Before I went to the factory... we did everything manually. The computer does everything today. Also, fashion isn't sold in the same way. There are the big groups. There are very few people like us outside of the machine.

WWD: You've always held that clothes aren't what make a woman interesting or seductive.

S.R.: Not at all. No, no. A dress will never make a woman sexy, fatale, magnificent, mysterious. It's a way of walking, of standing, or existing, the way you give your hand or your regard. That's what makes the dress. A woman and a dress, very often, fight against each other because they are not at the same place. Sometimes you see the woman moving the belt around. She is making the robe her own. She needs that. Otherwise the dress doesn't exist.

WWD: Recently you've changed the way you work by hiring another designer, Gabrielle Greiss, whom you appointed creative director of women's wear. Has the experience been enriching?

S.R.: I worked all alone for 35 years. And, now, for the last five years, I've starting working with a team. It was a decision. I knew I needed to accept that if this name was to exist and the brand was to exist in time. I needed someone near me who had something of me and something of her own as well. Fashion takes so much energy. You are on your feet all the time in front of a model. That's why I have bad knees today. You're on your knees in front of the model. Dialogue is very important. For instance, I go to see *La Traviata* and Gabrielle and the team will see Snoop Doggy Dogg. The next day we weave something from that. We mix a new culture.

WWD: What do you appreciate most about Gabrielle?

S.R.: She understands what I love. The style Rykiel I don't even know what it is. But she keeps me in line.

WWD: Describe the chemistry between you and your daughter, Nathalie, who is president of the house?

S.R.: It's fantastic. It's paradise. It's strange because we have the same words and the same way to say things and to like or dislike something.

WWD: Has it been difficult remaining an independent, family-owned firm in today's fashion environment?

S.R.: Of course it's been difficult. It's something I've always wanted. There are a lot of things we can't do since we don't belong to a group. But we have different facilities. We decide to do something and we do it.

WWD: In a way you've worn many different hats. Do you consider yourself a businesswoman, too?

S.R.: I'm not a formidable business-woman. I've been lucky. When I started I wondered if all of these women weren't crazy. In the beginning I wanted to dress myself and I didn't want to wear the same costume as all of the other women. I wanted to dress in special clothes. And then other women wanted the same thing. It was disturbing.

I'm not a businesswoman. But I'm attentive and I'm careful. Creation entails a lot of work. The creator is someone who doesn't stop running inside of his or her head. It's Roland Barthes who said that.

WWD: Is creating a difficult process for you?

S.R.: I've always suffered. Before each collection I'm desperate with fear.

WWD: You like to put books in the windows of your shops. What role does literature play in your creative process?

S.R.: I'm inspired by words. The first word I put on a sweater was "sensuous" because *WWD* elected me one of the most sensuous women in the world. I didn't even know what it meant. We sold so many of those sweaters. Writing on a sweater is so beautiful.

WWD: What else inspires you?

S.R.: At the moment I'm really interested in Jeff Koons. I love what he does.

WWD: What is the future of Sonia Rykiel?

S.R.: It's to be strong and know how to surround ourselves with the right people. I think there is a future for a house like ours, with a way of acting that's different. I love this métier. It's what makes me happiest.

—*Robert Murphy*

THAKOON PANICHGUL
Q&A with Thakoon

SEPTEMBER 9, 2008

Thakoon Panichgul took a breather from preshow overdrive to field some questions from *WWD*. Just last month, Michelle Obama wore the designer's floral Radzimir kimono dress for her husband's acceptance speech at the Democratic National Convention. In addition, he has signed to do Target's next diffusion line.

WWD: What is the most nerve-racking aspect about fashion week?

THAKOON PANICHGUL: Not having time to get a haircut.

WWD: What was the most valuable lesson you have learned in the past year?

T.P.: Go with my gut.

WWD: What do you wish people understood better about the way you work?

T.P.: It is multilayered, especially in this day and age, being a young designer.

WWD: How did you find out Michelle Obama would wear your dress on the Democratic National Convention's closing night?

T.P.: I found out while I was watching it on live television.

WWD: Which of your skills as a fashion editor [at *Harper's Bazaar*] served you well as a designer?

T.P.: I realize how important fine-tuning and editing are in the design process.

WWD: How do you measure success?

T.P.: I measure it on a personal level based on my personal goals and the expectations I set for myself.

WWD: Does being independent allow you to be more nimble in this economic climate or is it more challenging?

T.P.: I really believe that everyone has to be mindful during this economic period, whether you are independent or backed by a large group.

WWD: Are you in talks with anyone about buying your company?

T.P.: Luckily, we have some very strong supporters that have been with us from the beginning. Together, we are always discussing new ways to grow the business.

WWD: Any plans for freestanding stores? Secondary lines? One-offs?

T.P.: My own store would be a dream. I would be able to create my own entire world.

WWD: In another life, what would you be?

T.P.: A beekeeper.

—*Rosemary Feitelberg*

MARC JACOBS
Q&A with Marc Jacobs

OCTOBER 12, 2009

As a designer continually under the spotlight's glare—be that of the runway or the gossip columns—Marc Jacobs has his own perspective on the mystique in fashion. *WWD* executive editor Bridget Foley talked with Jacobs right before the Paris collections about luxury, reality TV and the similarity of designers and sports stars.

WWD: Fashion once upon a time was cloaked in mystique. Now we have obsessive media coverage with an industry where designers and editors are on display 24 hours a day. How do you think we got there?

MARC JACOBS: When I saw this [question] all I could think of was something someone said to me once, an off-handed comment about 10 years ago: "Do you remember what it was like when it was a big deal to go to Paris and buy perfume and to bring your wife or your girlfriend? French perfume, because it wasn't available anywhere except for in Paris." Now, everything is available everywhere. I don't know whether it's worthwhile to moan about whether this is a good thing or a bad thing—it's just the way it is. Life changes, and the Internet and the media have been a big part of the change that exists now. It's just better to accept things for what they are and enjoy them.

The idea of luxury and exclusivity [now] comes in another form. I think luxury isn't necessarily about exclusivity; it's about the quality of the design and the quality of the make. And I think the idea of people being exposed, whether it's stylists who have their reality shows or whatever, is just the way of the world. It's every chef, every stylist, every hairdresser, everybody who's doing plastic surgery. We're in a period where people are entertained by what they consider to be the real lives of people in different professions, etc. And fashion has also reached this kind of proportion like football or sport, you know—a spectator sport. So just like you had Joe Namath back in the Seventies promoting stockings, or shaving cream or whatever, you now have designers promoting life jackets and whatever else they do.

WWD: Does it make fashion more egalitarian?

M.J.: I don't know if it makes the actual product more egalitarian; it demystifies the experience. Any behind-the-scenes look is always telling of the fact that these are all real people doing real jobs and who work really hard. Again, I don't know that that makes the end result more accessible. It just makes the ideas more accessible.

WWD: Does that mean more pressure on the end result and design process?

M.J.: It's a catch-22 situation. That may exist. There's also this status—people know what it takes to make these things and they're recognized for having them. People like to show off.

WWD: It sounds like you think it's a good thing?

M.J.: I had lunch with Yves Carcelle [recently] talking about the Vuitton business. One thing that is so different about Vuitton than any of the other retailers, and any of the other luxury brands—Vuitton never goes on sale. That's a huge risk—and I guess an expense—in these challenging economic times, but apparently it's really worked to their advantage, because it's maintained a certain exclusivity. So they've managed to maintain, through their way of retailing through their rules, a certain cachet.

WWD: This 24 hours a day life on camera...do you think that it just may not be a good thing for fashion, or that fashion can make it a good thing?

M.J.: Again, good or bad thing is a judgment—and I just think it's unnecessary to do that. I read this article about the Standard Hotel and how people were lining up all around the Meatpacking District because they could watch people undressing, having sex [through the windows] and all this stuff. And you know what? The hotel is full; people want to stay there. So a voyeur doesn't mean anything without an exhibitionist. It takes all kinds.

Rachel Zoe is a good friend of mine. The reality show wouldn't have been renewed for another season if people didn't want to know that Rachel Zoe was this crazy stylist. So it is what it is.

WWD: Is there any mystique left in fashion or anywhere else in the world?

M.J.: I don't know. To me, as a working designer, I think fashion has great mystique. I mean, I have no idea what we're going to be showing in two weeks [at Louis Vuitton]. So for me the mystery remains the same. What people's reaction to it will be remains the same—I have no idea. So, there's always the possibility of surprise. It just may not come in the same form as it did before.

You know, if we talked about the days of couture, and when Orbach bought rights to reproduce things from the couture—you can't compare 2009 to 1950. Everybody has instant access to information, and everybody gets to see the shows, and Zara is not buying rights from Christian Dior. That's the way of the world. And, again, to qualify or to judge whether it is good or bad is, in a spiritual sense, really futile.

—*Bridget Foley*

STELLA McCARTNEY

Q&A with Stella McCartney

NOVEMBER 17, 2009

Calling herself "an infiltrator" in the world of fashion, Stella McCartney, in a wide-ranging Q&A that touched on topics from her adherence to animal-free production to the decision process behind her corporate collaborations, offered insight into the challenges facing a nascent luxury brand.

The designer initially disputed the notion the economic crisis has had a negative impact on her work, calling it "creatively empowering," while noting that being a relatively small company has its advantages in tough times. "I feel very much like it's made me have to challenge myself as a designer and have to push myself and do a better job, and not take things for granted and not take the easy way out," McCartney said. "But, you know, we're a very agile company...and we run a pretty tight ship anyway. It's obviously a very difficult time for everybody, but in our business, it's been strangely—we're OK."

Pressed on how precisely she has approached her work since luxury spending took a nosedive, McCartney explained she sees every garment individually, rather than as an outfit, and therefore stays detail oriented. "I'm also very aware that I work for the customer, and I think that's very important at times like this, to not try to elevate yourself above the person who's going to pay your wage," she said. "I think that I'm the customer, and I really admire

people who go out and earn money and part with their own hard-earned money for our products."

Despite her intensely private persona, the designer—who has three children with her husband, entrepreneur Alasdhair Willis—veered away from business talk at times. Her kids, she pointed out, were a primary reason in deciding to collaborate with Gap on her recent babyGap and GapKids lines: "I just couldn't buy anymore kids' clothes, to be honest. I couldn't be bothered."

As for social media, McCartney noted her company participates in it, but she views it as "fluff. It's not our bread and butter." The designer has little time: "I have a lot going on....I also think there's merit to some things being left to the imagination."

McCartney also admitted that only recently has she felt entirely comfortable with her career choice—"I was a bit embarrassed by the word 'fashion'"—and that part of her adjustment has been dependent on sticking to her ideological as well as aesthetic guns. "I'm one of the school of designers that tries to do timeless pieces, pieces that will stay with you forever. It's important to have things that you can fall back on in your wardrobe," she said. Perhaps recognizing her designs have at times hewed to a more experimental customer as well, McCartney added: "It's important to be ridiculous in fashion occasionally."

Yet it is her commitment to "responsible luxury"—which McCartney said grew out of the way her parents, Sir Paul McCartney and the late Linda McCartney, raised her, on a rural farm in England—that has proven to be the biggest challenge in her work.

Prior to joining Gucci Group in 2001, McCartney said she was approached by Tom Ford, then the company's creative director, who was interested in McCartney becoming part of the company.

"I said, 'Great. OK.' I was really into it. He said, 'We're not going to do fur for you, Stella; we're gonna give up fur,' and I thought, that's amazing. And I told him, 'Well, you do know I don't do leather, either,' and his face just went white and his jaw dropped to the ground."

Nonetheless, Gucci Group approached her later and asked to invest in her company, and she now jointly owns it with Gucci. Still, McCartney said her standards have resulted in financial roadblocks. "I'm working with Italian factories that have been doing leather for years," she said (those factory owners think she's "less crazy" given her sell-through rate, McCartney noted dryly). "It costs us up to 70 percent more to make a pair of shoes than any other brand—we take that on the chin; we don't mark it up for the customer. Coming into the States, we have nearly a 30 percent import duty for nonleather goods, which I think of as kind of medieval." She added that about 50 million animals are killed each year to produce leather handbags and shoes, "which I'm sure nobody in this room wants to hear, but it's kind of a fact."

Given her well-known stance on the practice of using animals in fashion, McCartney said she remains committed to the expectations of Gucci Group—namely, creating luxury goods. "If my job first and foremost is to create luxurious, desirable, gorgeous items, and that is my job, and if that piece has to be sacrificed so much to the extent that it is no longer luxurious and desirable, then I will make the decision to probably not go with the organic fabric," she said.

And though McCartney declined to suggest leather be abolished from fashion—"That would be a ridiculous thing to say!"—she noted the slow move toward sustainable practices has frustrated her (she said even her London offices are solar- and wind-powered). "That's what I mean when the fashion industry can be a little unfashionable at times," the designer added. "All·other industries are having to think about how to push themselves."

Yet McCartney is disinterested in being known as an eco-friendly brand. She said she is happiest when customers don't realize her products are animal free, and that the blitz of corporate collaborations she has undertaken since linking with Adidas six years ago have been specifically chosen, in part, to expand her brand recognition. H&M, Adidas, a skin care line called Care with YSL Beauté and the Gap collections (as well as a LeSportsac capsule line) each have applied the McCartney name to brands with a wider audience than straightforward luxury offers, she explained.

"We really did it to have people get more access to the brand at a more affordable price point," she said of the H&M deal. "I think the main thing for me when we get asked to do stuff is to really choose things from the heart. I don't like to be hypocritical, just as a person." McCartney couldn't escape the question of how, particularly in this era of celebrity-saturated fashion, she copes with that famous last name, as well as the lingering whispers her name has offered significant tailwind for her ascent.

"It is what it is. At the end of the day, though, I don't think it really matters," she said. "I think staying power is the key. You've got to work your ass off. And you've got to be relatively good at something, I think, to go the distance."

Which is not to imply she's unaware of the trend in famous offspring entering the business. "I do joke with my celebrity friends, 'Everybody is a designer,' and I do joke, 'Don't you try it! Don't you step on my toes!'"

McCartney emphasized her own well-known mother, who died in 1998, represents the look she has tried to convey since her first collection at Central Saint Martins in 1995. "It was an attitude. I always say that our brand is naturally sexy and naturally confident and modern, and the natural word is very important to us," said McCartney, who wears little makeup and noted her mother eschewed it as well. "At the same time, you know, I was hugely influenced by my dad's Savile Row suits," McCartney said.

So much so that she took tailoring lessons in the evenings from a Savile Row designer while still in school. Thereafter, McCartney said, she even dabbled in editorial at *Vogue* ("I knew I didn't want to do that") as well as public relations ("I knew I definitely didn't want to do that"). Indeed, with her talk being live streamed to fashion students, McCartney said that beyond her number-one credo—hard work—adaptability is key to doing well in what she called "a fickle business."

"You have to believe in yourself, you have to be talented and if you don't think you're in the right area of the industry, don't be afraid to change directions," she said. Regarding her own penchant for following her gut when it comes to collaborations, McCartney remarked that a certain humility is valuable, too: "I would say hardly anyone knows of Stella McCartney, really. I once got told by a friend of mine that nobody else really cares as much as you do about yourself."

As for a perennial question—whether she will design men's wear, given that Savile Row background—McCartney told the audience she is considering it, increasingly since so many people seem to inquire about it. "I've always said I don't want to be a huge brand, but as time goes by, we're sort of slowly moving...," McCartney trailed off. "I'd like it to build, build brick on brick. I think that I would like the brand to still be here in the future. I would like it to build on the foundations we have now, the same belief system. I want to build a strong, dedicated clientele of women who really love the brand."

—*Sarah Haight*

VERA WANG
Vera Wang: A Life in Fashion

MAY 12, 2010

From the moment she unlaced her competitive figure skates for the last time, Vera Wang set her sights on a life in fashion.

In the 40-plus years since, hers has been a singular ride, one that took her first to *Vogue* magazine, where she learned that no one disturbed the calm of Mr. Penn's set with chatter, to Ralph Lauren,

where she experienced the creative joys of limitless resources, and finally, 20 years ago, to her own company.

From its modest beginnings as a small bridal boutique, Vera Wang the firm has grown into an important licensing-based operation, and Vera Wang the designer, into a major force. Long the go-to goddess for aisle-bound superstars, as of this fall, Wang begins a relationship with the marrying masses via her recent deal with David's Bridal.

In ready-to-wear, she has dared to be different, adhering steadfastly to her luxe-casual bohemian aesthetic—even though she acknowledges that a more mundane approach might play better at retail. But then, Wang didn't get into this business for the money.

"For me, fashion was sheerly for the love," she says. "It was never about the money. And unfortunately, now it has to be. That's the big adjustment I had to make in my life. You can't survive with a fashion company if you don't make any money. That's just a silly little reality we all want to sweep under the rug, but it's true."

TWENTY YEARS IN BUSINESS— A MOMENT FOR REFLECTION. YOU'VE ALSO LOOKED BACKWARD FOR SOME RECENT SPEAKING ENGAGEMENTS. ANY INTRIGUING SELF-REVELATIONS?

As I looked through, it became very apparent that my life has been defined far more by my failures to attain things, my goals or desires or hopes or dreams, than by anything you could perceive as success.

THAT SOUNDS HARSH.

I fell in love with figure skating when I was about six. I worked my ass off. Skating was my life. It was more than just a passing fantasy. I was always fourth [in competition] and they only took three.... So when I didn't make the [1968 Olympic] team, this was such a part of my life, I was devastated. That was the first lesson I learned in life.

WHAT WAS THE LESSON?

That nobody's going to get your dreams. It's not necessarily about winning or having your dream come true. It's about what you learn along the way. It's a process; it's not just the end result. And then it happened again at *Vogue.*

WHAT HAPPENED AT *VOGUE*?

I started after college as a rover, and then became Polly Mellen's assistant.

WHAT WAS POLLY LIKE?

Oh, killer. Killer. And she knows it. She was a total perfectionist. She was an artist in her own right and, like many artists, they have to work themselves in a fevered pitch to get the result. What I learned from watching Polly was that Polly made the model feel like a queen.

BUT THERE WAS A LESSON OF DISAPPOINTMENT?

I was there for 17 years. I became a senior editor. Eventually, I just didn't see where I was going. I did some really nice work with most of the photographers of that era. But I wasn't shooting with Penn and I wasn't getting Avedon because Polly was getting them. And so I decided to leave.

AND EVENTUALLY, AFTER SEVERAL YEARS WORKING AS AN ACCESSORIES DESIGNER FOR RALPH LAUREN, YOUR FATHER DECIDED TO BACK YOU IN BUSINESS. WHY DID HE INSIST ON BRIDAL?

It would be manageable, he thought. He said, "The inventory level seems low. You custom-make a dress, it's controllable. A nice boutique."

SO RATHER THAN A PASSION, BRIDAL WAS MERELY A WAY INTO FASHION DESIGN?

It became my passion because as I got better at it and I began to grow it, I could express myself in a way that I hadn't been able to in a long time. I've put everything into it for 20 years. I trained myself on the job. I didn't know how to work in lace. One day I just said, "I'm going to master the technique of lace, whether I have to cut it out, piece it, drape it, line it." Bridal became my passion....It didn't start that way.

WHAT DID YOU BRING TO BRIDAL THAT WAS MISSING?

I think I brought a fashion sense that changed bridal. I think we really changed the vocabulary of it. I've spent 20 years of my life doing that and investing in it financially and with physical energy.

WHAT WAS YOUR FIRST BIG CELEBRITY WEDDING?

The first really big one was Max Kennedy's, Ethel Kennedy's son. The bride, Victoria, was heaven. She was a law student and she was beautiful. I didn't go, but from what I heard, the dress was destroyed within 10 minutes because they were playing football after the ceremony. Victoria Kennedy was the first really big name, social-slash-celebrity, and from there on we got very lucky.

WHY DO YOU THINK YOU CONNECTED SO STRONGLY WITH THE CELEBRITY SET? THERE WERE AND ARE OTHER MAJOR NAMES IN BRIDAL....

I think what connected was the single-mindedness of it. There was nothing else. I could focus all that energy into how to cut a veil. I didn't have an empire. I looked for inspiration just as I would for ready-to-wear, in film or something else that resonated for me.

LET'S MOVE TO WHERE YOU ARE NOW. HOW DO YOU ASSESS YOUR BUSINESS TODAY?

My business today is definitely based on the licensing model. That's where we have grown the most, that's where we've spent a lot of energy, and I think we've been very successful. I don't want to ever appear like

I think I'm really successful because a) it isn't true, and b) whenever I say I'm feeling good, the next day I come down with strep throat. It's been a good model for us, but we've also worked hard at it. I think my licensees have grown to depend on my participation, which is a challenge because I'm one person. But I do control those businesses carefully, as much as I can.

WHAT HAVE BEEN THE BIGGEST CHALLENGES?

Each one of the businesses is different, and I've had to come up to speed on all. I've had to understand what the market will bear and yet I try not to let go of my own aesthetic. It's that constant challenge that is very, very difficult. At Wedgewood alone, there are 15 categories that I have to satisfy— the crystal, the sub-crystal, the plates, the gifting, the picture-frame business.

YOU'VE LEARNED A LOT ABOUT ARENAS FAR REMOVED FROM FASHION.

Stationery—that's worse than 500 ready-to-wear collections: the shape of the flap, the proportion of the envelope square, the myriad [details]. You learn here's the price point for that and here's the price point for that. If you add a ribbon or tie, it's that much more. It's the specificity of it all that is boggling. I'm not in one business, I'm in 30 little ones.

TABLETOP, FLATWARE, GIFTS, STATIONERY.

As a brand, it's certainly related to the bridal part of the business. So much a part of the bridal experience is invitations. Nobody got mattresses, but 70 percent of the mattress business is when [people] get married. We do sheets, we do towels, why wouldn't we do the mattress underneath? I'm sort of a bed fanatic. I spend a lot of time in bed.

IT SEEMS A GREAT DEAL RADIATES FROM BRIDAL.

[It's about] the credibility, the dedication, the singular energy, the fact that we work with brides, we fit brides. This isn't ready-to-wear—you really are involved. You have to deliver a perfect dress. They don't have three in the closet—they're depending on you. That responsibility never escapes me in bridal, and I think [it crosses over] to all the licensees. I mean, I said to Wedgewood, "I want the weight of the stainless to be heavy because there's nothing worse than a fork you can bend, and most people don't use sterling." I said, "Make sure that the stainless is heavy enough that people feel there's value." Defending all that on every level is a full-time job.

WHILE MOST DESIGNERS START WITH READY-TO-WEAR, YOUR COLLECTION IS ONLY SIX YEARS OLD. WHAT IS ITS GREAT CHALLENGE FOR YOU?
It's trying to push a contemporary—I don't mean a contemporary business—but a more contemporary, younger feel. Why should women at any age, young or old, have to dress old? It's been challenging.

WHY SO CHALLENGING?
Because does anyone care? We understand, but are there 12 people [who understand]? And, then, the question of [growth]: I know what I could do to be bigger, but something in me doesn't allow me to do it.

PLEASE EXPLAIN.
I would have to do dresses with really tight waists and skinny skirts, and I'd probably have to make them fairly boring, if they're going to be commercially successful. And do more evening for mermaids. And certainly more color—bright color probably, bright prints. But are you going to be honest to yourself or are you going to be doing what you think is formulaic? Those aren't small questions. I think that every designer today faces that on the upper end.

SUCH REALIZATION MUST BE FRUSTRATING.
I understand stores' needs. But I question myself: Am I, at this stage of the game, true to who I am? I try to walk the fine line. I try to make black go to different places—that's what I was trying to do the last time.

FOR MOST DESIGNERS, READY-TO-WEAR IS THE NUCLEUS AROUND WHICH THEY BUILD THEIR BRANDS. FOR YOU, THE BRIDAL IS THE NUCLEUS. HOW IMPORTANT IS RTW TO YOUR BUSINESS?
It is [important] because it expresses who I really am as a woman, as a person and as a designer. It's important for me to be able wear my own clothes, which is not a small thing to me after all the years of work and investment. I like to wear my knits. I like to wear my T-shirts. I'm doing things, finally, that are real to me.

BUT HOW IMPORTANT IS IT TO THE HEALTH OF YOUR BUSINESS, TO THE BRAND? ALMOST ACROSS THE BOARD, DESIGNER READY-TO-WEAR IS NOT WHERE THE MONEY IS.
I can afford it. And it enables me to be constantly challenged. A lot of what I do is about attitude. That's what I love most in clothing: It gives attitude. When you're wearing a blousy dress, you feel so different than when you're wearing a narrow dress. When you're wearing a knit, it's very different from wearing a tight top and little blazer. The clothes that lend that sense of who [women] can express themselves as can only come from ready-to-wear. That can't come from bridal. Evening, to some extent, but evening is very formulaic. Also, it's an older aesthetic.

HOW DIFFICULT IS IT TO BALANCE YOUR CASUAL ATTITUDE WITH THE REALITIES OF THE BUSINESS?
That's always been my problem—how do you reconcile who you are as a person and as, I would say, a fashion professional after all these years? And what do you have to do to be really successful, if it doesn't come naturally to you?

YOU'VE TALKED ABOUT YOUR LIFE HAVING BEEN DEFINED BY THINGS THAT DIDN'T GO AS PLANNED. RELATING THAT TO THE BUSINESS, GETTING ESTABLISHED IN CONTEMPORARY HAD BEEN PROBLEMATIC.
We've tried three times, the most recent time with Lavender.

WHAT HAPPENED?
I'll tell you what happened. We got too big too fast—too much distribution. And then the economy turned and the combination of the two—a double whammy. Lavender was only a year-and-a-half old, and I just said this isn't the time to continue this.

YOU'VE SAID IT'S "ON HIATUS." DO YOU WANT TO BRING IT BACK?
We're planning on bringing it back, but how we're bringing it back is another issue.

WOULD IT BE LESS EXPENSIVE?
Yes, it has to be. And it would depend on whether we do it with a partner as a joint venture, or whether we own it and we produce it with the factories we know in China, or whether we license it. Those are three totally different alternatives and we've been busy in the last year trying to figure that out.

CONVERSELY, KOHL'S IS WORKING.
I'll tell you why—because Kohl's has tremendous distribution. I'm able to be myself within the world of Kohl's, the context of Kohl's. They're really moving into fashion—that's been their big goal. That was the whole reason they brought me on. And they've always had a great juniors business.

OTHERWISE, BESIDES LAVENDER, HOW HAS THE RECESSION IMPACTED THE VERA WANG BUSINESS?
It affected bridal. At the same time, I made sure that I got away from any fabrics that were $40 to $50 a yard. You have to also realize that Neiman's and Saks closed bridal doors. In the major cities—L.A. or Dallas or Chicago—that's where I was. When you're at the upper end and you lose, let's say, 15, 16 doors in the key cities in the U.S., that's a bit of a blow. I heard it from *WWD* before I heard it from the buyer.

WERE YOU ANGRY?
It wasn't about being angry—I was just so worried. How was I going to replace businesses in Chicago and L.A.? That's partly why we opened [a store]. When Barneys shut its [bridal] boutique that was [just] us, that's when I started to look [for a store] in L.A.

WHAT DO YOU SEE AS THE RECESSION'S RESIDUAL EFFECTS, BOTH BOTTOM LINE AND PSYCHOLOGICALLY?

Financially, I was OK because I have a very, very good licensing business. But in terms of our business, we had to shave costs; we had to adjust everything. We had to change some leases. For example, I had a bigger store slated for L.A. because I was doing bridal and ready-to-wear, and bridal takes a lot of room. I gave up on that lease and took the smaller store, which is the one we're in now. But—I can't do alterations out of that store. I had to get another, less expensive space for alterations, which brings in other issues in terms of functionality and how you get it done. Welcome to my world. I've had to make the toughest decisions. I'm actually very proud to say this because I like change in clothes, but I don't like change in my life. We've had to make big changes, but I think we're in a good place. We're in a solid place. I'm not being boastful or anything, because you know, I'm never going to be Ralph.

IN BETWEEN *VOGUE* AND OPENING THAT FIRST BRIDAL SHOP, YOU WORKED FOR RALPH, WHAT WAS THAT LIKE?

I was design director for accessories. I just adored it because you could just be creative. You don't have to worry about getting it made, you don't have to worry about pricing it, you don't have to worry about whether we can duplicate this [or] are we spending too much money? It was kind of like being in a candy store. The amount of product we created—it's just inconceivable.

TALK ABOUT YOUR RELATIONSHIP WITH MARIO [GRAUSO].

Mario knows me very well. He is the strategic person and my right arm. He worked here years ago as vice president when Chet [Hazzard, the original president of Vera Wang] was so sick. [Hazzard died of AIDS in 2005.]

IT MUST HAVE BEEN EMOTIONALLY WRENCHING, AND DIFFICULT FOR A FLEDGLING BUSINESS.

There were months at a time maybe when Chet couldn't really come to work. But his life I knew was coming to work. He couldn't get on planes and fly every week to China or to L.A., so many things, we kept things at the status quo.

HOW DO YOU VIEW CHET'S LEGACY?

Chet supported me emotionally as a friend, as a brother. He was just there for me as a human being, and I needed that. I really didn't have anyone else there. On a business level, it was challenging. Part of it had to do with his health, for sure. Part of it had to deal with, you know, it takes a certain amount of experience—can I be honest?—to run even a small company. And that wasn't Chet's background. Yes, he had some licensing, yes he did. But I think he was unable to visualize strategically and implement—not taking away from his own emotional support of me—he couldn't implement significant growth.

WHAT'S NEXT FOR VERA WANG?

Retail is a very important component for us. I don't need 30 stores. I'm not trying to be an empire at the upper end, but I would like four or five stores in America. After that, what we want to do is a line somewhere between high and low. I think there's room for women in America to have something that isn't at Kohl's and isn't more elitist.

WOULD YOU LIKE YOUR DAUGHTERS, CECILIA AND JOSEPHINE, TO GO INTO THE BUSINESS?

Only if they want to. I would like them to do something that gives them discipline. When I went to *Vogue* as an assistant, I'd come home and say to my father, "I went to Sarah Lawrence. I almost have a master's in art history and I'm doing messenger slips." And he'd say to me, "You have no idea what you're learning. So go do those messenger slips." That's the kind of family I came from.

DO YOU FEEL AT ALL DAUNTED? SO MANY PEOPLE IN FASHION SAY THAT STARTING OUT, THEY WERE TOO IGNORANT TO BE SCARED.

I was ignorant and scared. I may have been a neophyte bridal designer, but I wasn't a neophyte in fashion. Because when you work for *Vogue,* you see businesses come and go. And when you work for Ralph, you see what it takes.

—*Bridget Foley*

IMAGE CREDITS

Credits are to be read as left page first, top left corner clockwise, then right page, top left corner clockwise.

FRONT MATTER:

Karl Lagerfeld, 1987, *WWD*, Courtesy of Fairchild Archive

Photographs by Peter Riesett, from *Drawing Fashion: The Art of Kenneth Paul Block*, Published by Pointed Leaf Press, LLC. Copyright © 2007 Kenneth Paul Block, Illustration, 1972

Miuccia Prada for Miu Miu, Pre-Fall 2010, Photo by Giovanna Pavesi, *WWD*, Courtesy of *WWD*

Miuccia Prada for Miu Miu, Pre-Fall 2010, Photo by Giovanna Pavesi, *WWD*, Courtesy of *WWD*

Miuccia Prada for Miu Miu, Pre-Fall 2010, Photo by Giovanna Pavesi, *WWD*, Courtesy of *WWD*

WWD Cover, 1910, Courtesy of Fairchild Archive

Ralph Lauren, Spring 2008, Photo by Kyle Ericksen, *WWD*, Courtesy of *WWD*

Oscar de la Renta, 1972, Photo by Pierre Schermann, *WWD*, Courtesy of Fairchild Archive

Frida Giannini for Gucci, Fall 2009, Photo by Davide Maestri, *WWD*, Courtesy of *WWD*

Marc Jacobs for Perry Ellis, Fall/Winter 1992, Photo by George Chinsee, *WWD*, Courtesy of *WWD*

Olivier Theyskens for Nina Ricci, Fall 2007, Photo by *WWD* Archive, Courtesy of *WWD*

André Courrèges, 1968, Photo by Pierre Schermann, *WWD*, Courtesy of Fairchild Archive

Christian Lacroix, Fall 1987, Photo by Philippe Costes, *WWD*, Courtesy of Fairchild Archive

Gabrielle Chanel, Fall 1968, Photo by Paris Press International, *WWD*, Courtesy of Fairchild Archive

DECADES:

Andy Warhol, Baroness Guy de Rothschild & Unknown Guest, 1972, Photo by Pierre Schermann, *WWD*, Courtesy of Fairchild Archive

1910s:

Suffragettes, 1913, © The Granger Collection, New York

Titanic, 1912, © Popperfoto/Getty Images

Theda Bara, 1915, © Bettmann/Corbis

Burberry Trench Coat, 1917, © The Granger Collection, New York

Pickford Film Poster, 1918, © The Granger Collection, New York

WWD Front Page, October 13, 1917, Courtesy of Fairchild Archive

Chanel Sport Suit, 1917, Courtesy of Fairchild Archive

1920s:

Amelia Earhart, 1928, © Hulton-Deutsch Collection/Corbis

"Night," 1928, George Barbier, Courtesy of The Bridgeman Art Library

Clara Bow, 1920s, © Bettmann/Corbis

WWD Front Page, January 3, 1927, Courtesy of Fairchild Archive

Hattie Carnegie sketch, 1927, *WWD*, Courtesy of Fairchild Archive

1930s:

Duke & Duchess of Windsor, 1937, © Bettmann/Corbis

Elsa Schiaparelli Coat, © Philadelphia Museum of Art/CORBIS

WWD Front Page, December 7, 1933, Courtesy of Fairchild Archive

Greta Garbo, *Inspiration*, 1931, © Bettmann/Corbis

Fashion sketch, 1932, Courtesy of Fairchild Archive

Depression Breadline, 1930s, © Bettmann/Corbis

Katherine Hepburn, 1938, Photo by Alfred Eisenstaedt, Time & Life Pictures/Getty Images

1940s:

Fashion sketch, 1943, Courtesy of Fairchild Archive

WWD Front Page, June 6, 1944, Courtesy of Fairchild Archive

Lana Turner, 1942, © Bettman/Corbis

Claire McCardell sketch, Courtesy of Fairchild Archive

Lastex Undergarments, 1940s, © Bettmann/Corbis

Betty Grable, 1943, Painting by Frank Powolny, © The Granger Collection, New York

Théâtre de la Mode, London, 1945, Photo by Reg Speller, Getty Images/Hulton Archive

1950s:

Lucille Ball, *I Love Lucy*, 1955, Getty Images

Air Raid Drill, 1958, © *Seattle Post-Intelligencer* Collection

James Dean, *Rebel Without a Cause*, 1955, Courtesy of Everett Collection

Cocktail Dress, 1954, Courtesy of Fairchild Archive

Audrey Hepburn, *Funny Face*, 1957, Courtesy of Everett Collection

WWD Front Page, April 18, 1956, Courtesy of Fairchild Archive

Marilyn Monroe, *All About Eve*, 1950, Courtesy of Everett Collection

1960s:

WWD Front Page, July 13, 1960, Courtesy of Fairchild Archive

Janis Joplin, Woodstock, 1969, © Elliott Landy/Corbis

Illustration by Kenneth Paul Block, Babe Paley in Mainbocher, Amanda Burden in Sami, *WWD*, Courtesy of Fairchild Archive

Jackie Kennedy, 1965, © Elliott Landy/Corbis

Monokini, Rudi Gernreich, Spring 1968, Photo by Claxton William, WWD, Courtesy of Fairchild Archive

Braniff Airlines Flight Attendant, 1965, © Bettmann/Corbis

Twiggy, 1966, Courtesy of Popperfoto/Getty Images

Mary Quant, 1967, Photo by George Freston, Courtesy of Getty Images/Hulton Archive

Washington Monument Demonstration, 1969, Photo by Fred W. McDarrah, Courtesy of Getty Images

1970s:

Punk Fashion, 1977, Photo by Tim Jenkins, *WWD*, Courtesy of Fairchild Archive

Yoko Ono, 1973, Photo by Peter Simins, *WWD*, Courtesy of Fairchild Archive

Green Suit, 1972, Photo by Pierre Venant, *WWD*, Courtesy of Fairchild Archive

Studio 54, 1978, © Michael Norcia/Sygma/Corbis

Diana Ross, 1970, Photo by Eli Silverberg, *WWD*, Courtesy of Fairchild Archive

WWD Front Page, October 26, 1970, Courtesy of Fairchild Archive

Diane Keaton, Photo by Allen Rosen, *WWD*, Courtesy of Fairchild Archive

1980s:

Nancy Reagan, 1982, Photo by Marianne Barcellona, *WWD*, Courtesy of Fairchild Archive

Wedding of Lady Diana Spencer and Prince Charles, July 29, 1981, Photo by Anwar Hussein, Courtesy of Getty Images

Bruce Willis & Demi Moore, 1989, Photo by Jim Smeal, Courtesy of WireImage

WWD Front Page June 24, 1987, Courtesy of Fairchild Archive

AIDS Quilt, 1987, © Jean Louis Atlan/Sygma/Corbis

Nan Kempner, 1985, Photo by Tony Palmieri, *WWD*, Courtesy of Fairchild Archive

Madonna, 1985, Photo by Jim Steinfeldt, Courtesy of Getty Images

1990s:

Gwyneth Paltrow & Giorgio Armani, 1996, Photo by Dave Allocca, Time & Life Pictures/Getty Images

Rock C, DJ Jazzy Jeff & Fresh Prince, 1990, Photo by Steve Pyke, Courtesy of Getty Images

Princess Diana, 1997, Photo by Tim Graham, Courtesy of Getty Images

Isaac Mizrahi, Spring 1993 (Christy Turlington, Kate Moss & Naomi Campbell), Photo by Ron Galella, Courtesy of WireImage

Seattle Grunge, 1993, © Carrarro Mauro/Corbis Sygma

WWD Front Page, July 19, 1999, Courtesy of Fairchild Archive

2000s:

Sex and the City, 2004, Photo by Richard Corkery, *NY Daily News* via Getty Images

WWD Front Page, January 21, 2009, Courtesy of Fairchild Archive

Lady Gaga, 2007, Photo by Josie Miner, *WWD*, Courtesy of Fairchild Archive

WWD Front Page, September 12, 2001, Courtesy of Fairchild Archive

Fall 2010 Runway Show on iPhone, Photo by Steve Eichner, *WWD*, Courtesy of *WWD*

THE DESIGNERS:
Marc Jacobs, 2009, Photo by Stephane Feugere, *WWD*, Courtesy of *WWD*

ADOLFO:
Adolfo, Fall 1983, Photo by Tony Palmieri, *WWD*, Courtesy of Fairchild Archive
Gloria Vanderbilt in Adolfo, 1972, Photo by Guy Delort, *WWD*, Courtesy of Fairchild Archive
Adolfo, 1972, Illustration by Steven Stipelman, *WWD*, Courtesy of Fairchild Archive
Adolfo, Fall 1985, Photo by Thomas Iannaccone, *WWD, Courtesy* of Fairchild Archive

AZZEDINE ALAÏA:
Azzedine Alaïa, Spring 2003, Photo by Giovanni Giannoni, *WWD*, Courtesy of *WWD*
Azzedine Alaïa, Spring 1984, Photo by Guy Marineau, *WWD*, Courtesy of Fairchild Archive
Azzedine Alaïa, Courtesy of Fairchild Archive
Azzedine Alaïa, Spring 2003, Photo by Giovanni Giannoni, *WWD*, Courtesy of Fairchild Archive

GIORGIO ARMANI:
Giorgio Armani for Armani Privé. Fall 2005, Photo by Giovanni Giannoni, *WWD*, Courtesy of *WWD*
Giorgio Armani for Armani Privé. Spring 2010, Photo by Giovanni Giannoni. *WWD*, Courtesy of *WWD*
Giorgio Armani, Fall 1985 RTW, Photo by Guy Marineau, *WWD*, Courtesy of Fairchild Archive
Giorgio Armani, Fall 1978, Photo by Gianni Lami, *WWD*, Courtesy of Fairchild Archive
Giorgio Armani for Emporio Armani, Fall 2010, Photo by Giovanni Giannoni, *WWD*, Courtesy of *WWD*
Giorgio Armani for Armani Privé. 2009, Photo by Donato Sardella, *WWD*, Courtesy of *WWD*
Giorgio Armani, Fall 1992, Photo by Art Streiber, *WWD*, Courtesy of Fairchild Archive
Giorgio Armani for Armani Privé, Fall 2009, Photo by Stephane Feugere, *WWD*, Courtesy of *WWD*

CHRISTOPHER BAILEY:
Christopher Bailey for Burberry Prorsum, 2009, Photo by Talaya Centeno, *WWD*, Courtesy of *WWD*
Christopher Bailey for Burberry, Spring 2004, Photo by Mauricio Miranda, *WWD*, Courtesy of *WWD*
Christopher Bailey for Burberry Prorsum, Fall 2002, Photo by Mauricio Miranda, *WWD*, Courtesy of *WWD*
Christopher Bailey for Burberry Prorsum, 2008, Photo by Kristen Somody Whalen, *WWD*, Courtesy of *WWD*
Christopher Bailey for Burberry Prorsum, Spring 2010, Photo by Giovanni Giannoni, *WWD*, Courtesy of *WWD*

CRISTÓBAL BALENCIAGA:
Cristóbal Balenciaga, 1964, *WWD*, Courtesy of Fairchild Archive
Cristóbal Balenciaga, 1964, *WWD*, Courtesy of Fairchild Archive
Cristóbal Balenciaga, 1963, Illustration by Sandra Leichman, *WWD*, Courtesy of Fairchild Archive
Cristóbal Balenciaga,1962, Illustration Sandra Leichman, *WWD*, Courtesy of Fairchild Archive
Photographs by Peter Riesett, from *Drawing Fashion: The Art of Kenneth Paul Block*, Published by Pointed Leaf Press, LLC. Copyright © 2007 Kenneth Paul Block, Duchess of Windsor, 1962
Photographs by Peter Riesett, from *Drawing Fashion: The Art of Kenneth Paul Block*, Published by Pointed Leaf Press, LLC. Copyright © 2007 Kenneth Paul Block, Diana Vreeland, Babe Paley and C.Z. Guest, 1964

PIERRE BALMAIN:
Pierre Balmain, 1956, *WWD*, Courtesy of Fairchild Archive
Pierre Balmain, 1950, *WWD*, Courtesy of Fairchild Archive

GEOFFREY BEENE:
Geoffrey Beene, 1977, Photo by Pierre Schermann, *WWD*, Courtesy of Fairchild Archive
Geoffrey Beene, 1981, Photo by John Bright, *WWD*, Courtesy of Fairchild Archive
Geoffrey Beene, 2005, Photo by Giovanni Giannoni, *WWD*, Courtesy of *WWD*
Geoffrey Beene, Fall 1973 RTW, Photo by Pierre Schermann, *WWD*, Courtesy of Fairchild Archive

BILL BLASS:
Bill Blass, Spring/Summer 1972, Photo by Nick Machalaba, *WWD*, Courtesy of Fairchild Archive
Photographs by Peter Riesett, from *Drawing Fashion: The Art of Kenneth Paul Block*, Published by Pointed Leaf Press, LLC. Copyright © 2007 Kenneth Paul Block. Illustration, 1982
Blass, Resort 1982, *WWD*, Courtesy of Fairchild Archive
Bill Blass, Spring/Summer 1973, Photo by Pierre Schermann, *WWD*, Courtesy of Fairchild Archive

MARC BOHAN:
Marc Bohan, 1965, *WWD*, Courtesy of Fairchild Archive
Marc Bohan, 1964, *WWD*, Courtesy of Fairchild Archive
Marc Bohan, 1966, *WWD*, Courtesy of Fairchild Archive
Marc Bohan for Christian Dior Couture, Fall 1973, Photo by Reginald Gray, *WWD*, Courtesy of Fairchild Archive

CALLOT SOEURS:
Callot Souers, 1918, *WWD*, Courtesy of Fairchild Archive
Callot Souers, 1913, *WWD*, Courtesy of Fairchild Archive
Callot Souers, 1926, *WWD*, Courtesy of Fairchild Archive
Callot Souers, 1917, *WWD*, Courtesy of Fairchild Archive

PIERRE CARDIN:
Pierre Cardin, 1978, *WWD*, Courtesy of Pierre Cardin Archives
Pierre Cardin, 1962, *WWD*, Courtesy of Fairchild Archive
Pierre Cardin, 1972, *WWD*, Courtesy of Fairchild Archive
Pierre Cardin, 1965, *WWD*, Courtesy of Fairchild Archive
Pierre Cardin, 1968, *WWD*, Courtesy of Fairchild Archive

HATTIE CARNEGIE:
Hattie Carnegie, 1951, *WWD*, Courtesy of Fairchild Archive
Hattie Carnegie, 1941, *WWD*, Courtesy of Fairchild Archive

BONNIE CASHIN:
Bonnie Cashin, 1969, Illustration by Anneliese, *WWD*, Courtesy of Fairchild Archive
Bonnie Cashin, Fall/Winter 1973, Sal Traina, *WWD*, Courtesy of Fairchild Archive
Bonnie Cashin, 1964, *WWD*, Courtesy of Fairchild Archive
Bonnie Cashin, Spring/Summer 1973, Sal Traina, *WWD*, Courtesy of Fairchild Archive
Bonnie Cashin, 1974, *WWD*, Courtesy of Fairchild Archive

OLEG CASSINI:
Oleg Cassini, 1962, *WWD*, Courtesy of Fairchild Archive
Oleg Cassini, 1962, *WWD*, Courtesy of Fairchild Archive
Oleg Cassini, 1965, *WWD*, Courtesy of Fairchild Archive
Oleg Cassini, 1972, Peter Simins, *WWD*, Courtesy of Fairchild Archive

ROBERTO CAVALLI:
Roberto Cavalli, Fall 2010, Photo by Davide Maestri, WWD, Courtesy of *WWD*
Roberto Cavalli, Spring 2001, *WWD*, Courtesy of *WWD*
Roberto Cavalli, Spring 2003, Photo by Giovanni Giannoni, *WWD*, Courtesy of *WWD*
Roberto Cavalli, Spring 2009, Photo by Giovanni Giannoni, *WWD*, Courtesy of *WWD*
Roberto Cavalli, Spring 2005, Photo by Mauricio Miranda, *WWD*, Courtesy of *WWD*

HUSSEIN CHALAYAN:
Hussein Chalayan, Spring 2008, Photo by Chris Moore, *WWD*, Courtesy of *WWD*
Hussein Chalayan, Spring 2010, Photo by Dominique Maître, *WWD*, Courtesy of *WWD*
Hussein Chalayan, Spring 2009, Photo by Dominique Maître, *WWD*, Courtesy of *WWD*
Hussein Chalayan, Spring 2007, Photo by Giovanni Giannoni, *WWD*, Courtesy of *WWD*

GABRIELLE CHANEL:
Gabrielle Chanel, 1962, Photo by Douglas Kirkland, *WWD*, Courtesy of Fairchild Archive
Gabrielle Chanel, 1959, *WWD*, Courtesy of Fairchild Archive
Gabrielle Chanel, Fall 1968, Photo by Paris Presse Internationale, *WWD*, Courtesy of Fairchild Archive
Gabrielle Chanel, Illustrations from the following years: 1917, 1927, 1929, 1931, 1937, 1966, 1960, 1959, 1958, *WWD*, Courtesy of Fairchild Archive

LIZ CLAIBORNE:
Liz Claiborne, 1977, Photo by Kichisaburo Ogawa, *WWD*, Courtesy of Fairchild Archive
Liz Claiborne, Spring 1983, Photo by Tony Palmieri, *WWD*, Courtesy of Fairchild Archive

Liz Claiborne, 1971, *WWD*, Courtesy of Fairchild Archive
Liz Claiborne, 1970, Photo by Nick Machalaba, *WWD*, Courtesy of Fairchild Archive

FRANCISCO COSTA:
Francisco Costa for Calvin Klein, Spring 2007, Photo by George Chinsee, *WWD*, Courtesy of *WWD*
Francisco Costa for Calvin Klein, Fall 2010, Photo by Kyle Ericksen, *WWD*, Courtesy of *WWD*
Francisco Costa for Calvin Klein, Spring 2010 RTW, Photo by Steve Eichner, *WWD*, Courtesy of *WWD*
Francisco Costa for Calvin Klein, Fall 2005, Photo by Steve Eichner, *WWD*, Courtesy of *WWD*
Francisco Costa for Calvin Klein, Spring 2006, Photo by Robert Mitra, *WWD*, Courtesy of *WWD*
Francisco Costa for Calvin Klein, Fall 2007, Photo by Thomas Iannaccone, WWD, Courtesy of *WWD*
Francisco Costa for Calvin Klein, Resort 2006, Photo by John Aquino, *WWD*, Courtesy of *WWD*

ANDRÉ COURRÈGES:
André Courrèges, Photo: 1967, *WWD*, Courtesy of Fairchild Archive
André Courrèges, 1968, *WWD*, Courtesy of Fairchild Archive

OSCAR DE LA RENTA:
Oscar de la Renta, Fall 2010, Photo by George Chinsee, *WWD*, Courtesy of *WWD*
Oscar de la Renta, Spring 2009, Photo by Thomas Iannaccone, *WWD*, Courtesy of *WWD*
Oscar de la Renta, Spring 2010 RTW, Photo by John Aquino, *WWD*, Courtesy of *WWD*
Oscar de la Renta, Fall 2008 Bridal, Photo by John Aquino, Steve Eichner, *WWD*, Courtesy of *WWD*
Oscar de la Renta, Spring 2009, Photo by George Chinsee, *WWD*, Courtesy of *WWD*
Oscar de la Renta, Pre-Fall 2010, Photo by George Chinsee, *WWD*, Courtesy of *WWD*

CHRISTIAN DIOR:
Christian Dior, 1950, *WWD*, Courtesy of Fairchild Archive
Christian Dior, 1947, *WWD*, Courtesy of Fairchild Archive

DOLCE & GABBANA:
Domenico Dolce & Stefano Gabbana, Spring 2010 RTW, Photo by Mauricio Miranda, *WWD*, Courtesy of *WWD*
Domenico Dolce & Stefano Gabbana, Spring 2009, Photo by Stephane Feugere, *WWD*, Courtesy of *WWD*
Domenico Dolce & Stefano Gabbana, Fall 2001, Photo by Giovanni Giannoni, *WWD*, Courtesy of *WWD*
Domenico Dolce & Stefano Gabbana, D&G Fall 2003, Photo by Giovanni Giannoni, *WWD*, Courtesy of *WWD*
Domenico Dolce & Stefano Gabbana, Fall 2005, Photo by Giovanni Giannoni, *WWD*, Courtesy of *WWD*
Domenico Dolce & Stefano Gabbana, Fall 2000, Photo by Giovanni Giannoni, *WWD*, Courtesy of *WWD*

ALBER ELBAZ:
Alber Elba for Lanvin, Fall 2006, Photo by Giovanni Giannoni, *WWD*, Courtesy of *WWD*
Alber Elbaz for Lanvin, Fall 2004, Photo by Giovanni Giannoni, *WWD*, Courtesy of *WWD*
Alber Elbaz for Lanvin, Fall 2008, Photo by Giovanni Giannoni, *WWD*, Courtesy of *WWD*
Alber Elbaz for Lanvin, Spring 2007, Photo by Giovanni Giannoni, *WWD*, Courtesy of *WWD*
Alber Elbaz for Lanvin, Fall 2010, Photo by Giovanni Giannoni, *WWD*, Courtesy of *WWD*

PERRY ELLIS:
Perry Ellis, Fall 1983, *WWD*, Photo by George Chinsee, Courtesy of Fairchild Archive
Perry Ellis, Fall 1982, *WWD*, Photo by George Chinsee, Courtesy of Fairchild Archive
Perry Ellis, Fall 1986, *WWD*, Photo by George Chinsee, Courtesy of Fairchild Archive
Perry Ellis, Fall 1979, *WWD*, Photo by George Chinsee, Courtesy of Fairchild Archive
Perry Ellis, Spring 1978, *WWD*, Photo by George Chinsee, Courtesy of Fairchild Archive
Perry Ellis, Fall 1981, Photo by Dustin Pittman, *WWD*, Courtesy of Fairchild Archive

JACQUES FATH:
Jacques Fath, 1949, *WWD*, Courtesy of Fairchild Archive
Jacques Fath, 1954, *WWD*, Courtesy of Fairchild Archive
Jacques Fath, 1957, *WWD*, Courtesy of Fairchild Archive

GIANFRANCO FERRÉ:
Gianfranco Ferré, Spring 2006, Photo by Giovanni Giannoni, *WWD*, Courtesy of *WWD*
Gianfranco Ferré for Christian Dior, Fall 1990 Couture, Photo by Christopher Simon Sykes, Courtesy of Fairchild Archive
Gianfranco Ferré for Christion Dior, Fall 1990 Couture, Photo by James Graham, *WWD*, Courtesy of Fairchild Archive
Gianfranco Ferré for Christian Dior, Fall 1990 Couture, Photo by Christopher Simon Sykes, *WWD*, Courtesy of Fairchild Archive

TOM FORD:
Tom Ford for Gucci, Spring 2003, Photo by Davide Maestri, *WWD*, Courtesy of *WWD*
Tom Ford for Yves Saint Laurent, Spring 2004, Photo by Giovanni Giannoni, *WWD*, Courtesy of *WWD*
Tom Ford for Gucci, Fall 2003, Photo by Giovanni Giannoni, *WWD*, Courtesy of *WWD*
Tom Ford for Gucci, Fall 2003, Photo by Giovanni Giannoni, *WWD*, Courtesy of *WWD*

JAMES GALANOS:
James Galanos, 1961, *WWD*, Courtesy of Fairchild Archive
James Galanos, Fall 1967, Photo by Richard Swift, *WWD*, Courtesy of Fairchild Archive
James Galanos, 1967, Photo by Guy Delort, *WWD*, Courtesy of Fairchild Archive
James Galanos, 1963, *WWD*, Courtesy of Fairchild Archive

JOHN GALLIANO:
John Galliano, Fall 2009, Photo by Stephane Feugere, *WWD*, Courtesy of *WWD*
John Galliano, Fall 2002, Photo by Giovanni Giannoni, *WWD*, Courtesy of *WWD*

John Galliano, Spring 2004, Photo by Giovanni Giannoni, *WWD*, Courtesy of *WWD*
John Galliano, Spring 2005, Photo by Giovanni Giannoni, *WWD*, Courtesy of *WWD*
John Galliano, Fall 2004, Photo by Giovanni Giannoni, *WWD*, Courtesy of *WWD*
John Galliano, Spring 2008, Photo by Giovanni Giannoni, *WWD*, Courtesy of *WWD*
John Galliano for Christian Dior Haute Couture, Fall 2010, Photo by Giovanni Giannoni, *WWD*, Courtesy of *WWD*
John Galliano for Christian Dior Haute Couture, Fall 2009, Photo by Giovanni Giannoni, *WWD*, Courtesy of *WWD*
John Galliano for Christian Dior Haute Couture, Fall 2010, Photo by Giovanni Giannoni, *WWD*, Courtesy of *WWD*
John Galliano for Christian Dior Haute Couture, Fall 2010, Photo by Giovanni Giannoni, *WWD*, Courtesy of *WWD*
John Galliano for Christian Dior Haute Couture, Fall 2010, Photo by Giovanni Giannoni, *WWD*, Courtesy of *WWD*

JEAN PAUL GAULTIER:
Jean Paul Gaultier, Spring 2010 Couture, Photo by Giovanni Giannoni, *WWD*, Courtesy of *WWD*
Jean Paul Gaultier for Hermès, Fall 2010 RTW, Photo by Dominique Maître, *WWD*, Courtesy of *WWD*
Jean Paul Gaultier, Fall 2002, Photo by Giovanni Giannoni, *WWD*, Courtesy of *WWD*
Jean Paul Gaultier, Spring 2010, Photo by Giovanni Giannoni, *WWD*, Courtesy of *WWD*
Jean Paul Gaultier, Spring 2009, Photo by Giovanni Giannoni, *WWD*, Courtesy of *WWD*

NICOLAS GHESQUIÈRE:
Nicolas Ghesquière for Balenciaga, Spring 2008 RTW, Photo by Giovanni Giannoni, *WWD*, Courtesy of *WWD*
Nicolas Ghesquière for Balenciaga, Spring 2008, Photo by Delphine Achard, *WWD*, Courtesy of WWD
Nicolas Ghesquière for Balenciaga, Spring 2006, Photo by Delphine Achard, *WWD*, Courtesy of *WWD*
Nicolas Ghesquière for Balenciaga, Fall 2006, Photo by Giovanni Giannoni, *WWD*, Courtesy of *WWD*
Nicolas Ghesquière for Balenciaga, Fall/Winter 2010, Photo by Giovanni Giannoni, *WWD*, Courtesy of *WWD*
Nicolas Ghesquière for Balenciaga, Pre-Spring 2008, Photo by Dominique Maitre, *WWD*, Courtesy of *WWD*

FRIDA GIANNINI:
Frida Giannini for Gucci, Spring 2010 RTW, Photo by Mauricio Miranda, *WWD*, Courtesy of *WWD*
Friday Giannini for Gucci, Fall 2010, Photo by Delphine Achard, *WWD*, Courtesy of *WWD*
Frida Giannini for Gucci, Fall 2007, Photo by Davide Maestri, *WWD*, Courtesy of *WWD*
Frida Giannini for Gucci, Spring 2010, Photo by Mauricio Miranda, *WWD*, Courtesy of *WWD*
Frida Giannini for Gucci, Photo: Evan Rachel Wood, 2009, Photo by Steve Eichner, *WWD*, Courtesy of *WWD*
Frida Giannini for Gucci. Fall 2008, Photo by Giovanni Giannoni, *WWD*, Courtesy of *WWD*

HUBERT DE GIVENCHY:
Hubert de Givenchy, 1963, *WWD*, Courtesy of Fairchild Archive
Hubert de Givenchy, 1954, *WWD*, Courtesy of Fairchild Archive
Hubert de Givenchy, 1958, *WWD*, Courtesy of Fairchild Archive
Hubert de Givenchy, Spring 1976 RTW, Photo by Guy Marineau, *WWD*, Courtesy of *WWD*
Hubert de Givenchy and Audrey Hepburn, *WWD*, Courtesy of Fairchild Archive

MADAME GRÈS:
Grès, Fall Couture 1977, Photo by Guy Marineau, *WWD*, Courtesy of Fairchild Archive
Grès, 1960, *WWD*, Courtesy of Fairchild Books
Grès, 1966, *WWD*, Courtesy of Fairchild Books

HALSTON:
Halston, Fall 1981, Photo by John Bright, *WWD*, Courtesy of Fairchild Archives
Halston, Spring 1975, Photo by Pierre Schermann, *WWD*, Courtesy of Fairchild Archives
Halston, Spring 1975, Photo by Pierre Schermann, *WWD*, Courtesy of Fairchild Archives
Halston, Fall/Winter 1973 RTW, Photo by Peter Simins, *WWD*, Courtesy of Fairchild Archives

CAROLINA HERRERA:
Carolina Herrera, Spring 1992, Photo by David Turner, *WWD*, Courtesy of Fairchild Archive
Carolina Herrera, Fall 2007 Briday, Photo by John Aquino, *WWD*, Courtesy of *WWD*
Carolina Herrera, Spring 1987, Photo by Thomas Iannaccone, *WWD*, Courtesy of Fairchild Archive
Carolina Herrera, Resort 2011, Photo by Thomas Iannaccone, *WWD*, Courtesy of *WWD*
Carolina Herrera, Spring 2002, Photo by George Chinsee, *WWD*, Courtesy of *WWD*
Carolina Herrera, Spring 1989, Photo by Thomas Iannaccone, *WWD*, Courtesy of *WWD*

TOMMY HILFIGER:
Tommy Hilfiger, Fall 2009, Photo by George Chinsee, *WWD*, Courtesy of *WWD*
Tommy Hilfiger, Fall 2003, Photo by John Aquino, *WWD*, Courtesy of *WWD*
Tommy Hilfiger, Fall 2002, Photo by David Turner, *WWD*, Courtesy of *WWD*
Tommy Hilfiger, Fall 2010 RTW, Photo by Robert Mitra, *WWD*, Courtesy of *WWD*

MARC JACOBS:
Marc Jacobs, Spring 2009, Photo by John Aquino, *WWD*, Courtesy of *WWD*
Marc Jacobs, Fall 2009, Photo by George Chinsee, *WWD*, Courtesy of *WWD*
Marc Jacobs, Fall 1985, *WWD*, Courtesy of *WWD*
Marc Jacobs for Louis Vuitton, Spring 2010, Photo by Giovanni Giannoni, *WWD*, Courtesy of *WWD*

CHARLES JAMES:
Charles James, 1951, *WWD*, Courtesy of Fairchild Archives
Charles James, 1946, *WWD*, Courtesy of Fairchild Archives
Charles James, 1944, *WWD*, Courtesy of Fairchild Archives
Charles James, 1948, *WWD*, Courtesy of Fairchild Archives

BETSEY JOHNSON:
Betsey Johnson, Fall 2001, Photo by Robert Mitra, *WWD*, Courtesy of *WWD*
Betsey Johnson, Spring 2006, Photo by Talaya Centeno, *WWD*, Courtesy of *WWD*
Betsey Johnson, Spring 2002, Photo by David Turner, WWD, Courtesy of *WWD*
Betsey Johnson for Alley Cat, Spring/Summer 1973, Photo by Sal Traina, *WWD*, Courtesy of Fairchild Archive

NORMA KAMALI:
Norma Kamali, 1976, *WWD*, Courtesy of Fairchild Archive
Norma Kamali, Spring 1981, Photo by Steve Landis, *WWD*, Courtesy of Fairchild Archive

DONNA KARAN:
Donna Karan, Spring 1992, *WWD*, Courtesy of Fairchild Archive
Donna Karan, Fall 2010, Photo by Steve Eichner, WWD, Courtesy of *WWD*
Donna Karan, Fall 1986, *WWD*, Courtesy of Fairchild Archive
Donnar Karan, Fall 1989, *WWD*, Courtesy of Fairchild Archive

REI KAWAKUBO:
Rei Kawakubo for Comme des Garçons, Spring 2009, Photo by Giovanni Giannoni, *WWD*, Courtesy of *WWD*
Rei Kawakubo for Comme des Garçons, Spring 2010, Photo by Giovanni Giannoni, *WWD*, Courtesy of *WWD*
Rei Kawakubo for Comme des Garçons, Spring 2009, Photo by Giovanni Giannoni, *WWD*, Courtesy of *WWD*

ANNE KLEIN:
Anne Klein, 1971, *WWD*, Courtesy of Fairchild Archive
Anne Klein, 1968, Illustration by Kenneth Paul Block, *WWD*, Courtesy of Fairchild Archive
Anne Klein, Fall 1972, Photo by Peter Simins, *WWD*, Courtesy of Fairchild Archive

CALVIN KLEIN:
Calvin Klein Fall/Winter 1981, *WWD*, Courtesy of Fairchild Archive
Calvin Klein, 1982, Photo by Michael Hitchcock, *WWD*, Courtesy of Fairchild Archive
Calvin Klein, Spring 1997, *WWD*, Courtesy of Fairchild Archive
Calvin Klein, Fall/Winter 1992, *WWD*, Courtesy of Fairchild Archive
Calvin Klein, Fall/Winter 1991, *WWD*, Courtesy of Fairchild Archive
Calvin Klein, Fall/Winter 1987, Photo by John Aquino, *WWD*, Courtesy of Fairchild Archive

MICHAEL KORS:
Michael Kors, Spring 2006, Photo by Robert Mitra, *WWD*, Courtesy of WWD
Michael Kors, Fall 2009, Photo by George Chinsee, *WWD*, Courtesy of WWD
Michael Kors, Spring 2010 RTW, Photo by Giovanni Giannoni, WWD, Courtesy of *WWD*

CHRISTIAN LACROIX:
Christian Lacroix, Fall 1987 Couture, Photo by Philippe Costes, *WWD*, Courtesy of Fairchild Archive

Christian Lacroix, Spring 2009 Haute Couture, Photo by Giovanni Giannoni, *WWD*, Courtesy of *WWD*
Christian Lacroix for Patou Couture, Spring 1987, Photo by Philippe Costes, *WWD*, Courtesy of Fairchild Archive
Christian Lacroix, Fall/Winter 2009, Photo by Giovanni Giannoni, *WWD*, Courtesy of *WWD*

KARL LAGERFELD:
Karl Lagerfeld for Chanel, Resort 2010, Photo by Davide Maestri, *WWD*, Courtesy of *WWD*
Karl Lagerfeld for Chanel, Fall 2010 RTW, Photo by Giovanni Giannoni, *WWD*, Courtesy of *WWD*
Karl Lagerfeld for Chanel Haute Couture, Spring 2009, Photo by Giovanni Giannoni, *WWD*, Courtesy of *WWD*
Karl Lagerfeld for Fendi, Fall 2010 RTW, Photo by Giovanni Giannoni, *WWD*, Courtesy of *WWD*
Karl Lagerfeld for Chanel, Fall 1983, Photo by Guy Marineau, *WWD*, Courtesy of Fairchild Archive
Karl Lagerfeld for Spring 2010, Photo by Dominique Maitre, *WWD*, Courtesy of *WWD*
Karl Lagerfeld for Chanel, Resort 2008, Photo by Steve Eichner and Stephane Feugere, *WWD*, Courtesy of *WWD*
Karl Lagerfeld for Chanel Couture, Spring 2009, Photo by Giovanni Giannoni and Stephane Feugere, *WWD*, Courtesy of *WWD*

HELMUT LANG:
Helmut Lang, Fall 2004, Photo by Giovanni Giannoni, *WWD*, Courtesy of *WWD*
Helmut Lang, Spring 2001, Photo by Thomas Iannaccone, *WWD*, Courtesy of *WWD*
Helmut Lang, Fall 2010, Photo by Thomas Iannaccone, *WWD*, Courtesy of *WWD*
Helmut Lang, Spring 2003, Photo by Giovanni Giannoni, *WWD*, Courtesy of *WWD*

JEANNE LANVIN:
Jeanne Lanvin, 1936, *WWD*, Courtesy of Fairchild Archive
Jeanne Lanvin, 1936, *WWD*, Courtesy of Fairchild Archive
Jeanne Lanvin, 1936, *WWD*, Courtesy of Fairchild Archive
Jeanne Lanvin, 1936, *WWD*, Courtesy of Fairchild Archive

RALPH LAUREN:
Ralph Lauren, Spring 2010, Photo by Thomas Iannaccone, *WWD*, Courtesy of WWD
Ralph Lauren, Fall 2009, Photo by Thomas Iannaccone, *WWD*, Courtesy of WWD
Ralph Lauren, Spring/Summer 1989 RTW, Photo by George Chinsee, *WWD*, Courtesy of Fairchild Archive
Ralph Lauren, Fall/Winter 1984 RTW, Photo by Thomas Iannaccone, *WWD*, Courtesy of Fairchild Archive
Ralph Lauren, Fall 2009, Photo by Thomas Iannaccone, *WWD*, Courtesy of WWD
Ralph Lauren, Spring 2007, Photo by John Aquino, *WWD*, Courtesy of *WWD*
Ralph Lauren, Fall 2009, Photo by Robert Mitra, *WWD*, Courtesy of *WWD*

MAINBOCHER:
Mainbocher, 1936, *WWD* Courtesy of Fairchild Archive
Mainbocher, 1947, *WWD* Courtesy of Fairchild Archive

Mainbocher, 1947, *WWD* Courtesy of Fairchild Archive

Mainbocher, 1942, *WWD* Courtesy of Fairchild Archive

MARTIN MARGIELA:

Martin Margiela, Spring 2006 RTW, Photo by Giovanni Giannoni, *WWD*, Courtesy of *WWD*

Martin Margiela, Spring 2007 RTW, Photo by Giovanni Giannoni, *WWD*, Courtesy of *WWD*

Martin Margiela, Spring 2009 RTW, Photo by Giovanni Giannoni, *WWD*, Courtesy of *WWD*

Martin Margiela, Spring 2010, Photo by Giovanni Giannoni, *WWD*, Courtesy of *WWD*

Martin Margiela, Spring 2007 RTW, Photo by Giovanni Giannoni, *WWD*, Courtesy of *WWD*

Martin Margiela, Fall 2007 RTW, Photo by Dominique Maître, *WWD*, Courtesy of *WWD*

CLAIRE McCARDELL:

McCardell, 1943, *WWD*, Courtesy of Fairchild Archive

McCardell, 1941, *WWD*, Courtesy of Fairchild Archive

McCardell, 1941, *WWD*, Courtesy of Fairchild Archive

McCardell, 1943, *WWD*, Courtesy of Fairchild Archive

STELLA McCARTNEY:

Stella McCartney, Spring 2010 RTW, Photo by Giovanni Giannoni, *WWD*, Courtesy of *WWD*

Stella McCartney, Fall 2010, Photo by Giovanni Giannoni, *WWD*, Courtesy of WWD

Stella McCartney, Spring 2010 RTW, Photo by Giovanni Giannoni, *WWD*, Courtesy of *WWD*

Stella McCartney, Fall 2007 RTW, Photo by Giovanni Giannoni, *WWD*, Courtesy of *WWD*

Stella McCartney, Spring 2004, Photo by Giovanni Giannoni, *WWD*, Courtesy of *WWD*

ALEXANDER McQUEEN:

Alexander McQueen, Spring 2005, Photo by Giovanni Giannoni, *WWD*, Courtesy of *WWD*

Alexander McQueen, Spring 2003, Photo by Giovanni Giannoni, *WWD*, Courtesy of *WWD*

Alexander McQueen, Fall/Winter 2009, Photo by Delphine Achard, *WWD*, Courtesy of *WWD*

Alexander McQueen, Spring 2004, Photo by Giovanni Giannoni, *WWD*, Courtesy of *WWD*

Alexander McQueen, Fall 2008, *WWD*, Courtesy of *WWD*

OTTAVIO & ROSITA MISSONI:

Ottavio & Rosita Missoni, Fall 1973, Photo by Beppe Semmola, *WWD*, Courtesy of Fairchild Archive

Ottavio & Rosita Missoni, 1972, *WWD*, Courtesy of Fairchild Archive

Ottavio & Rosita Missoni in Their Designs, Spring 1973, Photo by Pierre Schermann, *WWD*, Courtesy of Fairchild Archive

Ottavio & Rosita Missoni, Spring 1977, Photo by Gianni Lami, *WWD*, Courtesy of Fairchild Archive

ISAAC MIZRAHI:

Isaac Mizrahi, Fall 1989, Photo by George Chinsee, *WWD*, Courtesy of Fairchild Archive

Isaac Mizrahi, Fall 2009, Photo by John Aquino, WWD, Courtesy of *WWD*

Isaac Mizrahi, Spring 2010 RTW, Photo by Robert Mitra, WWD, Courtesy of *WWD*

Isaac Mizrahi, Spring 1991, Photo by George Chinsee, *WWD*, Courtesy of Fairchild Archive

Isaac Mizrahi, Spring 2007 Couture, Photo by Thomas Iannaccone, *WWD*, Courtesy of *WWD*

CAPTAIN EDWARD MOLYNEUX:

Captain Edward Molyneux, 1964, *WWD*, Courtesy of Fairchild Archive

Captain Edward Molyneux, 1936, *WWD*, Courtesy of Fairchild Archive

Captain Edward Molyneux, 1946, *WWD*, Courtesy of Fairchild Archive

Captain Edward Molyneux, 1936, *WWD*, Courtesy of Fairchild Archive

CLAUDE MONTANA:

Claude Montana, Fall 1984, Photo by Michel Maurou, *WWD*, Courtesy of Fairchild Archive

Claude Montana, Spring 1983, Photo by Guy Marineau, *WWD*, Courtesy of Fairchild Archive

Claude Montana, Spring 1981, Photo by Michel Maurou, *WWD*, Courtesy of Fairchild Archive

Claude Montana, Fall 2002 RTW, Stephane Feugere, *WWD*, Courtesy of *WWD*

Claude Montana, Fall 1984, Photo by Guy Marineau, *WWD*, Courtesy of Fairchild Archive

THIERRY MUGLER:

Thierry Mugler, Fall 1995, Photo by Frédérique Dumoulin, *WWD*, Courtesy of *WWD*

Thierry Mugler, 1992, *WWD*, Courtesy of Fairchild Archive

Thierry Mugler, Fall 1983 RTW, Photo by Guy Marineau, *WWD*, Courtesy of Fairchild Archive

Thierry Mugler, Fall 1995, Photo by Frédérique Dumoulin, *WWD*, Courtesy of *WWD*

NORMAN NORELL:

Norman Norell, 1963, *WWD*, Courtesy of Fairchild Archive

Norman Norell, 1963, Illustration by Sandra Leichman, *WWD*, Courtesy of Fairchild Archive

Norman Norell, 1963, Illustration by Sandra Leichman, *WWD*, Courtesy of Fairchild Archive

Norman Norell & His Design, Spring 1973, Photo by Sal Traina, *WWD*, Courtesy of Fairchild Archive

RICK OWENS:

Rick Owens, Spring 2004, Photo by Giovanni Giannoni, *WWD*, Courtesy of *WWD*

Rick Owens, Spring 2007, Photo by Giovanni Giannoni, *WWD*, Courtesy of *WWD*

Rick Owens, Spring 2009, Photo by Giovanni Giannoni, *WWD*, Courtesy of *WWD*

Rick Owens, Fall 2005, Photo by Giovanni Giannoni, *WWD*, Courtesy of *WWD*

Rick Owens, Fall 2010, Photo by Giovanni Giannoni, *WWD*, Courtesy of *WWD*

THAKOON PANICHGUL:

Thakoon Panichgul, Fall 2010, Photo by George Chinsee, *WWD*, Courtesy of *WWD*

Thakoon Panichgul, Spring 2010, Photo by Thomas Iannaccone, *WWD*, Courtesy of *WWD*

Thakoon Panichgul, Fall 2008, Photo by George Chinsee, *WWD*, Courtesy of *WWD*

Thakoon Panichgul, Fall 2009, Photo by Thomas Iannaccone, *WWD*, Courtesy of *WWD*

Thakoon Panichgul, Spring 2009, Photo by Robert Mitra, *WWD*, Courtesy of *WWD*

JEAN PATOU:

Jean Patou, 1936, *WWD*, Courtesy of Fairchild Archive

Jean Patou, 1936, *WWD*, Courtesy of Fairchild Archive

Jean Patou, 1936, *WWD*, Courtesy of Fairchild Archive

Jean Patou. 1925, *WWD*, Courtesy of Fairchild Archive

PHOEBE PHILO:

Phoebe Philo for Céline, Spring 2010, Photo by Giovanni Giannoni, *WWD*, Courtesy of *WWD*

Phoebe Philo for Chloé, Fall 2006, Photo by Delphine Achard, *WWD*, Courtesy of *WWD*

Phoebe Philo for Céline, Spring 2010, Photo by Giovanni Giannoni, *WWD*, Courtesy of *WWD*

Phoebe Philo for Chloé, Spring 2007, Photo by Giovanni Giannoni, *WWD*, Courtesy of *WWD*

Phoebe Philo for Chloé, Fall 2006, Photo by Delphine Achard, *WWD*, Courtesy of *WWD*

STEFANO PILATI:

Stefano Pilati for Yves Saint Laurent, Spring 2009, Photo by Dominique Maitre, *WWD*, Courtesy of *WWD*

Stefano Pilati for Yves Saint Laurent, Spring 2007, Photo by Giovanni Giannoni, *WWD*, Courtesy of *WWD*

Stefano Pilati for Yves Saint Laurent, Fall 2009 RTW, Photo by Giovanni Giannoni *WWD*, Courtesy of *WWD*

Stefano Pilati for Yves Saint Laurent, Spring 2010 RTW, Photo by Giovanni Giannoni, *WWD*, Courtesy of *WWD*

Stefano Pilati for Yves Saint Laurent, Fall 2008, Photo by Giovanni Giannoni, *WWD*, Courtesy of *WWD*

PAUL POIRET:

Paul Poiret, 1925, *WWD*, Courtesy of Fairchild Archive

Paul Poiret, 1910, *WWD*, Courtesy of Fairchild Archive

Paul Poiret, 1911, *WWD*, Courtesy of Fairchild Archive

Paul Poiret, 1910, *WWD*, Courtesy of Fairchild Archive

ZAC POSEN:

Zac Posen, Spring 2008, Photo by John Aquino, WWD, Courtesy of *WWD*

Zac Posen, Fall 2009, Photo by Thomas Iannaccone, *WWD*, Courtesy of *WWD*

Zac Posen for Pologeorgis, Fall 2010, Photo by Davide Maestri, *WWD*, Courtesy of *WWD*

Zac Posen, Spring 2007, Photo by Steve Eichner, *WWD*, Courtesy of *WWD*

Zac Posen, Spring 2007, Photo by Giovanni Giannoni, *WWD*, Courtesy of *WWD*

MIUCCIA PRADA:

Miuccia Prada, Fall 2009, Photo by Giovanni Giannoni, *WWD*, Courtesy of *WWD*

Miuccia Prada for Miu Miu, Pre-Fall 2009, Photo by Sakis Lalas, *WWD*, Courtesy of *WWD*

Miuccia Prada, Fall 2002, *WWD*, Courtesy of *WWD*

Miuccia Prada, Spring 2005, Photo by Mauricio Miranda, *WWD*, Courtesy of *WWD*

Miuccia Prada, Fall 2000, Photo by Giovanni Giannoni, *WWD*, Courtesy of *WWD*

Miuccia Prada, Pre-Fall 2009, Photo by Giovanni Pavesi, *WWD*, Courtesy of *WWD*

PROENZA SCHOULER:
Lazaro Hernandez and Jack McCollough for
Proenza Schouler, Resort 2011, Photo by
Robert Mitra, *WWD*, Courtesy of *WWD*
Lazaro Hernandez and Jack McCollough for
Proenza Schouler, Fall 2010, Photo by Robert
Mitra, *WWD*, Courtesy of *WWD*
Lazaro Hernandez and Jack McCollough for
Proenza Schouler, Fall 2005, Photo by
Giovanni Giannoni, *WWD*, Courtesy of *WWD*
Lazaro Hernandez and Jack McCollough for
Proenza Schouler, Fall 2008, Photo by
Giovanni Giannoni, *WWD*, Courtesy of *WWD*
Lazaro Hernandez and Jack McCollough for
Proenza Schouler, Spring 2007, Photo by Kyle
Ericksen, *WWD*, Courtesy of *WWD*

EMILIO PUCCI:
Emilio Pucci, The Look of the Seventies, 1969,
WWD, Courtesy of *WWD*
Emilio Pucci, Cruise Collection 1966, Illustration
by Kenneth Paul Block, *WWD*, Courtesy of
WWD
Pucci, 1965, Illustration by Sandra Leichman,
WWD, Courtesy of *WWD*
Pucci, 1964, *WWD*, Courtesy of Fairchild Archive

PACO RABANNE:
Paco Rabanne, Fall 2001 RTW, Photo by
Stephane Feugere, *WWD*, Courtesy of *WWD*

RODARTE:
Kate and Laura Mulleavy for Rodarte, Spring
2009 RTW, Photo by George Chinsee, *WWD*,
Courtesy of *WWD*
Kate and Laura Mulleavy for Rodarte, Fall 2009,
Photo by George Chinsee, *WWD*, Courtesy
of *WWD*
Kate and Laura Mulleavy for Rodarte, Spring 2007
RTW, Photo by John Aquino, *WWD*, Courtesy
of *WWD*
Kate and Laura Mulleavy for Rodarte, Spring
2008 RTW, Photo by George Chinsee, *WWD*,
Courtesy of *WWD*
Kate and Laura Mulleavy for Rodarte, Fall 2008,
Photo by Robert Mitra, *WWD*, Courtesy of
WWD

NARCISO RODRIGUEZ:
Narciso Rodriguez, Spring 2009 RTW, Photo by
Thomas Iannaccone, *WWD*, Courtesy of *WWD*
Narciso Rodriguez, Fall 2005 RTW, Photo by
Robert Mitra, *WWD*, Courtesy of *WWD*
Narciso Rodriguez, Spring 2003, Photo by George
Chinsee, *WWD*, Courtesy of *WWD*
Narciso Rodriguez, Fall 2010 RTW, Photo by
Robert Mitra, *WWD*, Courtesy of *WWD*

SONIA RYKIEL:
Sonia Rykiel, Spring 2010, Photo by Giovanni
Giannoni, *WWD*, Courtesy of *WWD*
Sonia Rykiel, Fall 2004, Photo by Dominique
Maître, *WWD*, Courtesy of *WWD*
Sonia Rykiel, Spring/Summer 1973, Photo by
Reginald Gray, *WWD*, Courtesy of Fairchild
Archive
Sonia Rykiel, Fall 2006, Photo by Giovanni
Giannoni, *WWD*, Courtesy of *WWD*
Sonia Rykiel, Fall 1002, Photo by Giovanni
Giannoni, *WWD*, Courtesy of *WWD*

YVES SAINT LAURENT:
Yves Saint Laurent, Fall 1972 Haute Couture,
Photo by Reginald Gray, *WWD*, Courtesy of
Fairchild Archive
Yves Saint Laurent, Le Smoking 1988, *WWD*,
Courtesy of Fairchild Archive
Yves Saint Laurent, 1976, *WWD*, Courtesy of
Fairchild Archive
Yves Saint Laurent, Spring 2002 Haute Couture,
Look from 1965, Photo by Giovanni Giannoni,
WWD, Courtesy of *WWD*
Yves Saint Laurent, 1979 Picasso Collection,
WWD, Courtesy of Fairchild Archive
Yves Saint Laurent, Spring 2002 Haute Couture,
Look from 1966, Photo by Giovanni Giannoni,
WWD, Courtesy of *WWD*

JIL SANDER:
Jil Sander, Fall/Winter 1996, Photo by Davide
Maestri, *WWD*, Courtesy of Fairchild Archive
Jil Sander, Spring 1990, *WWD*, Courtesy of
Fairchild Archive
Jil Sander, Fall/Winter 1996, Photo by Davide
Maestri, *WWD*, Courtesy of Fairchild Archive
Jil Sander, Spring 1989, Photo by Volonte, *WWD*,
Courtesy of Fairchild Archive
Jil Sander, Spring 2004, Photo by Giovanni
Giannoni, *WWD*, Courtesy of *WWD*

GIORGIO DI SANT'ANGELO:
Designer Giorgio di Sant'Angelo, 1968, Photo
by Pierre Schermann, *WWD*, Courtesy of
Fairchild Archive
Photographs by Peter Riesett, from *Drawing
Fashion: The Art of Kenneth Paul Block*,
Published by Pointed Leaf Press, LLC.
Copyright © 2007 Kenneth Paul Block.
Illustration, 1971
Giorgio di Sant'Angelo, Spring 1976 RTW, Photo
by Nick Machalaba, *WWD*, Courtesy of
Fairchild Archive
Giorgio di Sant'Angelo, 1974, Photo by Pierre
Schermann, *WWD*, Courtesy of Fairchild
Archive

ARNOLD SCAASI:
Arnold Scaasi, Spring 1984, *WWD*, Courtesy of
Fairchild Archive
Arnold Scaasi, Fall 1986, *WWD*, Courtesy of
Fairchild Archive
Arnold Scaasi, 1967, Illustration by Anneliese,
WWD, Courtesy of Fairchild Archive
Arnold Scaasi, Spring 1984, *WWD*, Courtesy of
Fairchild Archive
Arnold Scaasi, Spring 1973, Photo by Peter
Simins, *WWD*, Courtesy of Fairchild Archive

ELSA SCHIAPARELLI:
Schiaparelli, 1966, *WWD*, Courtesy of *WWD*
Schiaparelli, 1945, *WWD*, Courtesy of Fairchild
Archive
Schiaparelli, 1936, *WWD*, Courtesy of Fairchild
Archive

RAF SIMONS:
Raf Simons for Jil Sander, Fall 2009, Photo by
Giovanni Giannoni, *WWD*, Courtesy of *WWD*
Raf Simons for Jil Sander, Spring 2007 RTW,
Photo by Davide Maestri, *WWD*, Courtesy of
WWD
Raf Simons for Jil Sander, Fall 2008 RTW, Photo
by Giovanni Giannoni, *WWD*, Courtesy of
WWD
Raf Simons for Jil Sander, Spring 2008, Photo by
Davide Maestri, *WWD*, Courtesy of *WWD*
Raf Simons for Jil Sander, Spring 2010, Photo by
Davide Maestri, *WWD*, Courtesy of *WWD*
Raf Simons for Jil Sander, Fall 2006 RTW, Photo
by David Yoder, *WWD*, Courtesy of *WWD*

WILLI SMITH:
Willi Smith, Fall 1972 RTW, Photo by Pierre
Schermann, *WWD*, Courtesy of Fairchild
Archive
Willi Smith, Fall 1973 RTW, Photo by Nick
Machalaba, *WWD*, Courtesy of Fairchild
Archive

STEPHEN SPROUSE:
Stephen Sprouse, Fall 1988, *WWD*, Courtesy of
Fairchild Archive
Stephen Sprouse, Fall 1985, Photo by Thomas
Iannaccone, *WWD*, Courtesy of Fairchild
Archive
Stephen Sprouse, Holiday Collection 1984,
Photo by Amy Meadows, *WWD*, Courtesy of
Fairchild Archive
Stephen Sprouse, Fall 1986 RTW, *WWD*, Courtesy
of Fairchild Archive

ANNA SUI:
Anna Sui, Spring/Summer 1993, Photo by
Thomas Iannaccone, *WWD*, Courtesy of
Fairchild Archive
Anna Sui, Spring 1994 RTW, *WWD*, Courtesy of
Fairchild Archive
Anna Sui, Fall 2006, Photo by Robert Mitra, *WWD*,
Courtesy of *WWD*

OLIVIER THESKYENS:
Olivier Theskyens for Nina Ricci, Spring 2009,
Photo by Giovanni Giannoni, *WWD*, Courtesy
of *WWD*

RICCARDO TISCI:
Riccardo Tisci for Givenchy, Spring 2009, Photo
by Giovanni Giannoni, *WWD*, Courtesy of
WWD
Riccardo Tisci for Givenchy, Spring 2010, Photo
by Giovanni Giannoni, *WWD*, Courtesy of
WWD
Riccardo Tisci for Givenchy, Pre-Fall 2010, Photo
by Robert Mitra, *WWD*, Courtesy of *WWD*
Riccardo Tisci for Givenchy, Fall 2008, Photo by
Giovanni Giannoni, *WWD*, Courtesy of *WWD*

EMANUEL UNGARO:
Emanuel Ungaro, Spring 1988, Photo by Jean-
Louis Coulombel, *WWD*, Courtesy of Fairchild
Archive
Emanuel Ungaro, Fall 1988 Couture, *WWD*,
Courtesy of Fairchild Archive
Emanuel Ungaro, Fall 1996, Photo by Cédric
Dordevic, *WWD*, Courtesy of Fairchild Archive
Emanuel Ungaro, Spring 1995, Photo by Cédric
Dordevic, *WWD*, Courtesy of Fairchild Archive
Emanuel Ungaro, 1968, *WWD*, Courtesy of
Fairchild Archive

VALENTINO:
Lee Radziwell in Valentino, Photo by Stephane
Feugere, WWD, Courtesy of *WWD*
Valentino, 1970, *WWD*, Courtesy of Fairchild
Archive
Valentino, Fall 1968, Photo by Pierre Schermann,
WWD, Courtesy of Fairchild Archive
Valentino, Fall 2006, Photo by Giovanni Giannoni,
WWD, Courtesy of *WWD*

Valentino, Spring 1973 RTW, Photo by Gianni Lami, *WWD*, Courtesy of Fairchild Archive

DRIES VAN NOTEN:

Dries Van Noten, Spring 2009, Photo by Giovanni Giannoni, WWD, Courtesy of *WWD*

Dries Van Noten, Spring 2004, Photo by Giovanni Giannoni, *WWD*, Courtesy of *WWD*

Dries Van Noten, Fall 2008, Photo by Dominique Maitre, *WWD*, Courtesy of *WWD*

Dries Van *WWD*, Fall 2003, Photo by Giovanni Giannoni, *WWD*, Courtesy of *WWD*

Dries Van Noten, Spring 2006, Photo by Giovanni Giannoni, *WWD*, Courtesy of *WWD*

DONATELLA VERSACE:

Donatella Versace, Spring 2009, Photo by Giovanni Giannoni, *WWD*, Courtesy of *WWD*

Donatella Versace, Fall 2004, Photo by Giovanni Giannoni, *WWD*, Courtesy of *WWD*

Donatella Versace, Fall 2006, Photo by Giovanni Giannoni, *WWD*, Courtesy of *WWD*

Donatella Versace, Fall 2002, Photo by Giovanni Giannoni, *WWD*, Courtesy of *WWD*

Donatella Versace, Spring 2000, Photo by Giovanni Giannoni, *WWD*, Courtesy of *WWD*

GIANNI VERSACE:

Gianni Versace, Spring 1993 RTW, Photo by Donato Sardella, *WWD*, Courtesy of Fairchild Archive

Gianni Versace, Spring 1984 RTW, Photo by Tim Jenkins, *WWD*, Courtesy of Fairchild Archive

Gianni Versace, Spring 1993 RTW, Photo by Donato Sardella, *WWD*, Courtesy of Fairchild Archive

Gianni Versace, Fall 1990, Photo by Art Streiber, *WWD*, Courtesy of Fairchild Archive

Gianni Versace, Fall 1990, Photo by Art Streiber, *WWD*, Courtesy of Fairchild Archive

Gianni Versace, Fall 1990, Photo by Art Streiber, *WWD*, Courtesy of Fairchild Archive

Gianni Versace, Fall 1990, Photo by Art Streiber, *WWD*, Courtesy of Fairchild Archive

Gianni Versace, Fall 1990, Photo by Art Streiber, *WWD*, Courtesy of Fairchild Archive

MADELEINE VIONNET:

Madeleine Vionnet, 1961, *WWD*, Courtesy of Fairchild Archive

Madeleine Vionnet, 1969, *WWD*, Courtesy of Fairchild Archive

DIANE VON FURSTENBERG:

Diane von Furstenberg, Fall 2009, Photo by Robert Mitra, *WWD*, Courtesy of *WWD*

Diane von Furstenberg, Spring 2010 RTW, Photo by George Chinese, *WWD*, Courtesy of WWD

Diane von Furstenberg, 1973, Drawn by Kenneth Paul Block, *WWD*, Courtesy of *WWD*

Diane von Furstenberg, Spring 1973 RTW, Photo by Nick Machalaba, *WWD*, Courtesy of Fairchild Archive

ALEXANDER WANG:

Alexander Wang, Spring 2010, Photo by John Aquino, *WWD*, Courtesy of *WWD*

Alexander Wang, Fall 2010, Photo by Steve Eichner, *WWD*, Courtesy of *WWD*

Alexander Wang, Fall 2009, Photo by John Aquino, *WWD*, Courtesy of *WWD*

Alexander Wang, Fall 2008, Photo by Robert Mitra, *WWD*, Courtesy of *WWD*

VERA WANG:

Vera Wang, Portrait, 2008, Photo by Pasha Antonov, *WWD*, Courtesy of *WWD*

Vera Wang, Fall 2008 RTW, Photo by Kyle Ericksen, *WWD*, Courtesy of *WWD*

Vera Wang, Fall 2006 Bridal, Photo by Thomas Iannaccone, *WWD*, Courtesy of WWD

Vera Wang, Fall 2009 RTW, Photo by Giovanni Giannoni, *WWD*, Courtesy of *WWD*

Vera Wang, 2010, Photo by Patricia Heal, *WWD*, Courtesy of *WWD*

VIVIENNE WESTWOOD:

Vivienne Westwood and Her Designs, 1977, Photo by Tim Jenkins, *WWD*, Courtesy of Fairchild Archive

Vivienne Westwood, Spring 2003 RTW, Photo by Giovanni Giannoni, *WWD*, Courtesy of *WWD*

Vivienne Westwood, Fall 1994, Photo by Lee Strickland, *WWD*, Courtesy of *WWD*

Vivienne Westwood, Fall 2001, Photo by Stephane Feugere, *WWD*, Courtesy of *WWD*

Vivienne Westwood, Red Label, Fall 2010, Photo by Giovanni Giannoni, *WWD*, Courtesy of *WWD*

JASON WU:

Jason Wu, Spring 2010, Photo by Giovanni Giannoni, *WWD*, Courtesy of *WWD*

Jason Wu, Fall 2006, Photo by Giovanni Giannoni, *WWD*, Courtesy of *WWD*

Jason Wu, Fall 2008, Photo by Talaya Centeno, *WWD*, Courtesy of *WWD*

Jason Wu, Fall 2010, Photo by Robert Mitra, *WWD*, Courtesy of *WWD*

Jason Wu, Smithsonian 2010, Photo by Kyle Samperton, *WWD*, Courtesy of *WWD*

Jason Wu, Spring 2009, Photo by Giovanni Giannoni, *WWD*, Courtesy of *WWD*

YOHJI YAMAMOTO:

Yohji Yamamoto, Spring 2003, Photo by Stephane Feugere, *WWD*, Courtesy of *WWD*

Yohji Yamamoto, Fall 2009, Photo by Giovanni Giannoni, *WWD*, Courtesy of *WWD*

Yohji Yamamoto, Spring 2008, *WWD*, Courtesy of *WWD*

Yohji Yamamoto, Fall 2010, Photo by Giovanni Giannoni, *WWD*, Courtesy of *WWD*

Yohji Yamamoto, Fall 2003, Photo by Giovanni Giannoni, *WWD*, Courtesy of *WWD*

INTERVIEWS:

Yves Saint Laurent, 1965, *WWD*, Courtesy of Fairchild Archive

Lucien Lelong, 1925, *WWD*, Courtesy of Fairchild Archive

Jacques Fath, 1941, Photo by Albin Guillot/Roger Viollet/Getty Images

Pierre Balmain, 1972, Photo by Gray Reginald, *WWD*, Courtesy of Fairchild Archive

Gabrielle Chanel & James Brady, *WWD*, Courtesy of Fairchild Archive

Valentino Garavani, 1970, *WWD*, Courtesy of Fairchild Archive

Giorgio di Sant'Angelo Spring 1976 RTW, Photo by Nick Machalaba, *WWD*, Courtesy of Fairchild Archive

Yves Saint Laurent, 1974, Photo by Reginald Gray, WWD, Courtesy of Fairchild Archive

Diane Von Furstenberg, 1973, Photo by Harry Morrison, WWD, Courtesy of Fairchild Archive

Calvin Klein, 1973, Photo by Nick Machalaba, *WWD*, Courtesy of Fairchild Archive

Madeleine Vionnet, 1961, *WWD*, Courtesy of Fairchild Archive

Hubert de Givenchy, Fall/Winter 1973, Photo by Reginald Gray, *WWD*, Courtesy of Fairchild Archive

Halston, 1964, *WWD*, Courtesy of Fairchild Archive

Giorgio Armani, Spring 1978 RTW, Photo by Tim Jenkins, *WWD*, Courtesy of *WWD*

Karl Lagerfeld for Chanel, Fall 1983 RTW, Photo by Guy Marineau, *WWD*, Courtesy of Fairchild Archive

Ralph Lauren, 1977, Photo by Nick Machalaba *WWD*, Courtesy of Fairchild Archive

Pierre Cardin, Creation Cardin, Fall 1983, Photo by Jean Luce Hure, *WWD*, Courtesy of Fairchild Archive

Bill Blass, 1972, Photo by Peter Simins, *WWD*, Courtesy of Fairchild Archive

Rei Kawakubo, 2009 Beatles Collection, *WWD*, Courtesy of *WWD*

Perry Ellis, Fall 1986, *WWD*, Courtesy of Fairchild Archive

Christian Lacroix, Fall 1987 Couture, Photo by Thierry Bouët, *WWD*, Courtesy of Fairchild Archive

Gianni Versace, Fall 1990 RTW, Photo by Art Streiber, *WWD*, Courtesy of Fairchild Archive

John Galliano, Fall 2001 RTW, Photo by Giovanni Giannoni, *WWD*, Courtesy of *WWD*

Tommy Hilfiger, Fall 2009 RTW, Photo by Thomas Iannaccone, *WWD*, Courtesy of *WWD*

Helmut Lang, Fall 2002, Photo by David Turner, WWD, Courtesy of *WWD*

WWD McQueen, Spring 2000, Photo by Staff, WWD, Courtesy of *WWD*

Sonia Rykiel, 1972, Photo by Jean-Luce Hure, *WWD*, Courtesy of Fairchild Archive

Thakoon Panichgul for Hogan, Fall 2008 RTW, Photo by Davide Maestri, *WWD*, Courtesy of *WWD*

Marc Jacobs, Fall 1985 RTW, Photo by George Chinsee, *WWD*, Courtesy of Fairchild Archive

Stella McCartney for Chloé, Fall 2001 RTW, Photo by Giovanni Giannoni, *WWD*, Courtesy of *WWD*

Vera Wang, Spring 2010, Photo by Giovanni Giannoni, *WWD*, Courtesy of *WWD*

BACK MATTER:

Carolina Herrera, Fall 2009, Photo by Robert Mitra, *WWD*, Courtesy of *WWD*

Bill Blass, 1962, Photo by Tony Palmieri, *WWD*, Courtesy of Fairchild Archive

INSIDE COVER ENDPAPER:
1ST ROW (left to right):

Christian Lacroix, Fall 2006, Photo by Stephane Feugere, WWD, Courtesy of *WWD*

Julie Christie, 1966, Photo by Desmond O'Neil, *WWD*, Courtesy of *WWD*

Donna Karan, 2003, Photo by George Chinsee, *WWD*, Courtesy of *WWD*

Jean Paul Gaultier, Photo by WWD Archives, *WWD*, Courtesy of *WWD*

Proenza Schouler, Spring 2010, Photo by George Chinsee, *WWD*, Courtesy of *WWD*

Katherine Graham and Truman Capote, 1966, Photo by Ray "Scotty" Morris, *WWD*, Courtesy of Fairchild Archive

Pierre Cardin, *WWD*, Courtesy of Fairchild Archive

Giorgio di Sant'Angelo and Calvin Klein, 1976, Photo by Nick Machalaba, *WWD*, Courtesy of Fairchild Archive

Christian Lacroix, Fall 1988, Photo by Philippe Costes, *WWD*, Courtesy of *WWD*

Rudi Gernreich, Spring/Summer '68, Photo by Sal Traina, *WWD*, Courtesy of Fairchild Archive

2ND ROW:

Geoffrey Beene, 1973, Photo by Pierre Schermann, *WWD*, Courtesy of Fairchild Archive

Alexander McQueen, 2010, Photo by Staff, *WWD*, Courtesy of *WWD*

Jackie Kennedy, 1967, Photo by Sal Traina, *WWD*, Courtesy of Fairchild Archive

Giorgio Armani, Fall 2010, Photo by David Yoder, *WWD*, Courtesy of *WWD*

Roy Halston, 1968, Photo by Nick Machalaba, *WWD*, Courtesy of Fairchild Archive

Vivienne Westwood, Fall 2010, Photo by Giovanni Giannoni, *WWD*, Courtesy of *WWD*

Betsey Johnson, Photo by Dan D'Errico, *WWD*, Courtesy of Fairchild Archive

Christian Dior, Spring 2008, Photo by Giovanni Giannoni, *WWD*, Courtesy of *WWD*

Jill Sander, 1993, Photo by Cédric Dordevic, *WWD*, Courtesy of *WWD*

Christian Dior, Spring 2009, Photo by Giovanni Giannoni, *WWD*, Courtesy of *WWD*

3RD ROW:

Yves Saint Laurent, 1973, Photo by Reginald Gray, *WWD*, Courtesy of Fairchild Archive

Oscar de la Renta, 1988, Photo by Dan D'Errico, *WWD*, Courtesy of Fairchild Archive

John Galliano for Christian Dior, Photo by Giovanni Giannoni and Stephane Feugere, *WWD*, Courtesy of *WWD*

Yves Saint Laurent, 2008, Photo by *WWD* Archives, *WWD*, Courtesy of *WWD*

Tom Ford for Gucci, Fall 2004, Photo by Giovanni Giannoni, *WWD*, Courtesy of *WWD*

East Village Fashion, 1972, Photo by Murray Feierberg, WWD, Courtesy of Fairchild Archive

Hubert de Givenchy, 1975, Photo by Reginald Gray, *WWD*, Courtesy of Fairchild Archive

Halston, 1973, Photo by Nick Ackerman, *WWD*, Courtesy of Fairchild Archive

Raf Simons for Jil Sander, Spring 2010 RTW, Photo by Davide Maestri WWD, Courtesy of *WWD*

Marc Jacobs, Spring 1987, Photo by George Chinsee, *WWD*, Courtesy of Fairchild Archive

4TH ROW:

Miuccia Prada, 1994, Photo by Davide Maestri, *WWD*, Courtesy of *WWD*

Jean Paul Gaultier, Spring 2010, Photo by Giovanni Giannoni, *WWD*, Courtesy of *WWD*

CZ, Photo by Tony Palmieri, *WWD*, Courtesy of Fairchild Archive

Marc Jacobs, Spring 2009, Photo by Steve Eichner, *WWD*, Courtesy of *WWD*

Karl Lagerfeld, Photo by David Turner, *WWD*, Courtesy of Fairchild Archive

Valentino, Spring 2008, Photo by Giovanni Giannoni, *WWD*, Courtesy of *WWD*

Marc Bohan, Spring 1969, Photo by Reginald Gray, *WWD*, Courtesy of Fairchild Archive

Dolce & Gabbana, Fall 2010, Photo by David Yoder, *WWD*, Courtesy of *WWD*

Oscar de la Renta, Spring 1973, Photo by Pierre Schermann, *WWD*, Courtesy of Fairchild Archive

Nicolas Ghesquière, Fall 2010, Photo by Giovanni Giannoni, *WWD*, Courtesy of *WWD*

5TH ROW:

Issac Mizrahi, Fall 2009, Photo by John Aquino, *WWD*, Courtesy of *WWD*

Bonnie Cashin, Spring 1973 RTW, Photo by Sal Traina, *WWD*, Courtesy of Fairchild Archive

Alexander McQueen and Sarah Jessica Parker, 2006, Photo by Jimi Celeste, *WWD*, Courtesy of *WWD*

Coco Chanel and Verdura, Circa 1969, *WWD*, Courtesy of *Fairchild Archive*

Giorgio Armani, Spring 2005, Photo by Giovanni Giannoni, *WWD*, Courtesy of *WWD*

Donna Karan, Spring 1986, Photo by Thomas Iannaccone, *WWD*, Courtesy of Fairchild Archive

Roberto Cavalli, *WWD*, Courtesy of WWD

Gianni Versace, Valentino, Giorgio Armani, and Gianfranco Ferré, 1992, Photo by Art Streiber, *WWD*, Courtesy of Fairchild Archive

John Galliano for Christian Dior, Fall 2009, Photo by Giovanni Giannoni and Stephane Feugere, WWD, Courtesy of *WWD*

Vivienne Westwood, 1977, Photo by Tim Jenkins, *WWD*, Courtesy of Fairchild Archive

BACK COVER ENDPAPER:

1ST ROW (left to right):

Marc Bohan for Christian Dior, Fall 2009, Photo by Giovanni Giannoni, *WWD*, Courtesy of *WWD*

Donna Karan, 2008, Photo by Thomas Iannaccone, *WWD*, Courtesy of *WWD*

Anna Sui, Spring 1995, Photo by George Chinsee, *WWD*, Courtesy of *WWD*

Tommy Hilfiger, Fall 2002, Photo by David Turner, *WWD*, Courtesy of *WWD*

Rei Kawakubo, *WWD*, Courtesy of *WWD*

Karl Lagerfeld for Chanel, Spring 2009, Photo by Giovanni Giannoni and Stephane Feugere, *WWD*, Courtesy of *WWD*

Pat Buckley and Nan Kempner, Fall 1973, Photo by Nick Machalaba, *WWD*, Courtesy of Fairchild Archive

Zac Posen, Fall 2009, Photo by Steve Eichner, *WWD*, Courtesy of *WWD*

Bill Blass, Spring/Summer 1973, Photo by Ed Azzopardi, *WWD*, Courtesy of Fairchild

Rodarte, Spring 2010, Photo by John Aquino, *WWD*, Courtesy of *WWD*

2ND ROW:

Betsey Johnson, Fall 2010, Photo by Pasha Antonov, *WWD*, Courtesy of *WWD*

Valentino and Giancarlo Giametti, Photo by Tony Palmieri, *WWD*, Courtesy of Fairchild Archive

Sonia Rykiel, Spring 2009, Photo by Giovanni Giannoni, *WWD*, Courtesy of *WWD*

George Plimpton, *WWD*, Courtesy of Fairchild Archive

Christian Lacroix, Fall 2008, Photo by Giovanni Giannoni, WWD, Courtesy of *WWD*

Guests at Adolfo, Fall 1983, Photo by Pierre-Gilles Vidoli, WWD, Courtesy of Fairchild Archive

Maggie Gyllenhaal, 2005, Photo by Donato Sardella, *WWD*, Courtesy of *WWD*

Mia Farrow and Robert Redford, 1973, Photo by Sal Traina, *WWD*, Courtesy of Fairchild Archive

Betsy Bloomingdale, 1972, Photo by *WWD* Archive, *WWD*, Courtesy of *WWD* Archive

Ottavio and Rosita Missoni, 1972, *WWD*, Courtesy of Fairchild Archive

3RD ROW:

Andy Warhol, Photo by Pierre Schermann, *WWD*, Courtesy of Fairchild Archive

Diane von Furstenberg, 2008, Photo by Giovanni Giannoni, *WWD*, Courtesy of *WWD*

Rudi Gernreich, 1966, Photo by Max Shapiro, *WWD*, Courtesy of Fairchild Archive

Michael Kors, Fall 2009, Photo by Kyle Ericksen, WWD, Courtesy of *WWD*

Steve McQueen and Ali MacGraw, 1972, Photo by Nick Ackerman, *WWD*, Courtesy of Fairchild Archive

John Galliano, Fall 2005, Photo by Giovanni Giannoni, *WWD*, Courtesy of *WWD*

Anne Klein, Fall/Winter 1972, Photo by Peter Simins, *WWD*, Courtesy of Fairchild Archive

Marc Jacobs, Spring 1994, Photo by Thomas Iannaccone, *WWD*, Courtesy of *WWD*

Adolfo, Photo by Gort, *WWD*, Courtesy of Fairchild Archive

Christian Dior, Spring 2010, Photo by Giovanni Giannoni, *WWD*, Courtesy of *WWD*

4TH ROW:

Ralph Lauren, Fall/Winter 1983, Photo by Tony Palmieri, *WWD*, Courtesy of Fairchild Archive

Julie Christie, 1967, Photo by Otn, *WWD*, Courtesy of Fairchild Archive

John Galliano for Christian Dior, Fall 2010, Photo by Giovanni Giannoni, *WWD*, Courtesy of *WWD*

Illustrator Kenneth Paul Block and Gloria Vanderbilt, Photo by Tony Palmieri, *WWD*, Courtesy of Fairchild Archive

Carolina Herrera, 2009, Photo by Steve Eichner, *WWD*, Courtesy of *WWD*

André Courrèges, 1972, Photo by Reginald Gray, *WWD*, Courtesy of Fairchild Archive

Calvin Klein, Fall 2009, Photo by George Chinsee, *WWD*, Courtesy of *WWD*

Giorgio di Sant'Angelo, 1974, Photo by Pierre Schermann, *WWD*, Courtesy of Fairchild Archive

Ralph Lauren, Spring 2008, Photo by George Chinsee, *WWD*, Courtesy of *WWD*

Adolfo, Spring 1984, *WWD*, Courtesy of Fairchild Archive

5TH ROW:

Anne Klein, 1972, Photo by Pierre Venant, *WWD*, Courtesy of Fairchild Archive

Roy Halston, Holiday 1979, Photo by Dustin Pittman, *WWD*, Courtesy of Fairchild Archive

Valentino, Spring 1972, Photo by Gianni Lami, *WWD*, Courtesy of Fairchild Archive

Jean Paul Gaultier for Hermès, Spring 2008, Photo by Giovanni Giannoni, *WWD*, Courtesy of *WWD*

Pierre Cardin, Fall/Winter 1973, Photo by Reginald Gray, *WWD*, Courtesy of Fairchild Archive

Roberto Cavalli, Photo by Kyle Ericksen, *WWD*, Courtesy of *WWD*

Ungaro, Photo by Sal Traina, *WWD*, Courtesy of Fairchild Archive

Alexander McQueen, Fall 2009, Photo by Giovanni Giannoni, *WWD*, Courtesy of *WWD*

Arnold Scaasi, Resort 1973, Photo by Peter Simins, *WWD*, Courtesy of Fairchild Archive

Giorgio Armani, Fall 2008, Photo by Delphine Achard, *WWD*, Courtesy of *WWD*

INDEX

2009

ACKNOWLEDGMENTS

Mining the fragile archives of this daily newspaper has brought to life the complexity of the effort its founders laid out so well in their "Our Excuse for Being" statement, printed in the very first issue. This project has underscored the passion and talent of the writers, editors, photographers and illustrators who have contributed to the paper these past 100 years. We salute them, one and all. While it would be impossible to capture the full scope of *Women's Wear Daily*, or the depth and breadth of the designers it has covered in a single volume, *WWD: 100 Years, 100 Designers* illustrates the richness of both...and makes us want more.

Many people have contributed to this book and deserve our deepest thanks:

Etta Froio, Bridget Foley and Ed Nardoza shared their invaluable editorial point of view, ultimate insider's wisdom and encyclopedic knowledge of the paper and the designers it has covered. Molly Monosky and her team in the Fairchild Publications Archives found and scanned hundreds and hundreds of articles, illustrations and photographs; their knowledge and passion has impressed us daily. The management team at Fairchild Fashion Group, Gina Sanders, Peter Kaplan, Will Schenck and Melissa Brecher, celebrate this brand every day, and their support and encouragement for this project has been greatly appreciated. And thanks, too, to the dedicated *WWD* editorial team—Carrie Provenzano, Andrew Flynn, Bobbi Queen, Tara Bonet-Black, Maureen Morrison-Shulas and Peter Sadera—who contributed their great ideas and effort.

Editor: Laurie Sprague
Creative Director/Book Designer: Carolyn Eckert
Editorial Development Director, Fairchild Books: Jennifer Crane
Editor-in-Chief, *WWD*: Ed Nardoza
Executive Edtor, *WWD*: Bridget Foley
Contributing Senior Executive Editor, *WWD*: Etta Froio
Fashion Writer, *WWD*: Venessa Lau
Editorial Assistant, *WWD*: Tara Bonet-Black
V. P. & General Manager, Fairchild Books: Elizabeth Tighe
Production Editor, Fairchild Books: Jessica Rozler
Design/Photo Research & Project Coordinators: Andrea Lau, Sarah Silberg
Art Research/Coordinators: Carly Grafstein, Suzette Lam
Photo & Art Researchers: Avital Aronowitz, Lindsay Aveilhe, Elizabeth Greenberg, Ashley Kolodziej, Alexandra Rossomando, Lauren Vlassenko
Decades Editor: Katherine Wessling
Associate Archivist, Fairchild Publications: Molly Monosky
Editorial Research Assistants: Jessica Bowers, Lexi Karpel, Sabrina Marzaro
Archive Associates: Ryan Blomberg, Helen Schumacher, Samantha Vuignier
Archive Scanners/Retouchers: Leonard Greco, Jeremy Merriam
Production Assistant: Jeff Klingman
Page Composition: Torborg Davern, Erin Fitzsimmons, Tom Helleberg

FAIRCHILD BOOKS
Executive Editor: Olga T. Kontzias
Production Director: Ginger Hillman
Director of Sales & Marketing: Brian Normoyle

Copyright © 2011 Fairchild Books,
A Division of Condé Nast.
Fairchild Books
750 Third Avenue
New York, NY 10017

All rights reserved. No part of this book covered by the copyright hereon may be reproduced or used in any form or by any means—graphic, electronic, or mechanical, including photocopying, recording, taping, or information storage and retrieval systems—without written permission of the publisher.

Library of Congress Catalog Card Number: 2010934956
ISBN: 978-1-60901-252-6
GST R 133004424
Printed in the United States of America
TP08

1962